An Introduction to Population

CHANDLER PUBLICATIONS IN SOCIOLOGY

Leonard Broom, *General Editor*
Charles M. Bonjean, *Advisory Editor*

An Introduction to Population

Kenneth C. W. Kammeyer
University of Kansas

CHANDLER PUBLISHING COMPANY
An Intext Publisher
SAN FRANCISCO • SCRANTON • LONDON • TORONTO

Contents

Preface

Course enrollments and other obvious signs indicate that population as a field of study is currently experiencing a sudden surge of popularity among college students. The reason for this is clear enough: Population has been linked to those other catchwords, "ecology" and "environment." "The population explosion," or overpopulation, is now being viewed by many as the primary cause of "damage to our ecological system," or the "plundering of our environment." Whether or not this charge is accurate, many people have become interested in population—particularly in how and why it grows and declines. This small book is an introduction to the study of population, and in part, it tries to provide answers for these questions. Hopefully, it will also provide some additional information and ideas about population.

This book also considers how population has been, and can be, studied. Historically there have been different reasons for studying or being interested in population, and the same is true today. However, even if the objective is simply to explain variations in population growth or decline, or to understand population movements and distribution, the methods and the theories employed for these purposes vary greatly. In Chapter 1 there is a discussion of how some students of population explain variations in population events (births, deaths, migration) in terms of social, cultural, psychological, biological, or other systems of variables, while others explain demographic events in terms of other demographic factors. I have tried to give some indication of both the advantages and weaknesses of these different approaches, but on the whole, the orientation of this book is weighted toward the social, cultural, and social-psychological explanations of population.

This book is an introduction to population in the sense that it introduces the ways in which population is studied; it gives attention to the data being used by students of population; it offers some emergent conceptual frameworks, particularly for the study of migration and fertility; and it attempts to summarize some of the more important knowledge about population processes and particular populations. I hope that this introduction will encourage many readers to go beyond this book, for many topics can be explored in much greater depth, and many questions about population dynamics must still be answered.

* * * *

Acknowledging the help that people have given me in the preparation of this book is a pleasant responsibility. First, it has been a great pleasure to work with the Chandler staff. From the time of our first discussion of this book they have been both patient and helpful. Leonard Broom and Chuck Bonjean, the consulting editors for Chandler publications in sociology, have given more time and attention to this manuscript that I ever imagined they could. I have been greatly aided by their continued willingness to read and criticize the successive drafts of the manuscript.

The University of Kansas has provided a particularly conducive atmosphere for my work. I am especially grateful for the semester I spent as a research associate with the Institute for Social and Environmental Studies. The Institute Director, Bob Aangeenbrug, was always ready to provide any support I needed. This assistance included the help of Sheryl Farney as an editorial assistant. Her work saved me many hours—I want to thank her and all the members of the Institute staff who helped me.

Quite a number of my colleagues and friends helped me or listened to me at one time or another as I worked on this book. They include Stan Eitzen, Gary Maranell, Lew Mennerick, Sheila Miller, David Mitchell, George Nielson, Beth See, Jim Weiss, and Norm Yetman. I want to note here that I appreciate their friendship and their help.

As the several versions of this manuscript have been written, many hours have been spent by some hard-working typists. Foremost among them is Barbara Johnson, who does such a good job because, in addition to her skill, she takes your job and makes it her own; she takes your deadline and meets it. She has never failed me, nor have the other girls in her office: Debbie Huff, Linda Hoffman, and Patricia Bartee. Nancy Baron, of Portland State University, also worked through one draft of this manuscript, and she too took the kind of personal interest that is necessary to get the job done. I sincerely thank all of these helpful and skilled people.

Finally, my wife Alyce deserves recognition for the kind of help and support she provides. She often gives my ideas a much more critical assessment than my students, but in the end her review of my work is almost always "It's good, I like it." At the risk of revealing some latent male chauvinism, I appreciate that kind of help and support.

K. C. W. K.

Lawrence, Kansas
March, 1971

An Introduction to Population

Chapter **1** The Study of Population

TYPES OF STUDY

The subject of this book is human population. The important questions about populations have to do with how and why they change, particularly in size, location, and composition. The scientific study of these questions characterizes the field of *demography.*

But demography is a general term, one that is used to refer to many different kinds of population research and analysis. A useful distinction can be made between two divisions of demography: *formal demography* and *population studies.*[1] An example will help to highlight some of the essential differences between formal demography and population studies. Consider first the approach of a formal demographer who wishes to estimate the size of a country's population over the next twenty years. How would he approach the question, what kind of information would he require, and what techniques would he employ? Initially, he would want to compile as much information as he could on the present composition of the population, particularly the age composition. Knowing the age and sex composition would allow him to estimate the number of women who would be in the childbearing ages during the coming decades. Knowledge about the age composition of the population would also enable the formal demographer to anticipate the number of deaths that would occur over the next twenty years, if he had detailed information on the rates of death at all different ages. He would also need information on birth rates in order to predict the future size of the population. Again, as in the case of mortality, he could make a better prediction if he had the specific fertility rates that prevailed for women at different childbearing ages. These birth rates could then be applied to the anticipated age composition of the population so that an estimate could be made of the number of new children to be born into the population. A final factor that might enter into the formal demographer's prediction equation would be the amount of migration into and out of the population.

If a formal demographer had all this information, and if all prevailing rates remained unchanged, he could make an excellent prediction of the future size of the population. Of course, one of the problems in formal demography is that birth rates, death rates, and migration patterns do not remain always the same, but tend to change. A cohort of married couples may have fewer, or more, babies than a previous cohort. Mortality can suddenly decline for specific age groups, as when infant mortality is greatly diminished by some

1

medical discovery. Migration into the population can decrease or increase dramatically, for instance when new legislation cuts off or opens up immigration. Or, migration rates can vary according to changing economic conditions. Yet, while all of these problems can cause the formal demographer's predictions to be in error, he is often able to make very useful estimates about the size and composition of future populations.

This example illustrates that the formal demographer works entirely within the realm of population facts. Population composition, age-specific fertility, age-specific mortality, and migration are *all* demographic factors. The most distinctive feature of formal demography is that the factors which are viewed as "causal," or "independent," variables and the factors which are the "effect," or "dependent," variables, are exclusively from the province of demography. Put simply, in formal demography some population variables are used to explain changes in some other population variables.

In addition, although not necessarily an intrinsic characteristic, formal demography is characterized by techniques of analysis that are quantitative. There is a strong emphasis on the measurement of demographic rates and mathematical models for analysis. In practice, the data of formal demography come largely from censuses and vital-registration systems.[2]

In contrast to formal demography there is the approach of *population study*. The key to population study is that nondemographic factors are used to explain and predict variations in demographic variables. Thus the phenomena to be investigated remain the same as in formal demography: Changes in birth rates, death rates, migration rates, and the composition and size of populations are still the basic variable factors that are explained. These demographic events can, however, be explained by many factors—factors that are quite different from the demographic variables used by the formal demographer. There are social variables, psychological variables, cultural, historical, medical, and physiological variables, to name a few. The choice of which nondemographic variables to focus on depends largely upon the orientation and the expertise of the researcher. A sociologist quite naturally emphasizes the importance of prominent social and cultural variables. He often gives special attention to the structural features of the society, such as social classes and minority groups. He may also study the impact that the norms (the informal rules of conduct), the values, and the social roles of the society have on population phenomena.

By comparison, medical and biological scientists engaged in population studies may emphasize the causal importance of medical and physiological factors. For example, the incidence of certain diseases may increase sterility, which will obviously influence the birth rate. (Venereal diseases have such an effect on fertility.) More obviously, there are many medical and physiological factors that influence the death rates for different age and sex categories in a population.

Other nondemographic variables that are occasionally used to explain variations in population include psychological, genetic, geographical, historical, and political factors. A study in which a nondemographic factor is the independent variable used to explain some demographic fact is a *population study Type I*.

There is a second kind of population study (*Type II*), in which the population factors are the explanatory, or independent, variables, used to explain variations in nondemographic variables. For example, a researcher might use the age composition of a population to explain variations in some behavior, such as voting patterns in a community election. One part of a community, with a high proportion of families who no longer have school-age children, may oppose school-bond referenda, while another part of the community, where there are many children, may support such measures. In this instance, a knowledge of the demographic composition of the community would help to explain voting behavior. In a very strict sense, Type II studies may be considered outside the scope of demography, for their objective is to explain variations in phenomena other than population. However, many inquiries of this type are conducted by demographers, and certainly the results are of interest to students of population.

Table 1 presents the distinguishing characteristics and some examples of formal demography and population studies, Types I and II.

Many times in this book the results and findings of formal demography are presented, but generally emphasis and attention are not on the formal demographic approach. Rather, the approach is that of population study, Type I, and the orientation is basically sociological. But it is sociological in a very broad sense, encompassing social, cultural, and social-psychological phenomena.[3] The principal theme in this book is that the nature of social life is an important, if not primary, factor in determining the births, deaths, and migration of a population.

THE HISTORY OF POPULATION STUDY

It is not possible in a few pages to do more than outline some of the historical highlights in the development of population study. But even a brief discussion will provide some understanding of several important antecedents to the present-day study of population. In particular, it will show the emergence of different population concerns over time.

Historically, three major interests have stimulated the study of population. Probably the earliest and most lasting concern has been with the effects

TABLE 1. CHARACTERISTICS AND EXAMPLES OF FORMAL DEMOGRAPHY; POPU-
LATION STUDIES, TYPE I; AND POPULATION STUDIES, TYPE II

Type of Study	Independent Variables	Dependent Variables
Formal Demography	*Demographic Variables (examples)*	*Demographic Variables (examples)*
	Age composition	Birth rate
	Birth rate	Age composition
	Age composition of in-migrants	Birth rate of the total population
Population Study, Type I	*Nondemographic Variables (examples)*	*Demographic Variables (examples)*
	Social class (sociological variable)	Birth rate
	Attitude toward maternal role (social-psychological variable)	Number of children
	Incidence of venereal disease (medical variable)	Number of children
	Cigarette smoking (medical variable)	Death rate
	Economic opportunities (economic variable)	Out-migration
Population Study, Type II	*Demographic Variables (examples)*	*Nondemographic Variables (examples)*
	Age composition	Voting behavior (political variable)
	In-migration	Social disorganization *(sociological variable)*
	Birth rate	Economic growth *(economic variable)*

of population size and composition on the well-being of the society. Second, with the beginnings of the scientific method, an interest emerged in applying the scientific-empirical approach to the study of population. The third major interest has been in developing a theory of population to explain why populations change.

These three concerns correspond roughly to three historical time periods. The first period covered a very broad span of time, from the early historical period to the eighteenth century. The second period, much shorter than the first, encompassed the seventeenth and eighteenth centuries and reflected the thinking of the European scientists and scholars called "political arithmeticians." The final historical reference point is even more clearly defined; it focuses on the publication of the *Essay on the Principle of Population* by Thomas Robert Malthus, at the beginning of the nineteenth century.[4]

These three historical foci occur chronologically, but there is also some obvious overlap, so the differentiation is only partially based on their order in time. Also, as with almost any attempt at classification, there is some over-simplification in this characterization of the history of the study of population.

Early Population Concerns

The early writings on population were largely contained in the works of social and political philosophers, and were primarily concerned with the effect that population had on political or economic systems. Some of the earliest discussions of the relationship between societal well-being and population appeared in the writings of the ancient Chinese philosophers.

Confucius and other Chinese scholars gave consideration to the ideal proportion between the land area and the number of people. Confucius held that it was the responsibility of the government to move people from over-populated to underpopulated areas. He also noted several factors that would tend to act as checks on population growth, numbering among them such things as insufficient food supply, war, premature marriage (which resulted in high infant mortality), and costly marriage ceremonies.[5]

Plato and Aristotle also discussed population, but specifically in the context of the ideal size of the Greek political unit, the city-state. The optimum population size of a city-state was that in which the well-being and the security of the citizens could be best maintained and the administration of the government could be carried out efficiently. Plato was most specific with regard to population size, setting the optimum number of citizens at 5040. However, since dependents and slaves were not counted as citizens, the actual number of people living in the city-state would have been much larger than 5040. The total population of such a political unit could have ranged up to ten times that number.

While Plato allowed that the number of citizens might possibly vary according to local circumstances and exigencies (for example, the availability of land and relations with neighboring groups), he nevertheless held firmly to the exact number of 5040 citizens, and believed that the state should exert efforts to maintain that number. The primary mechanism he suggested for retaining that precise number of citizens was the inheritance system. The land of a newly formed city-state was to be divided equally among the 5040 citizens. Each family was then to pass its allotment on to a single, preferred male heir. In Plato's words,

Let the possessor of a lot leave the one of his children who is best beloved, and only one, to be the heir of his dwelling . . . but of his other children, if he have more than one, he shall give the females in marriage . . . and the males he shall distribute as sons to those citizens who have no children, and are disposed to receive them. . . .[6]

If some citizen families appeared to be having too many or too few children, Plato considered it reasonable that the government and the elders of the society exert the pressures necessary to keep their number of offspring at the desired level. Such pressures were to include "rewards" and "stigmas," "advice" and "rebuke," but if all else failed the size of the population could be held at 5040 citizens by sending the surplus numbers to a colony.

Plato chose the number 5040 as the optimum size of the population partly because it is divisible by all numbers from one to ten. It is also divisible by the number twelve, which was particularly important to Plato, for he also suggested that the first division of the land of a city-state should be into twelve pie-shaped parts.

Aside from the practical administrative advantages of the divisibility of 5040, there are indications that Plato also saw religious or mystical significance in the number. He urged that the citizens honor and "observe the aforesaid number 5040 throughout life."[7] Speaking of the twelve portions into which the city-state would be divided, he said,

Now every portion should be regarded by us as a sacred gift of Heaven, corresponding to the months and to the revolution of the universe. Every city has a guiding and sacred principle given by nature, but in some the division or distribution has been more right than in others, and has been more sacred and fortunate. In our opinion, nothing can be more right than the selection of the number 5040, which may be divided by all numbers from one to twelve with the single exception of eleven.[8]

Aristotle, while less explicit than Plato about the exact number of citizens that should exist in a city-state, clearly supported the notion that the size of the population should be stabilized and controlled by the government. He specifically argued that a population could become too large to be properly governed. Aristotle noted that the number of citizens of a state might be used to judge the quality of a state, and he cautioned that "a great state is not the same thing as a state with a large population. . . . [I]t is difficult and perhaps impossible for a state with too large a population to have good legal government."[9]

Aristotle was concerned with controlling the size of the population, and viewed with some alarm a population that was too great for its resources or too large to allow for an orderly life. He advocated government control of the number of births per family, approved of abortion under certain circumstances, and recommended the exposure of any infant who was born deformed.[10]

Following the classical Hellenic period, the focus of the history of Western civilization becomes the Roman world. The Roman writers, concerned with a great empire, were principally interested in the practical problem of stimulating population growth. They tended to disapprove of celibacy, while they gave support to marriage and childbearing. Legislation was passed during the period of the Roman Empire which was aimed at stimulating both marriage and birth rates.[11]

One of the earliest writers who might be credited with developing a population theory was the fourteenth-century Arab social philosopher Ibn Khaldun (1332–1406). His theory of population was based on the idea that societies pass through stages of development which have an influence on the number of births and deaths. He believed that in the early part of its development a society experiences high fertility and low mortality, and thus a high population-growth rate (this phenomenon is now called *natural increase* by demographers—the difference between the number of births and the number of deaths in a society if the value is positive). According to Khaldun, a society would, as it passed into the later stage of existence, come to experience the opposite demographic conditions; that is, low fertility and high mortality. Khaldun's theory assumed that high fertility would occur in the early stages of the society because the people would be more confident and show more energy and enterprise. Toward the end of a society there would be famines, epidemics, rebellions, and disorders. All of these events would produce a widespread insecurity that would result in reduced fertility. Khaldun offered the hypothesis that during these later stages of a society "[h]ope sinks and procreation diminishes, for procreation is stimulated by high hopes and the resulting heightening of animal energies."[12]

Writings on population began to appear more frequently by the seventeenth century. Many European political and social philosophers offered their ideas on the influence that population might have on the society. Increasingly, the emphasis came to be placed on the relationship between population and the economy. Characteristic of this emphasis were the writings of the mercantilists of the seventeenth and eighteenth centuries.

The mercantilist philosophers argued that a large and growing population would lead to economic and military advantages for the state. They held that the accrual of wealth and power to the state—particularly manifested in the state's supply of precious metals—would be enhanced by a large and growing population. The aim of the mercantilists was not to increase per capita income, but to increase the aggregate national income over the total wage costs of production. They argued that a growing population, which would produce a growing labor force, would depress wage rates, make competition among workers keener, and thus increase the gap between wage costs and national income. Following this line of reasoning, the mercantilists advocated a high rate of population growth to enhance the economic goals of the state.[13]

With the possible exception of the cyclical population theory of Ibn Khaldun, early population writings are principally characterized by their concern with the relationship between population size and the goals or desired values of the state or society. Few efforts were made toward advancing theoretical propositions about population, except as they might relate to the goals of the state. In short, in the early writing on population, there was very little of what could be labeled scientific population theory; that is, propositions positing relationships between other factors and population phenomena. Also, the early writings on population presented little population data, and only rarely were there indications that empirical observations had been made or that any research had been conducted.

The Political Arithmeticians

The group of seventeenth-century scholars and writers who called themselves "political arithmeticians" were contemporaries of the mercantilist political philosophers. Indeed, some of the political arithmeticians could reasonably be included among the mercantilists, and it is likely that many were influenced by mercantilist ideas. The distinguishing factor as far as population study is concerned is that the political arithmeticians were empirical scientists; they were influenced by, and were a part of, the beginning of the scientific age. In the physical realm, scientific inquiry, with its emphasis on observation and experiment, was already firmly established by the seventeenth century. Scientists of the stature of Bacon, Galileo, Harvey, and Kepler had proven the utility of scientific observation for understanding the physical world. The political arithmeticians were the contemporaries of Sir Isaac Newton, who was establishing scientific inquiry even more firmly as the best means of verifying the uniformities and the laws of nature. Greatly influenced by these intellectual currents, the political arithmeticians recognized the potential of collecting and analyzing data in the social realm.

However, applying the scientific method to establish facts about human population was only one part of a dual motivation that the political arithmeticians had. The second motive was related to mercantilism, for many political arithmeticians acknowledged that they were setting out to measure the resources of the state or the crown in terms of land, capital, wealth, and *population.*

The double task of political arithmetic was well defined in the preface to a volume called *Natural and Political Observations . . . made Upon the Bills of Mortality,* published in 1662 and written by the first and most honored English political arithmetician, John Graunt (1620–1674). In this book, Graunt reported his findings on the London and English populations as he had derived them from the *Bills of Mortality*—weekly reports of the deaths that had occurred in the parishes of London. Graunt said in his preface:

The observations, which I happened to make (for I designed them not) upon the Bills of Mortality, have fallen out to be both Political, and Natural, some concerning Trade, and Government, others concerning the Air, Countries, Seasons, Fruitfulness, Health, Disease, Longevity, and the Proportions between the Sex, and Ages of Mankind.[14]

Because Graunt had made "political" observations, that is, observations that were relevant to the government, he dedicated his book in part to the Lord Privy Seal. However, because some of his conclusions were in the "natural" realm, he also dedicated his work to the president of the Royal Society of Philosophers. In short, the empirical inquiry of Graunt, like that of other political arithmeticians, had both a practical political purpose and a more strictly scientific purpose. Nevertheless, while the political arithmeticians had two motivations, their important contribution to the study of population was their insistence that conclusions be based on data.

Working from the *Bills of Mortality,* Graunt made a number of demographic observations, which, as generalizations, still retain considerable validity today. For example, Graunt noted that there was a heavy migration of persons from the country to the city and that this migration was usually made by "breeders," that is, persons in the reproductive ages. His observation that rural-to-urban migration was characteristically made by the younger age groups has held to be generally true up to the present time. Graunt also noted that the rate of population growth in rural areas exceeded that of the urban areas, and that the mortality rate was greater in urban places than in rural. He used christening data to show that more boys were born than girls, and that there was an extremely high death rate for infants and children in seventeenth-century England.

Graunt is credited with making one of the early and reasonably accurate estimates of London's population, and with constructing the first, albeit crude, *life table.* The life table, as it has subsequently developed, is used for estimating life expectancy under the death rates that prevail at different ages. It became an indispensable tool for the life-insurance industry that was emerging in Europe in the seventeenth century.

After Graunt, the next most well known political arithmetician was William Petty (1623–1687), who was not only a contemporary of Graunt, but also a close friend. Petty was slightly more representative of the mercantilist tradition, apparently carrying out most of his empirical inquiries to establish various facts about the population and wealth of London and England. Nevertheless, his concern for quantitative empirical data is evident, for his essays were heavily laced with tables and calculations in support of his observations and conclusions.[15]

Among the other prominent political arithmeticians of England and the Continent, several made special contributions. Gregory King (1648–1712), following Graunt, carried out a more extensive study of the total population of England and Wales. He used the hearth-tax returns to establish the number of dwellings in the country, and then estimated the average number of persons per home to determine the total population. A German political arithmetician named Johann P. Sussmilch (1708–1767) was a theologian by vocation who interpreted the population regularities he observed as evidence of a divine order. Most of the political arithmeticians had some proclivities toward a theological interpretation of their data with the result, as Mayer has pointed out in a recent essay, that, "while the demographic measurements of these writers were scientific, their causal interpretations were not."[16]

The political arithmeticians were distinguishable from the early writers on population because they relied on empirical data in making their observations. Their writings were not generally theoretical, but they were based on fact and data. The political arithmeticians, with their emphasis on fact-gathering by scientific methods, were the first scholars to establish one of the two essential components of modern population study. The other component—an adequate theory of population—was still lacking. The last of the three major historical landmarks in the development of demography was the introduction of a theory of population that has stimulated work in the field up to the present time; that is, the famous *Essay on the Principle of Population* by Thomas Robert Malthus.

Malthus

Much has been written about Thomas Robert Malthus (1766–1834), his theory, and his contribution to the study of population. When Malthus published his essay, there was an immediate reaction to what he had written and speculation about his purpose for having written it. Some of the reaction was positive; much was negative. A considerable part of the initial controversy and debate has continued in one form or another until the present day. The purpose here is not to offer an elaborate presentation and critique of Malthus's theory. Nor is it to consider all the many controversial issues that have surrounded the man and his writing. Rather, the purpose is to consider the position of importance that Malthus's work has occupied in the development of modern demography. Since the elements of Malthus's theory are relatively simple, and in all likelihood most readers have some familiarity with them already, the theory will be presented here only in its skeletal details.

Malthus started with some basic propositions about man and nature:

> I think I may fairly make two postulata.
> First, that food is necessary to the existence of men.
> Secondly, that the passion between the sexes is necessary, and will remain nearly in its present state.
> Assuming then, my postulata as granted, I say, that the power of population is indefinitely greater than the power in the earth to produce subsistence for man.
> Population, when unchecked, increases in a geometrical ratio [1, 2, 4, 8, 16, 32, 64]. Subsistence increases only in an arithmetical ratio [1, 2, 3, 4, 5, 6, 7]. A slight acquaintance with numbers will show the immensity of the first power in comparison of the second.
> By that law of our nature which makes food necessary to the life of man, the effects of these two unequal powers must be kept equal.
> This implies a strong and constantly operating check on population from the difficulty of subsistence.[17]

The checks on population growth that Malthus referred to in the last statement he labeled "positive checks." Positive checks limit the population size by increasing the death rate. Examples of the positive checks suggested by Malthus included famine, pestilence, infant mortality, war, and "vicious customs with respect to women."[18] These various evils Malthus called "misery and vice."

Malthus also suggested that "preventive checks," for example, delayed marriage or "moral restraint," might affect the size of the population by decreasing the birth rate. While he saw this kind of prudence and forethought as operating "in some degree through all ranks of society," he clearly did not expect much of it from the lower classes. He generally presumed that the combined forces of vice and misery (the positive checks) would be much more likely to shape their lot in life. As he put it, "The positive check to population . . . is confined chiefly, though not perhaps solely, to the lowest orders of society."[19]

Malthus was, and is, often attacked for the reactionary political views he expressed in his essay on population. His essay strongly opposed the Poor Laws of England and argued for their abolition. While some writers have sought to demonstrate that Malthus was not reactionary, it is clear from a reading of the *Essay* (particularly the first edition) that Malthus was expressing the values and views of the upper and upper-middle classes of English society.

There has been some tendency of late on the part of a few demographers to diminish or de-emphasize Malthus's contribution to, or influence on, the field of demography. An expression of this critical position has been made by Mayer:

It is remarkable that the Malthusian controversy, which produced an abundance of theoretical writings, had comparatively little direct influence on the development of formal demography . . . Only a few of the scholars who engaged in the theoretical discussions [during the middle decades of the nineteenth century] undertook any serious empirical studies.[20]

Davis has expressed similar feelings about Malthus's influence on modern scientific demography:

It is difficult to avoid the conclusion that the major advances in the science of population have come from improvements in the sources of information and in the techniques of analysis, rather than from the broad interpretations . . . The discrepancy was already clear with Malthus. He did not fully understand the progress in systematic demography that had been made at this time; yet it was his work that captured most attention, and it is his work that is still debated today in general population theory. Despite the outpouring of books, pamphlets, and articles on population theory . . . it is hard to cite a single scientific advance since Malthus's day that this literature has contributed to the subject.[21]

There are, on the other hand, noted demographers who take the position that Malthus made a singular and very positive contribution to the scientific study of population. Both Thompson and Lewis, and Petersen have come to almost identical conclusions. Thompson and Lewis write:

Malthus's primary contribution to the study of population, and one which in our opinion makes him the real father of modern population study, was his use of facts for the support of his general doctrine regarding the dynamics of population growth and change in relation to man's welfare. He is more responsible than anyone else for bringing population study within the field of social science.[22]

Petersen, although calling attention to many shortcomings of Malthus's work has concluded that

Malthus's *Essay on the Principle of Population,* in spite of its faults and limitations, marks the beginning of scientific demographic theory.[23]

The writers expressing these two opposing views on the contribution of Malthus have tended to emphasize different features of his work. The critics have reacted negatively to the scholarly and political furor surrounding Malthus in the nineteenth century. Clearly, much of the response to Malthus by his contemporaries was polemical, as was the *Essay* itself. It is also true that advances were being made in the techniques of formal demography during the nineteenth century, and that the debates about Malthus's ideas were quite separate from these developments. The work of the statisticians, the actuarials, and the census and vital-statistics analysts was leading to steady improvements in the techniques of formal demography. But demographic analysis unguided by theory would have been a sterile exercise. It was the singular contribution of Malthus that he advanced a theory of population and then began the process of supporting it with facts.

The theory that Malthus introduced may not have been the first population theory, and certainly many of the ideas it contained had been previously expressed.[24] Also, it cannot be argued that the theory was correct in all details. It did, however, offer an important hypothesis about the relationship between population and man's economic welfare. This hypothesis had relevance for the nineteenth century, and is not without significance today. Malthus's theory gave prominence and importance to population as a causal factor, and also, through the positive and preventive checks, sought to explain how and why populations grow and decline. While other and more detailed theories for explaining changes may be preferred today, it was the theory of Malthus that drew public and scholarly attention to the importance of population in social life.

SUMMARY

This chapter has emphasized that demography is a general term used to refer to the scientific study of population. The field can be divided into two component parts: formal demography and population studies. Formal demography is concerned with the interrelationships and causal connections between demographic variables only. Formal demography characteristically employs data from censuses and vital-registration systems. The procedures and techniques of formal demography are highly quantitative. Population studies are of two types. Population studies, Type I are those studies and analyses that employ some nondemographic factor to explain the changes and variations in demographic phenomena. Population studies, Type II are those studies in which demographic variables are used to explain nondemographic phenomena.

The brief treatment of the historical highlights in the development of the study of population offered a few examples of the earliest discussions of population issues. These early writings were largely concerned with the relationships between population size and the social or economic well-being of the society. The beginning of systematic empirical study of population was signaled by the work of the political arithmeticians of England and the European continent. The combination of theory and empirical inquiry on population was accomplished in a noteworthy fashion by Malthus. His contribution in this regard gives him a unique position in the history of the study of population.

Most of the material in the chapters that follow will reflect the knowledge and the understandings that have emerged from the scientific study of population since the time of Malthus. There will be a special emphasis on the research and the theories of sociologists and social psychologists, but other approaches will not be totally excluded.

In the chapter that follows the focus of attention will be on the single most persistent problem of demography: the data. The remaining chapters will deal first with the structure of populations, and then, in turn, with the three dynamic features of population: migration, mortality, and fertility. The final chapter will examine several questions related to world population, with special attention to the outlook for the future population of the world.

: : SELECTED READINGS AND MATERIALS

Basic Textbooks

Each of the following widely used texts provides a comprehensive exposition of the major areas of demographic interest.

Bogue, Donald J. *Principles of Demography.* New York, John Wiley and Sons, 1969.

Petersen, William. *Population,* 2nd edition. New York, Macmillan, 1969.

Thomlinson, Ralph. *Population Dynamics: Causes and Consequences of World Population Change.* New York, Random House, 1965.

Thompson, Warren S., and David T. Lewis. *Population Problems,* 5th edition. New York, McGraw-Hill, 1965.

General Collections of Articles and Essays

Ford, Thomas R., and Gordon F. DeJong, editors. *Social Demography.* Englewood Cliffs, N.J., Prentice-Hall, 1970.

Hauser, Philip M., and Otis Dudley Duncan, editors. *The Study of Population: An Inventory and Appraisal.* Chicago, University of Chicago Press, 1959. See especially Chapter 1, "The Nature of Demography."

Heer, David M., editor. *Readings on Population.* Englewood Cliffs, N.J., Prentice-Hall, 1968.

Kammeyer, Kenneth C. W., editor. *Population Studies: Selected Essays and Research.* Chicago, Rand-McNally, 1969. This collection of readings contains sections closely paralleling the present volume. For example, the papers that augment this first chapter are found in Section I, "The Study of Population."

Nam, Charles B., editor. *Population and Society: A Textbook of Selected Readings.* Boston, Houghton Mifflin, 1968.

Periodicals and Journals

Demography. Published by the Population Association of America. P.O. Box 14182, Benjamin Franklin Station, Washington, D.C. 20044.

Population Bulletin. Published by the Population Reference Bureau. The *Population Bulletin* and other materials on population published by the

Population Reference Bureau provide one of the most convenient sources of information on population, especially for the interested nonprofessional. Annual membership fee for the Population Reference Bureau is $8.00 ($5.00 for teachers). Population Reference Bureau, Inc., 1755 Massachusetts Ave., N.W. Washington, D.C. 20036.

Population Index. Published by the Office of Population Research, Princeton University; and the Population Association of America. This journal provides an ongoing bibliography of virtually everything published on population. Office of Population Research, Princeton University, Princeton, N.J. 08540.

Population Studies. Published by the Population Investigation Committee, London School of Economics, Houghton St., Aldwych, London W.C. 2, England.

: : NOTES

1. This distinction and the discussion that follows reflect the writings of Philip M. Hauser, O. D. Duncan, and William Petersen, even though the exact terms used by these writers differ from those employed here. See Philip M. Hauser, "Demography in Relation to Sociology," *American Journal of Sociology,* 65: 170 (1959); Philip M. Hauser and Otis Dudley Duncan, *The Study of Population: An Inventory and Appraisal* (Chicago: University of Chicago Press, 1959), pp. 3–4, 33–34; William Petersen, *Population,* 2nd edition (New York: Macmillan, 1969), pp. 2–3.

2. For some examples of the methods and findings of formal demography, the reader may examine Peter R. Cox, *Demography,* 3rd edition (Cambridge, England: Cambridge University Press, 1960); Nathan Keyfitz, *Introduction to Mathematics of Population* (Reading, Mass.: Addison-Wesley, 1968); Mortimer Spiegelman, *Introduction to Demography.,* rev. edition (Cambridge, Mass.: Harvard University Press, 1968).

3. In recent years the social-psychological approach has emerged as a particularly important perspective. In modern societies, where individual choice plays a large part in shaping the demographic events of people's lives, the role of personal and individual decision making is receiving much more attention from students of population. For the best recent statement on this point see Kurt W. Back, "New Frontiers in Demography and Social Psychology," *Demography,* 4: 90–97 (1967).

4. Thomas Robert Malthus, *An Essay on the Principle of Population as it Affects the Future Improvement of Society, with Remarks on the Speculations of Mr. Godwin, M. Condorcet and Other Writers* (London: Printed for J. Johnson in St. Pauls Churchyard, 1798. Reprinted by Macmillan, London, 1926).

5. Department of Social Affairs, Population Division, *The Determinants and Consequences of Population Trends* (New York: United Nations, ST/SOA/Ser. A/17, 1953), p. 21.

6. *The Dialogues of Plato,* translated by B. Jowett, 3rd edition (New York: Random House, 1937, by arrangement with Oxford University Press), pp. 506–507.

7. *The Dialogues,* p. 507.

8. *The Dialogues,* pp. 531–532. The numerological significance of 5040 has been remarked upon by Jowett, who observed also that 5040 is made up of the numbers one through seven multiplied times each other (factorial of seven). Reported by E. P. Hutchinson, *The Population Debate* (New York: Houghton-Mifflin, 1967), pp. 11–12.

9. Aristotle, *The Politics,* translated by H. Rackham (London: William Heinemann, 1932), p. 555.

10. Aristotle, pp. 103, 141, 555, 623–624.

11. United Nations, p. 22; and Hutchinson, p. 14.

12. Ibn Khaldun, *An Arab Philosophy of History,* translated by Charles Issawi (London: John Murray, 1950), pp. 96, 97.

13. Of course, the mercantilist argument about the relationship between the economy and population was not unopposed. Some writers argued that increases in the population would depress the economy. For a comprehensive treatment of this entire debate see Hutchinson, pp. 110–139.

14. John Graunt, *Natural and Political Observations mentioned in a following Index and made upon the Bills of Mortality* (London: 1662. Reprinted by Johns Hopkins Press, Baltimore, 1939), p. 6.

15. Sir William Petty, *Essays on Mankind and Political Arithmetic* (London: Cassell, 1894). This is a collection of Petty's essays written between 1682 and 1687, the year of his death.

16. Kurt Mayer, "Developments in the Study of Population," *Social Research,* 29: 296 (1962).

17. Malthus, pp. 11, 13, 14.

18. Malthus, p. 100.

19. Malthus, p. 71.

20. Mayer, p. 298.

21. Kingsley Davis, "The Sociology of Demographic Behavior," in *Sociology Today,* edited by Robert K. Merton, Leonard Broom, and Leonard S. Cottrell (New York: Basic Books, 1959), p. 313.

22. Warren S. Thompson and David T. Lewis, *Population Problems,* 5th edition (New York: McGraw Hill, 1965), p. 35.

23. Petersen, *Population,* p. 166.

24. For an excellent presentation of the pre-Malthusian writers who had advanced similar ideas, see Hutchinson, pp. 110–139.

Chapter 2 The Data

DEMOGRAPHY AS AN OBSERVATIONAL SCIENCE

The study of population is an empirical science, and the task of any science is to describe, explain, and predict the events connected with some phenomenon. To achieve these general goals there is a need for data. It is possible to classify the sciences on the basis of how their data are commonly obtained. One such categorization is to divide the sciences into two types: the "observational" and the "experimental."[1] The observational sciences are those whose data are produced by observing and recording events occurring naturally in the world. The experimental sciences are those in which the data are generally produced by experiments conducted in the laboratory under conditions controlled by the experimenter. *Demography is basically an observational science.*

The categories "observational science" and "experimental science" are abstractions, and like all abstractions they will not always fit the specific case perfectly. It is true that demographers have on occasion used experimental techniques to develop generalizations or test hypotheses about population. One example of experimental research goes back to the 1920s when Pearl, a biologist-demographer, conducted a series of studies on the growth patterns of insect populations under laboratory conditions.[2] Using the *Drosophila*, the common fruit fly, Pearl established that with a fixed food supply and in a finite environment the size of the insect population grew in a regular cyclical pattern. When a few insects were placed in a bottle with food, the population grew slowly at first, then increased rapidly, and finally reached a peak where it leveled off. The resulting growth curve, known as the *logistic curve*, is shown in Figure 1. Pearl believed that this growth curve could be used to characterize the growth of human populations as well as insects. While this idea was appealing to many demographers, it did not prove to be very effective for predicting the growth of either national populations or the world population.

A more recent application of the experimental research design can be found in a study of Puerto Rican family-planning programs.[3] In this research, the investigators sought to test experimentally some of the hypotheses that had been developed with more conventional survey-research methods. They conducted their experiments in a natural community setting instead of a laboratory, but the research design did allow them to observe the effects of a number of experimentally controlled factors. Essentially they sought to determine the effects of various educational techniques on the success of a family-planning

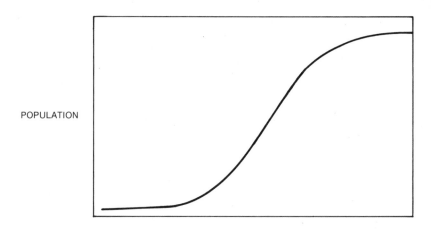

TIME

FIGURE 1. THE LOGISTIC CURVE

program. Different groups of Puerto Rican families were exposed to different modes of presentation and program content to see which would improve and increase their use of contraception. Follow-up studies conducted after completion of the educational programs measured the effectiveness of the various approaches by comparing the experimental families with a control group of families.

The experimental procedures used in the Puerto Rican study are more likely to be the type undertaken by demographers of the future than are the more precise laboratory experiments, but it is not likely that the controlled experiment will ever be a primary research technique of demography. In general, demography is like astronomy and meteorology in that most of the data in these sciences come from observations of naturally occurring events.

One of the characteristics of demography as an observational science is that the data are dispersed. The data are distributed and "spread out" in time and space. Demographers are concerned with events such as births, deaths, and migration, which are occurring over wide geographical areas. These same demographic events are spread out in time; that is, a great percentage of them have occurred in the historical past.

Because the data of population are widely dispersed in space, any single demographer can gather only a very small proportion of the data he needs to describe population phenomena or to test hypotheses and build generalizations. The births, deaths, and migration of people are occurring constantly and throughout the territory occupied by a population. New members of the population are being born, people are dying, and people are moving. Recording these naturally occurring events in any but the smallest society would be an impossible task for any one scientist. In order to have the population facts, the demographer must almost always use data gathered by other people. Most of the data he uses are gathered by people over whom he has no control, and under circumstances where he has no control. For example, the demographer often uses census data that have been collected by and primarily for the state. He also makes frequent use of the data assembled by the vital-registration systems of the society.

A good scientist must always be concerned with the quality of his data, but whenever he does not have personal control over the data-gathering process he must be especially on guard against the errors and inadequacies that lower data quality. To avoid the dangers of working with faulty data, demographers have given considerable attention to the techniques of census taking and the methods of registering vital statistics. Some of the techniques of census taking as well as the kinds of errors that are found in such data will be discussed below.

Another feature of the dispersed nature of demographic data concerns the demographer. There are relevant population data spread out over time as well as space, and these demographic events of the past are often even less accessible to the individual demographer. Even when the demographer needs only simple descriptive facts about populations of the past, he may find it difficult or impossible to get them. If no observations were made and recorded at the time of their occurrence, then the facts may have been lost forever. Today in most modern societies there is an abundance of facts and figures about most things, including population, but this widespread availability of data is a very recent development in the history of the world. Even some very simple demographic questions about American society in the eighteenth and nineteenth centuries can be answered only tentatively and with considerable guesswork. And there are still some countries that to this day do not have a trustworthy system for gathering and recording the data of the society.

To provide the needed historical data on population, the field of *historical demography* has developed.[4] In many ways this field, which is attracting historians, sociologists, and demographers, is reminiscent of political arithmetic in the seventeenth century. In fact, the parish record, a source of data for John Graunt, is again coming in for a good deal of attention. Even the motivations of the historical demographers parallel those of the early political arithmeticians. First, both groups of scholars are motivated primarily by an intellectual curiosity intensified by the difficulties and challenges involved with obtaining the data. Second, some concerns of both the political arithmeticians and the historical demographers are with practical, or applied, matters. While the political arithmeticians wanted to serve their government by providing information on the human and economic resources of the society, the practical concerns of today's historical demographers are more likely to be an interest in the demographic problems currently facing the world. On the assumption that there are some similarities between the economic and social conditions in European countries two hundred to four hundred years ago and the conditions now prevailing in many of the underdeveloped countries, some historical demographers have argued that it would be useful to have as much information as possible about the economic, social, and demographic histories of the earlier period.[5] An understanding of the relationship between economic development and population growth in Europe at that time may improve our understanding of similar, or contrasting, processes going on today in the underdeveloped societies.

There are increasing efforts by historical demographers to establish and improve the quality of their data and the methods for dealing with them. Among the most frequently used sources of data, parish records of births (christenings), marriages, and deaths are still proving to be the most useful. Historical demographers are particularly skillful at assessing and assembling these data, and drawing the maximum possible information from them. Consider, for example, the following population facts that have been established by historical demographers.

A high proportion of the English peasants, craftsmen, laborers, and others during the seventeenth and eighteenth centuries were first married in their late twenties or early thirties. This is a specific instance of what has been labeled the "European marriage pattern,"[6] which is a combination of late marriage and high rates of nonmarriage that prevailed in preindustrial Europe. It has now been established that many countries of Western Europe experienced late marriage and a high proportion of unmarried people for several centuries prior to 1800. This particular pattern, existing as it did in a preindustrial society, contrasts dramatically with other peasant societies of the past and the undeveloped societies of the present.

Another example of the fruitfulness of historical demography is found in a study of infant and general mortality in England for the three centuries prior to 1800.[7] For this research the technique of *family reconstitution* was used very effectively. Family reconstitution has been described as "the bringing together of scattered information about members of a family to enable its chief demographic characteristics to be described as fully as possible."[8] The technique is essentially a genealogical one, which traces the vital events of a family line over time. With the appropriate precautions it has been possible to establish a sufficient number of family lineages to draw certain demographic conclusions.

One finding of this particular study was that infant mortality (deaths occurring between birth and one year of age) between the sixteenth and nineteenth centuries was not always uniformly high, but instead fluctuated. For example, the first half of the eighteenth century appears to have had a higher infant-mortality rate than those determined for the one hundred-fifty years that preceded it (at least in the particular English parish producing the data). This study also found that the average expectation of life at birth was 43.2 years between 1538 and 1625, 36.9 from 1626 to 1699, and 41.8 from 1700 to 1774. One might have supposed that the expected life span has steadily increased through history, but the historical demographers have shown that this is not true.

Going back still further into antiquity, the problem of data becomes more acute, for even such sources as parish records date back only to the sixteenth century. The problem becomes one of establishing even the most elementary demographic facts for earlier periods of time. One of the most interesting efforts involves the use of tombstone data to estimate the average length of life in a society. Several years ago, research was reported by Durand in which he estimated the average length of life during the first and second centuries in the Roman Empire.[9] To make mortality estimates he used the information appearing on Roman funeral tablets. Durand had to make allowances for social-class differences in burials and the underrepresentation of children's deaths, as well as various overstatements and understatements of age, but having done so, he was able to make an estimate of the average length of life in the Roman Empire. His surprising conclusion was that the expectation of life at birth was between 25 and 30 years for the population of the Roman Empire. As Durand noted in reporting these high levels of mortality, no twentieth-century society has had a recorded mortality level which reflected such a short average length of life.

MODERN SOURCES OF POPULATION DATA

In the twentieth century the most common sources of population data have been vital-registration systems and censuses, and, for those countries where they exist, continuing registers of the population. While these traditional sources still prevail in the study of population, new research methodologies are being used more and more in recent years. Especially in the last fifteen years, population data have often been obtained by special surveys and other sociological inquiries. But it has taken quite a number of years for many demographers to accept and use these nontraditional data sources. Demographers have always had a large amount of "hard" population data readily available because census taking has long been a regular practice in European countries and the United States. The quality of census data may have left something to be desired, and the data may not have been in the most useful form, but with ingenuity and skill the census and vital-statistics data were made to yield information on a great many population questions.

This ready and voluminous source of population data had some significant effects upon the emergence of demography during the first three decades of the twentieth century. First, demography (or more exactly, formal demography) probably attracted scholars who had some propensity toward the use of statistical data and quantitative techniques. Second, since the field attracted and recruited people with these preferences, it is likely that a professional culture developed that, at least initially, resisted certain other kinds of data. While these other kinds of data—for example, those produced by social surveys, social experiments, and observation—might have been useful, they were not generally valued by demographers because they did not originate in the census or the vital-statistics reports. Data on the attitudes and values of people, and data on their interaction patterns were largely rejected by the formal demographers. In the process, they were overlooking variables that might have had great explanatory value. For example, such things as family role behavior, including power relations in the family and communication patterns between husbands and wives, have been shown in more recent research to be important in behavior related to fertility.[10] But because these kinds of data were not to be found in census volumes or vital-statistics reports, and because demographers were not enthusiastic about measuring attitudes and values, many potentially useful studies were not conducted until very recently.[11] Stycos has forcefully pointed out the implications of demographers' resistance to social-psychological data:

In a science dealing with three of the most basic human events and processes—birth, death, and migration—psychological, social, and cultural factors have been all but ignored as objects of scientific inquiry. It is probably fair to say, even now [1963] that we know more about what people expect, want, and do with respect to planting wheat or purchasing T.V. sets than with respect to having babies.[12]

It is worth noting that this aversion to nontraditional sources of population data has probably been reduced greatly among most demographers in recent years, largely because of the productiveness of researchers who have chosen to utilize the results of special surveys and other sociological studies. As a case in point, Blake used data from public-opinion polls to answer a variety of questions about fertility motivations.[13] These data were used quite effectively to establish that there were significant changes in fertility preferences after World War II which account for the higher fertility of that era.

The Continuous Population Register

The continuous population register is an excellent source of population data but is not widely used by demographers, primarily because it is found in so few countries. A continuous population register is a complete and ongoing record of the vital events in each individual's life (birth, permanent moves within the country, emigration, marriages, divorces, children, and death).

Such a comprehensive record for each individual is probably feasible only in countries with relatively small populations and a high degree of stability and literacy. Continuing registers are in fact found only in the smaller countries of Northern Europe (Belgium, Denmark, Finland, the Netherlands, Norway, and Sweden). Because the continuous population register is particularly useful for the study of internal migration, data from these countries are often used to test migration hypotheses.

The Registration of Vital Statistics

The vital events of a population are usually recorded by means of a registration system rather than a continuous population register. The political system makes legal requirements that births, deaths, marriages, and divorces must be registered with some official, generally at the local level. The parish records discussed above were the ecclesiastical forerunners of civil registration systems.

In the United States, the methods of acquiring population data through the census and a vital-registration system were greatly influenced by the establishment of a federal system of government which delegated a great many powers to the individual states. The Constitution provided for the election of a House of Representatives on the basis of population, and therefore called for an enumeration of the population at regular ten-year intervals. It was this feature of the federal system of government that assured the people of the United States a continuing body of population data from a regular census. But ironically this same federal system doomed the vital-registration system to inadequacy and incompleteness for many years, because it gave a great deal of power and autonomy to the individual states. Specifically, if the responsibility for a task was not indicated in the Constitution, it was left to the discretion of the individual states. The states could decide *if* the task was to be performed, and *how* it was to be performed. Since the United States Constitution did not provide for a uniform system of registering vital events, it was left to the individual states and other minor political subdivisions to carry out the task in whatever way they saw fit. The result was a system of widely varying and inconsistent methods. Such variety in the collection of vital statistics has made the task of accumulating data for the entire country difficult.

Compared to most modern countries, the American system of registering vital events has been very late in developing. The collection of death statistics on an annual basis started in 1900, but at that time only ten states and the District of Columbia were supplying information. In 1915, the national collection of birth statistics began, also with ten states and the District of Columbia. In 1933, for the first time all the states in the United States were submitting data on both births and deaths. The data on marriages and divorces are still obtained from only a portion of the states. As late as 1967, only 36 states were reporting information on marriage, and as few as 22 were providing information on divorce.[14]

Even now the freedom of individual states to set their own rules creates some problems for those who would use the data for scientific purposes. As a recent example, in the year 1963 the state of New Jersey did not record racial data on the birth and death registration forms. Removing the racial designation was apparently in response to the demands of civil-rights groups who viewed the recording of racial information as a form of institutionalized racism. It is understandable that many people would seek to eliminate racial designations from official forms, for such practices did originate in a time when most people believed that race was a sufficient reason for treating people differently. Yet, though one may sympathize with those who would prefer to eliminate the artifacts of prejudice, demographers cannot but regret it when there is a loss of important social data. Negroes and whites differ on many demographic characteristics, but the differences are generally produced by social and cultural factors, not racial factors. However, the fact that the demographic characteristics of racial groups are produced by social institutions often needs to be demonstrated. A case in point is the discussion of the relationship between racial segregation and infant mortality that will be presented in Chapter 5. If residential segregation is producing higher rates of infant mortality among the Negroes in American society, then the facts of the case must be firmly established. This can be facilitated if the racial designations are retained on the vital registration and census forms. At this moment in American history there are practical as well as theoretical reasons for retaining racial designations.

The History of the Census

Censuses covering the total population of a society are a relatively recent phenomenon—they probably go back not more than three hundred years. The populations of some societies of the world have still not been enumerated, and some large populations like that of the Chinese are only sporadically counted. (China had her first modern census in 1953, and has had none since.) But while total-population censuses are of relatively recent origin, some counting of the population goes far back into antiquity. Some historical records of inquiries into population numbers have been dated back to 4000 B.C., in Babylonia; 3000 B.C., in China; and 2500 B.C., in Egypt.

Most early censuses were probably taken for the purpose of assessing the manpower strength of the tribe, society, or empire. A biblical reference to the counting of a population is illustrative of this point:

> Satan stood up against Israel, and David said to Joab and the commanders of the army, "Go, number Israel, from Beersheba to Dan, and bring me a report, that I may know their number." But Joab said, "May the Lord add to his people a hundred times

as many as they are! Why then should my lord require this? Why should he bring guilt upon Israel?" But the king's word prevailed against Joab. So Joab departed and went throughout all Israel, and came back to Jerusalem. And Joab gave the sum of the numbering of the people to David. In all Israel there were one million one hundred thousand men who drew the sword, and in Judah four hundred and seventy thousand who drew the sword.

But God was displeased with this thing, and he smote Israel.[15]

There are two significant points found in this passage. First, it is clear that those who were counted were the "men who drew the sword." This population count was an assessment of the military strength and capabilities of the nation. Throughout most of history, counts of the population have been made for the purpose of assessing the military and/or economic resources—that is, the taxable population—of the society. The results of such censuses were viewed as military secrets, much as the counts of intercontinental ballistic missiles are kept secret by present-day governments.

The second significant point that may be drawn from the biblical passage is the indication, through God's displeasure, that counting the population was viewed as inherently evil. The reason why a census should be so viewed is unclear, though it might have been taken as an indication of too much concern with secular or worldly matters. Whatever the reason, it is probably true that the very presence of this negative attitude in the Bible kept the practice from developing in many societies of Western Europe for centuries.

Even today in the United States some religious groups refuse to cooperate with census takers because doing so seems to be paying too much homage to the state. Also, increasingly in recent years the census has been under attack from people who believe that it invades the privacy of the citizen and provides the government with information that could be used to control and manipulate the people. This recent campaign against the census has been fostered by ultraconservative propaganda organizations; editorials in newspapers, on radio, and on television; and a surprising array of Congressmen. By early in 1969, sixty-five bills had been introduced into the House of Representatives aimed at modifying and limiting the 1970 census.[16]

The Modern Census

Historians of population do not agree as to exactly which country should have the credit for conducting the first complete, and therefore modern, census. Some say it should be Canada since a complete census was carried out in the Province of Quebec in 1666, while others contend that Sicily and various other Italian states were the first to do so, in the fifteenth century. Sweden is usually credited with conducting the first modern nationwide census, in the year 1749.[17]

Beginning in 1790 in the United States, and 1801 in Great Britain, the census achieved the status of a regular governmental function. The place of the United States in this historical consideration is extremely important, for it was with the writing of the Constitution that the census at set intervals of time became a regular feature of the government.

Article I, Section 2 of the Constitution, as it was originally ratified, stated:

> Representatives and direct Taxes shall be apportioned among the several States . . . according to their respective Numbers, which shall be determined by adding to the whole Number of free Persons, including those bound to Service for a Term of Years, and excluding Indians not taxed, three fifths of all other Persons. The actual Enumeration shall be made within three Years after the first Meeting of the Congress of the United States and within every subsequent Term of ten Years, in such Manner as they shall by Law direct.

With the ratification of the 14th Amendment in 1868, the first sentence of this clause was modified so as to be consistent with the freeing of slaves.

Since the federal system of government of the United States gave lower-house representation to the states in proportion to their population, the ten-year, or decennial, census was firmly established. Furthermore, since the enumeration was for the purpose of apportioning representatives and direct taxes, the information gathered was necessarily public knowledge. In the United States the count of the population could not be a state secret as population figures had so often been in other countries.

The Constitution called for the census to be taken "in such a Manner as they [the Congress] shall by Law direct." This open-ended directive has made it possible for the census to expand greatly over the years. In the first census, taken in 1790, only six questions were asked, and the total report of the census was contained in fifty-six pages. Today the report runs to over fifty volumes. There are separate bound volumes for each state, a summary of the United States population, and many special-report volumes. The decisions about which questions will be asked and how they may best be asked are the result of a continuing dialogue among Census Bureau officials, legislators, business-men, social scientists, and other interested parties.

Types of Censuses

A few basic distinctions may be made about types of censuses. One distinction has to do with the place of residence of the persons enumerated. In a *de jure* census, each individual is classified as living at his usual place of residence. In contrast, the *de facto* census classifies a person according to the place where he is when counted. Because the United States census is concerned in part with establishing the population size of the various states, the *de jure* method is used. Several weeks are required to carry out the census, and it is not meaningful to count people as residents of the place where they just happen to be at the time they are counted. The *de facto* census works best if the population is rather small, and general directives can be issued instructing people to remain in their homes during the hours of the count (usually at night or on a weekend). It is obvious that even though a country may conduct a *de facto* census, the objective is usually to approximate the results of a *de jure* census, since the aim is to record people according to where they usually reside.

A second major distinction refers to the method by which the data are gathered. With the *householder method*, sometimes called *self-enumeration*, the citizen completes the questions on the census form himself. The alternative is the *canvasser method*, whereby the census taker or interviewer asks questions of the resident and records the answers. Until 1960 the United States census was a canvasser census, but since then it has been largely a householder census.

The 1970 United States Census

In the 1970 census the majority of Americans received census forms in the mail and were requested to return them in the same fashion. This was called the two-way mail method and was used for about sixty percent of the population. For the remaining forty percent—primarily those who lived outside of the major urbanized areas—the census forms were delivered by the post office, but were collected by a census taker. This was called the one-way method.

At four out of five households the census form was quite brief, asking only seven questions for each individual residing there, and thirteen questions relating to the house. For twenty percent of the households additional questions were asked about the residents and the house. Within this twenty percent there were two different forms, one going to fifteen percent of the households, the other and the most extensive form, going to only five percent of the households (see Appendix 5, the 1970 United States census forms). For those households in which the one-way mail method was used the census taker interviewed the householders who were being asked questions beyond the basic set. Thus, among this portion of the American population the canvasser form of census taking was partially retained.

Census Errors

Since the demographer is dependent upon census data, he must be cognizant of the errors that are likely to occur. Knowledge of such shortcomings may not actually allow the demographer to correct the data, but at least he can be aware of the areas in which he must be cautious.

Because of the vast accumulated experience of the Census Bureau, many readers may find it difficult to believe that serious errors can occur in the census of the United States. Unfortunately, errors do occur, but before documenting this assertion it should be emphasized that, taking into account the size of the population being enumerated, the United States Census is probably as accurate as any census in the world.

It is somewhat surprising to note that, while 180 million people were counted in 1960, an estimated 5.7 million people were missed.[18] More important than the absolute number of the persons missed by the census takers is the fact that those missed were not randomly distributed in the population, but were members of particular categories and groups.

Siegel, of the Census Bureau, reported that in 1960 about 98 percent of the resident White population was counted, but only about 90.5 percent of the resident non-White population was counted. (About 90 percent of the non-Whites were classified as Negroes by the Census Bureau; most of the remainder were Chinese, Japanese, American Indians, and Filipinos.) Siegel also noted that among the non-Whites the undercount was greater for the males than for the females. In 1960, 11 percent of the non-White males and 8 percent of the non-White females were not enumerated. The category most likely to be missed by the census takers was the non-White male group between the ages of 20 and 39 years; 17 percent, or one out of every six men in this group, was not included in the count of the United States population. It hardly needs to be stated that such an astounding degree of error makes the data for this particular age-sex group nearly useless for any demographic analysis. Furthermore, it has been pointed out that the significance of this undercount of non-Whites, many of whom come from the Black ghettos of our major cities, is "not simply a scholarly or ideological quibble; this is a social problem with powerful legal and ethical implications. The census is not simply a public service the government provides for sales managers, sociologists, and regional planners. It is a constitutional process whereby political representation in Congress is distributed."[19]

Other analysts of the census, including employees of the Census Bureau, have pointed out that there are errors in the census reports other than undercounts. For example, in follow-up surveys, in which highly trained interviewers reinterview samples of the population (this is called the Post-enumerative Survey), sizeable percentages of people are not classified in the same way by the interviewer as they were in the original census. An illustration of such misclassification may be found in the case of educational attainment level, as measured by the highest school grade completed. This seems to be a clear-cut piece of information, but Table 2 shows that a high percentage of the respondents were not in the same classification in the Post-enumerative Survey as they were in the initial census report.

TABLE 2.   PERCENT OF CENSUS RESPONDENTS NOT IN SAME EDUCA-
TIONAL CLASSIFICATION IN COMPARISON WITH POST-ENUMER-
ATION SURVEY. 1960 CENSUS

Educational Attainment	Percent *not* in the same class as the Post-enumeration Survey
1–2 years	59.62%
3–4 years	35.83%
5–6 years	33.14%
7 years	38.74%
8 years	23.79%
Elementary, total (not in the same specific class)	31.48%
High School 1 year	34.80%
High School 2 years	35.88%
High School 3 years	41.39%
High School 4 years	14.39%
High School, total (not in the same specific class)	23.56%
College 1 year	29.80%
College 2 years	27.40%
College 3 years	35.60%
College 4 years or more	5.48%
College, total (not in the same specific class)	19.09%
TOTAL	25.78%

Source: Donald Bogue, "The Pros and Cons of 'Self-Enumeration,'" *Demography*, 2: 617-618 (1965). (Reprinted by permission.)

It seems almost impossible, but more than one-fourth of the respondents were given a different educational-attainment level by the Post-enumerative Survey interviewer than they had been given on the basis of the original census form. Keep in mind that in 1960 the original census form was self-administered and therefore probably filled out by the respondent or a member of his family.

Table 2 was drawn from a larger analysis of the 1960 census conducted by Bogue from which he concluded that the self-enumeration procedures used in 1960 did little to improve the quality of American census data. In particular, Bogue emphasized that the current methods create some serious problems with regard to enumerating the lower economic groups in our society. It was among the poor and less educated that many of the errors were concentrated.[20]

Since many of the census errors appear to involve the poorly educated members of the society, the continued increase in the educational level of the United States and other developed countries will probably improve the quality of census data. In addition, there will probably be continued improvements in the procedures of census taking which will also increase the validity of the data. These trends might lead us to feel complacent about the problem of errors in the data. But there are many countries in the world where the educational and literacy levels are very low and the data-gathering organizations are quite inexperienced. These are the very countries that will be demographically most important in the coming decades. The lessons that have been learned from European and American census-taking experiences must be recognized and applied in the developing countries.

SUMMARY

The science of demography has been and continues to be for the most part an observational science. The observational sciences are those in which data come from naturally occurring events rather than being generated in the laboratory. Since the events that produce the data are spread out both spatially and temporally, the demographer cannot make the observations himself, but must rely on the recordings of others. The political arithmeticians faced this problem in the seventeenth century, and it is still the basic problem of present-day demographers, whether their interests are historical or contemporary.

The major traditional sources of population data are censuses, vital-registration systems, or, if available, continuing registers of the population. Demographers in the past often limited themselves to the kinds of studies that could be conducted with the data coming from these traditional sources. However, students of population are increasingly turning to special studies and surveys for data, particularly data on values, attitudes, and expectations. These kinds of population studies have resulted in great improvements in our knowledge of the human motivations affecting population behavior, and one could expect that the next decade will witness even more fruitful studies of this kind.

: : SELECTED READINGS AND MATERIALS

General

Barclay, George W. *Techniques of Population Analysis.* New York, John Wiley and Sons, 1958.

Hauser, Philip M., and Otis Dudley Duncan, editors. *The Study of Population: An Inventory and Appraisal.* Chicago, University of Chicago Press, 1959. Chapter 2, "The Data and Methods."

Heer, David M., editor. *Social Statistics and the City.* Cambridge, Mass., Joint Center for Urban Studies of the Massachusetts Institute of Technology and Harvard University, 1968.

Kammeyer, Kenneth C. W., editor. *Population Studies: Selected Essays and Research.* Chicago, Rand-McNally, 1969. Section II, "The Data of Demography."

Nam, Charles B., editor. *Population and Society: A Textbook of Selected Readings.* Boston, Houghton Mifflin, 1968. Chapter 1, "The Nature of Population Data."

Wolfenden, Hugh H., *Population Statistics and their Composition.* Revised edition. Chicago, University of Chicago Press, 1954.

Major Sources of Population Data

United Nations. *Demographic Yearbook.* New York, United Nations. Published annually. The *Yearbook* contains the basic demographic statistics for over 200 countries.

United States Bureau of the Census. *Statistical Abstract of the United States.* Washington, D.C., Government Printing Office. Published annually. The *Statistical Abstract* provides authoratative data on vital rates as well as much social and economic data.

United States Bureau of the Census. *United States Census of the Population, 1970.* The results of the census of the population taken in April 1970 will be published as a series of preliminary and final reports during 1970, 1971, and 1972. *Volume I. Characteristics of the Population* will consist of separate reports of the entire United States, each of the 50 states, the District of Columbia, Puerto Rico, Guam, Virgin Islands, American Samoa, Canal Zone, and The Trust Territory of the Pacific. For each of these 58 areas there will be four parts making up *Volume I:* A. *Number of Inhabitants;* B. *General Population Characteristics;* C. *General Social and Economic Characteristics;* and D. *Detailed Characteristics.* These four parts will first be issued as separate paperbound chapters; at a later time they will be assembled and issued in hard-cover volumes. *Volume II* will be a series of *Subject Reports,* to be issued in 1972. Each report will concentrate on a particular subject. For example, there will be *Special Reports* on national origin and race, fertility, families, migration, education, employment, unemployment, occupation, industry and income. A major portion of the results of the 1970 Census will also be on magnetic computer tape that will be made available to researchers at cost.

United States Public Health Service. *Vital Statistics of the United States.* *Volume I, Natality; Volume II, Mortality; Volume III, Marriage and*

Divorce. Washington, D.C., Government Printing Office. Published Annually.

: : NOTES

1. This distinction follows the discussion of Philip M. Hauser and Otis Dudley Duncan, *The Study of Population: An Inventory and Appraisal* (Chicago: University of Chicago Press, 1959), pp. 45–46.

2. Raymond Pearl, *The Biology of Population Growth* (New York: Knopf, 1925).

3. Reuben Hill, J. Mayone Stycos, and Kurt W. Back, *The Family and Population Control* (Chapel Hill: University of North Carolina Press, 1959).

4. Four recent publications signal the emerging importance of historical demography: D. V. Glass and D. E. C. Eversley, *Population in History* (Chicago: Aldine, 1965); Edward A. Wrigley, *An Introduction to English Historical Demography,* (New York: Basic Books, 1966); Edward A. Wrigley, *Population and History* (New York: McGraw-Hill, 1969); and *Daedalus,* issue titled *Historical Population Studies,* 97 (1968).

5. Roger Revelle, "Introduction," *Daedalus,* 97: 353–354 (1968).

6. J. Hajnal, "European Marriage Patterns in Perspective," in D. V. Glass and D. E. C. Eversley, pp. 101–143.

7. E. A. Wrigley, "Mortality in Pre-Industrial England: The Example of Colyton, Devon, Over Three Centuries." *Daedalus, op. cit.,* pp. 546–580.

8. Wrigley, *An Introduction,* p. 96.

9. John D. Durand, "Mortality Estimates from Roman Tombstone Inscriptions," *American Journal of Sociology,* 65: 372 (January 1960).

10. Hill, Stycos, and Back, pp. 142–162.

11. Demographers began to use social-psychological studies in 1939. This year marks the time when leading American demographers met to discuss and plan the first major social-psychological study of the factors affecting fertility. This meeting eventually led to the "Indianapolis Study of the Social and Psychological Factors Affecting Fertility" (See Chapter 6).

12. J. Mayone Stycos, "Obstacles to Programs of Population Control—Facts and Fancies," *Marriage and Family Living,* 25: 5 (1963).

13. Judith Blake, "Ideal Family Size Among White Americans: A Quarter of a Century's Evidence," *Demography,* 3: 154–173 (1966).

14. U.S. Bureau of the Census, *Statistical Abstract of the United States: 1967,* 88th edition (Washington, D.C.: U.S. Government Printing Office, 1967), pp. 45–46.

15. I Chronicles 21: 1–7. Revised Standard Version.

16. "The Census Inquisition," *Population Bulletin,* 25 (May 1969).

17. Hugh Wolfenden, *Population Statistics and Their Compilation* (Chicago: University of Chicago Press, 1954), p. 6

18. Jacob S. Siegel, "Completeness of Coverage of the Nonwhite Population in the 1960 Census and Current Estimates and Some Implications," in *Social Statistics and the City,* David Heer, ed. (Cambridge, Mass: Joint Center for Urban Studies of the Massachusetts Institute of Technology and Harvard University, 1968), p. 41. The following discussion is based on Siegel's analysis.

19. "The Census—What's Wrong With It, What Can Be Done," *Trans-Action,* 5: 49 (1968).

20. Donald Bogue, "The Pros and Cons of 'Self-Enumeration,'" *Demography,* 2: 624 (1965).

Chapter 3 Population Composition

This chapter examines the reasons why a consideration of population composition is often important. It presents some of the measures and tools that demographers employ to summarize the composition of a population, and describes some structural features of the United States population, past and present.

In practice, demographers typically deal with only a few characteristics. Their attention has most frequently been directed first toward age and sex composition, and then toward race, religion, and residence. Other important population characteristics are marital status, nationality, education, and occupation. Demographers have probably chosen to concentrate on these particular composition variables because each has been found to influence demographic behavior in some way. If a population characteristic has very little influence on fertility, migration, or mortality, it usually attracts little attention from demographers. Such characteristics as height, weight, hair color, or political-party affiliation do not typically interest them.

Actually, other features of some of these characteristics probably operate to make them widely used variables: the characteristics are readily ascertainable, relatively well defined, and accurately recorded. It was noted in Chapter 2 that traditional demographers have a preference for "hard" quantitative data. Age and sex, for example, are two characteristics that are usually recorded in statistical data and are conveniently available to demographers. As a result, there is a great deal of information about the interrelations between age and sex composition and other demographic phenomena. While no one would deny the importance of age and sex as demographic variables, it is relevant to ask, What would be learned if the degree of attention these variables have received had been devoted to the effects of some other characteristics? Would demographers be better able to explain and predict population patterns? For example, the decline in American fertility, which started in 1957 and continued for at least a decade, can be explained in part by a changing age structure. The early part of the decline (1957-1961) has been largely accounted for by the relatively small number of women in the most productive childbearing years, but since 1961 other factors seem to have been producing the decline in fertility.[1] While these other factors have not been identified precisely, they can be generally characterized as motivational. Demographers know very little about the distribution of fertility motivations in the population, and even less about their particular effect on fertility. This lack of information is partially attributable to the fact that motivational factors are not as conveniently available, nor as easily and reliably measurable as composition variables such as age and sex.

The treatment of composition variables in this book emphasizes their role as explanatory variables. The discussion later in this chapter shows that it is often necessary to hold composition variables constant when making certain kinds of comparisons of social rates. For example, in the illustration above it was necessary to take into account the changing age structure of the population in order to understand the decline in United States fertility rates since 1957. The changing age composition was a *partial* explanation for the decline in fertility after 1957.

AGE COMPOSITION AS A DEPENDENT VARIABLE

Composition variables can also be viewed as *dependent*, or *effect*, *variables*. Since this aspect of population composition does not receive much emphasis in the pages that follow, one illustration will be presented here. A very interesting case showing the effect of a demographic rate on a composition variable is the surprising influence that declining mortality may have on the average age of a population. A reduction of death rates can have the effect of making the average age of the population somewhat younger than it would have been if the rates had not declined. It may seem impossible that a decline in death rates could have the effect of lowering the average age of a population, but that is exactly what can happen. Coale has stated, with regard to the United States population, that, "[h]ad the risks of death prevailing in 1900 continued unchanged, and the other variables—rates of immigration and rates of childbearing per mother—followed the course they actually did, the average age of the population today would be greater than it is."[2] The reason that a declining death rate has this effect is relatively simple once it has been adequately analyzed. Any reduction in mortality rate will increase the average length of life of the total population. But reductions in mortality can occur at any place in the age structure. While all age levels have benefited from declining mortality in the United States, the improvements have not been evenly distributed. The greatest decline in death rates occurred among infants and very young children. When there are fewer deaths among children in the first few years of life, more young people are added to the population. In effect, each child saved during these early years is equivalent to an additional birth. Furthermore, in about twenty years these children, who might otherwise have died, will again add to the younger part of the population by having children of their own—and if mortality rates have continued to decline, an even higher proportion of their babies will live. In summary, if mortality rates decline and the average length of life increases primarily because of reductions in infant and childhood mortality, the effect of reduced mortality will be to produce a younger population.

In the United States and in European countries, the average age of the population did not in fact go down as mortality rates dropped. The average age of the population has gone up in the twentieth century, but the cause was not declining mortality; it was declining fertility. While a high proportion of babies lived, there were fewer babies born per mother, and this was the factor that caused the age of the population to increase.

AGE AND SEX COMPOSITION

Knowledge of the age and sex composition of a population is often very important for a proper understanding of societal phenomena, but this information is frequently overlooked or ignored by the nondemographer. When societies, or segments of a society, are compared with regard to the rate of some occurrence, one must assume either that the units being compared have roughly the same age and sex structure, or that age and sex are unrelated to the occurrence. The example provided by a classic sociological study will give some concreteness to this idea.

Suicide, Marital Status, and Age Composition

In 1897 the French sociologist Durkheim first published his study of suicide.[3] Durkheim was advancing a sociological explanation of suicide (as opposed to psychological or other explanations), and a key element in his theory was that persons who are socially integrated are less likely to commit suicide than persons who are not. For example, social integration may prevail when a person belongs to a highly cohesive religious community. Durkheim found that Jews and Catholics had lower rates of suicide than Protestants, and concluded that this was so because the two former religious groups were more integrated and more supportive of collective life. Following this line of thought, Durkheim examined the relationship between marital status and suicide rates. Using the data on suicides from all of France for the years 1873 to 1878, Durkheim found that 16,264 suicides were married persons and 11,709 were unmarried. Durkheim noted in his analysis that if one were to take these figures at face value one would conclude that being married (with all of its attendant burdens and responsibilities) increased the tendency toward suicide. But he observed that a very large number of unmarried persons were less than 16 years old, while almost all married persons were older. Furthermore—and this was the important point—up to the age of 16 the tendency to commit suicide was very slight. In other words, suicide was related to age, so that in any comparison of the suicide rates of the married and unmarried segments of the population, the different age structures of the two categories had to be taken into account. That is exactly what Durkheim did. According to his calculations, the unmarried persons above 16 had a suicide rate of 173 per million people, while the married persons above 16 had a rate of only 154.4 per million. By comparing the rates for married and unmarried people who were over 16 years of age, Durkheim had at least partially taken age into account. The figures supported his theory that the married would be more socially integrated and have a lower suicide rate. But Durkheim noted that even this analysis had assumed that all unmarried persons and married persons over 16 were of the same average age; that is, that the two populations had the same age structure. Durkheim guessed that this assumption was not true, and indeed it was not, for the average age of all unmarried men was about 27, of all unmarried women about 28, while the average age of married persons was between 40 and 45 years of age. Since, as Durkheim noted, suicide was not only rare among the young but increased progressively with age, one would expect the married people in the population to have a higher rate of suicide simply because they were, on the average, about 15 years older than the unmarried people. By taking the difference in age structure into account, Durkheim concluded that marriage reduced the danger of suicide by about one-half. It was the great care that Durkheim took to consider the age structure of the married and unmarried populations that allowed him to substantiate this part of his theory of suicide.

Age Composition and the Crime Rate

It may seem to the reader that the influence on behavior patterns of the age and sex structure of a population is so obvious that no thinking person would ever neglect it in his analysis. Yet one frequently finds instances where the age-sex composition of a population may be influential, but it is still neglected. Just as one example, it is fairly common knowledge that crimes, particularly crimes against property such as burglary, theft, and robbery, are more often committed by young men (ages 15-24) than any other age-sex category. Thus, any discussion of changing crime rates in a population should take into consideration significant changes in the age structure of the population. If more people are reaching the age of fifteen each year than reached that age in the immediately preceding years, the effect may be an increase in the proportion of the population in the 15-24 age group. Crime rates are generally reported on the basis of the number of crimes per 100,000 total population; thus, the rate ignores possible changes in the age structure. It is entirely possible that an increase in the number of crimes per 100,000 population may reflect, in part or wholly, the larger numbers of people in the age-sex category that contributes most to the crime rate generally. The United States is in fact experiencing a demographic situation in which large numbers of youngsters are reaching age fifteen each year, because the number of babies born per year increased quite dramatically in the years following 1945. Babies born in 1947 reached their fifteenth birthday in 1962, so each year since 1962 the United States may have had an increasing proportion of its population in the 15-24 age group. Naturally this proportion is also dependent on what has happened at other parts of the age scale. If the proportion of young men in the population has gone up, then the crime rate per 100,000 total population could also have gone up, even though for any specific age group the crime rate may not have changed.

It is not being argued that the crime rate in the United States has not in fact gone up. The point here is that unless age-structure changes are taken into account, or unless crime rates are reported for age-specific categories (say 15-24 age group), one cannot be certain that any real change has taken place. Incidentally, it must also be noted that crime rates may be greatly influenced by the manner in which crimes are reported to the authorities and the methods used to compile statistics.

Age Composition and Mortality

There are many instances in the study of population itself where an awareness of the age structure is essential. Often, when the vital rates (birth and death rates) of countries are compared, only the crude rates—the number of births or deaths per 1000 total population—are available. But the age structure of a society can significantly affect these demographic rates. For example, both the birth rate and the death rate may be influenced by the age structure. As a case in point, the crude death rate for the United States in 1969 was 9.6 (9.6 deaths per 1000 people in the population at midyear). This is a relatively low death rate, but there are a number of other countries around the world with similar or lower death rates. Some of these countries are less developed than the United States and might therefore be expected to have a higher mortality rate. The following countries had lower crude death rates than the United States: Malaysia, 8; Taiwan, 6; Costa Rica, 8; Jamaica, 8. Although all of these countries had a lower crude death rate than the United States, one may expect the average length of life of their people to be shorter. They have lower crude death rates because of their age structures. The United States has an older population than any of these countries, and thus experiences relatively more deaths in relation to its total population. An indication of the difference in age structures may be seen by comparing the percent of the total population under 15 years of age in these countries. For the United States, the figure was 30 percent in 1969, while the countries cited all ranged between 40 and 50 percent (Malaysia, 44 percent; Taiwan, 44 percent; Costa Rica, 48 percent; and Jamaica, 41 percent). The influence of the age structure on the crude death rate is clearly indicated by these comparisons. Generally, if a country has a young population, it will have a low crude death rate compared with countries with an older population.

Measures of Age and Sex Structure

There are several measures and graphic methods for describing or depicting the age and/or sex structure of a population. These tools are particularly useful when one wants to compare the populations of different societies or the population of the same society at various points in time.

Sex Ratio

An important and widely used measure is the *sex ratio*. The sex ratio is defined as the number of males in the population per 100 females. For example, a sex ratio of 102.4 would mean that there are 102.4 males for every 100 females in the population.

A number of factors influence the sex ratio of a population. Perhaps the most basic factor is the sex ratio at birth. There are more males born than females. Generally, the sex ratio at birth is above 102, and often it is as high as 105. Where living conditions are poor or difficult, the sex ratio at birth is likely to be somewhat lower, ranging down to the 102 level. It seems that under adverse living conditions the male fetus will not survive to birth as often as the female, and thus the sex ratio at birth will be lowered. This fact implies that the sex ratio at conception is even higher than 105, and that seems to be the case. Examination of fetuses that did not go to full term has revealed that the number of males aborted always exceeds the number of females; yet the number of males still exceeds females at birth.[4] Because females have better life chances than males after they have been born (see Chapter 5), the general conclusion with regard to sex and mortality is inescapable: from conception onward the female is more viable than the male.

A number of other factors often influence the balance between males and females in a given society or community. First, some cultural practices may be particularly hazardous for one sex or the other. Historically, there have been cultures that valued males more than females, and thus practiced some degree of female infanticide. Both India and China are examples of major cultures that have practiced female infanticide, though the degree of influence these practices have had on the sex ratio is not known.

Many societies follow the cultural practice of subjecting males, particularly the strongest and healthiest, to great hazards through dangerous hunting activities or fighting wars. Several countries of Western Europe have noticeable shortages of males at various age levels resulting from the losses of young men in World Wars I and II.

The sex ratio of a society, or a region within a society, may be greatly affected by the prevailing migration patterns. Generally speaking, whenever an area has been settled by migration that covered great distances, or where the journey was in some way arduous, the sex ratio is very high. (Immigration to the United States since World War II runs counter to this generalization [see Chapter 4].) On the other hand, if the migration route covered a relatively short distance, the sex ratio is likely to be below 100. An example of this situation is the urban center with a large rural hinterland. The flow of migration from the rural place to the urban place is often produced by the job market, particularly the need for many female employees. This may produce an overabundance of females in the city. The outstanding illustration of this phenomenon in American society is Washington, D.C., which had a sex ratio of 88.3 in 1960.

Occasionally a cultural practice can create an apparent sex imbalance where in reality none exists. An example can be found in what has been labeled the "marriage squeeze."[5] This colorful label refers to an imbalance between the number of males and females at the prime marriage ages of the two sexes. Generally, no serious imbalance would occur if the prime marriage age of the sexes were the same. However, in most societies females typically marry males older than themselves. In recent decades in the United States, women have been marrying men who average about two and one-half years older. For females the average age at first marriage is somewhat above 20, and for males it is nearly 23. As a result of this pattern, there will be an imbalance of the sexes at prime marriage age whenever there has been a pronounced increase or decrease in births about twenty years earlier. An increase in fertility will lead to a shortage of marriage-age males. But, a decrease in fertility will result in the opposite—a shortage of marriage-age females. A dramatic increase in fertility occurred in the United States in the 1940s when the "baby boom" produced many more children in 1947 than had been born during the last years of World War II. The result is that the females born during the years 1947 and 1948 exceed the males born in 1945 and 1946. By a recent estimate, 21 percent of the females born during one year of the baby boom (July 1946 through June 1947) will not be matched by males born two years earlier. Within this cohort of women, 400,000 are not matched by men of the age they would normally marry. The exact manner in which this culturally created sex imbalance will be resolved remains to be seen, but one recent investigation has suggested that the effects can already be detected in two trends that have developed in the 1960s. First, the proportion of young women who had not yet married increased between 1960 and 1966. Second, the average age for first marriages increased slightly between 1959 and 1966,[6] and has continued to increase through 1969. The average age at first marriage is now nearly 21 for women and over 23 for men.

This consideration of the "marriage squeeze" offers another illustration of how the formal demographer uses his approach to explain social trends. In this case, variations in the age at marriage and the proportion of the population marrying (patterns that have an influence on the birth rate) are explained by the age-sex composition of the population. But this illustration can also serve to show the division of labor that exists in demography. For a phenomenon like an increasing age at marriage, the formal demographers can examine various demographic factors, such as the age-sex composition, for their possible causal effects. At the same time, other researchers can use entirely different frames of reference, such as the sociological or the psychological, to explain the same phenomenon. Neither approach is wrong; perhaps it is not even possible to say which is "better." It is primarily a matter of appropriate skills, available data, and the frame of reference of the investigator. The ideal relationship between formal demography and population studies is a mutually supportive one.

Dependency Ratio

There are several ways of describing the age structure of a society. One was used in the comparison of national mortality rates, when differences in the percentage of the population under 15 years of age were used as an indication of the age structures of societies. In a rough way, this single percentage indicated that the less developed countries (Malaysia, Taiwan, Costa Rica, and Jamaica) had younger populations than the United States.

A more frequently employed measure of age composition is the *dependency ratio*. This measure takes into account persons of all ages. The entire age range is divided into three major age groups. The basis for the dependency ratio is the idea that certain age groups in the society are generally productive and other age groups are generally dependent upon the efforts of the productive group. Of course, the label "dependent" will always be somewhat arbitrary, since there will undoubtedly be exceptions. Nevertheless, it has become customary to describe the population under 15 and over 64 years of age as the *dependent population*. The people in the population aged 15 to 64 years are considered to be the *productive population*. It would be possible to argue that young people in many societies are dependent until they are eighteen or twenty years old, since very few people in modern industrial societies enter the labor market before that age. However, some do, and many teenage youths do begin to contribute something to the economic well being of their families, albeit generally less than they receive. A more compelling reason for retaining the cut-off point of 15 is found in the uses that are made of the dependency ratio. Generally, the purpose is comparison, and if societies around the world are being compared, the economic systems which require entry into the labor market during adolescence must be accounted for. So for comparative purposes the age 14 may be the best compromise as the upper limit of the dependent youthful years.

The dependency ratio compares the dependent and productive groups in the total population. Specifically, the dependency ratio is the number of persons under 15 years of age plus the number of persons 65 and over per 1000 persons between the ages 15 and 64. As a computation formula the dependency ratio is:

$$\frac{\text{No. of persons under 15 years of age} + \text{No. of persons 65 years and over}}{\text{No. of persons 15 to 64 years of age}} \times 1000$$

An interesting comparison of dependency ratios in the United States is the contrast between rural and urban populations shown in Table 3.

TABLE 3.   DEPENDENCY RATIOS IN THE UNITED STATES FOR RURAL AND URBAN POPULATIONS: 1950 AND 1960

Populations	Dependency Ratios	
	1950	1960
Rural	658	799
Urban	478	648

In both 1950 and 1960, the dependency ratios in rural places were higher than in urban places. The higher proportion of dependent people in rural areas was probably caused by both migration patterns and differential-fertility levels. Many young people from rural areas left for urban places when they reached adulthood, while those who did remain typically had higher-than-average fertility rates. Both patterns contributed to a high proportion of young and old dependents compared to the productive adults.

The other noteworthy feature of the figures in Table 3 is that the dependency ratio went up in both rural and urban places between 1950 and 1960. This effect may be attributed to two factors also: continuing high birth rates during most of the decade of the 1950s in both rural and urban populations, and improvements in mortality rates. The continued improvements in mortality include both greater average length of life and reduced infant mortality.

The Age-Sex Pyramid

One very graphic method used to depict the age and sex composition of a population simultaneously is called the *age-sex pyramid*, or the *population pyramid*, because of its typical triangular shape.

The age-sex pyramid is a variation of a graphic-presentation technique called the bar chart, in which the length of a bar represents a proportion of the total. A population pyramid for the United States population is presented in Figure 2. There are actually two population pyramids in Figure 2; one for the 1950 population is superimposed upon one for the 1960 population. The superimposition makes the interpretation of this particular pyramid somewhat more complicated than usual, but it also allows certain comparisons to be made more effectively. This particular population pyramid is divided into age intervals of one year. It is much more common to see population pyramids with intervals of five years, but obviously some details are obscured by the grosser age categories. Finally, this chart has absolute numbers along the baseline, while more commonly the scale on the baseline represents percentages of the total population. The form of the pyramid is exactly the same regardless of the number scale, since the bar length always represents a portion of the total. When a percentage scale is used along the baseline it simply facilitates making certain kinds of observations. For example, if the baseline is a percentage of the total, and one wants to know the percentage of the population that is male between 18 and 26, it is a simple matter to estimate the percentages represented by each bar (18 through 25) and to add them. On the other hand, for finding the number in this age-sex category, the absolute number scale such as that shown in Figure 2 is more useful.

An age-sex pyramid can display a variety of things about a population, but it can also reveal something about the quality of data. The data used to construct the pyramid in Figure 2 came from the 1950 and 1960 censuses of the United States, and, as was discussed in Chapter 2, census data are subject to error. For example, in many censuses, including the United States census of 1950, the age of a person has been obtained by asking, "How old was this person on his last birthday?" Whenever this question is used, some people round off their age, particularly to numbers ending in zero and five. This tendency—known as *age heaping*—has been especially noted at the older ages. The effect of age heaping can be best seen by examining the pyramid for the 1950 United States population (the grey bars) beginning at the bar for age 40. The bars for 40, 45, 50, 60, 65 and 70 are longer than the bars for the years just below and above each. In the data from earlier United States censuses, and the censuses of many underdeveloped countries, the tendency toward age heaping is even more pronounced than that shown here.[7]

An interesting variation of age heaping is found in the data from the 1960 census of the United States. For the 1960 data there is no evidence of age heaping at 40, 45, 50, and so on. What does stand out is the extraordinary length of the bar representing people aged 59 years. Why should this age have received an usually large response in 1960? The normal pattern of age heaping makes ages ending with the digit 9 the least popular. The answer lies in the form of the age question asked in the 1960 census. Instead of asking, "How old was this person on his last birthday?" the census form asked, "When was

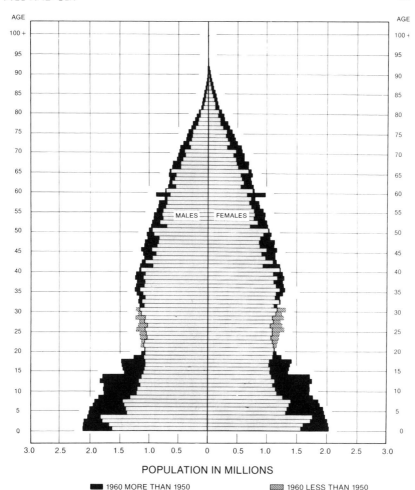

AGE

POPULATION IN MILLIONS

■ 1960 MORE THAN 1950   ▨ 1960 LESS THAN 1950

FIGURE 2. POPULATION OF THE UNITED STATES BY SINGLE YEARS OF AGE AND SEX: 1960 AND 1950. Source: U.S. Bureau of the Census. *U.S. Census of Population: 1960. Detailed Characteristics. United States Summary.* Final Report PC (1)—ID (Washington, D.C.: U.S.Government Printing Office, 1963), Part 1, Vol. I, p. xi.

this person born?" The result is an apparent variation on the age-heaping phenomenon: In 1960 many people responded that the year of their birth was 1900. Thus all those whose birthdays were after April—the time of the census —would be counted as 59 years of age. Apparently the years 1890, 1910, 1920, and so on did not receive the same overselection, since there was no visible age heaping at the corresponding ages. The 1960 method of determining age has removed most of the age heaping that has generally occurred, save for this one particular year.

There is yet another kind of census error that can be observed in Figure 2. This error is the tendency for children below the age of 1 year to go uncounted by the census.[8] The exact reason for this tendency is unclear, but again it has occurred in many censuses, suggesting that it is not just a cultural trait of the United States. The undercount of very young children may be observed in Figure 2 by noting the length of the bar at age 0-1 for the 1950 census and comparing it with the length of the bar for age 10-11 in 1960. It can be observed for both males and females that there were considerably more 10-year-olds in 1960 than there were "0-year-olds" in 1950. If there had been no immigration into the country, the number of ten-year-olds would have been less in 1960 than the number of 0-year-olds in 1950, since normally there would be some reduction in the numbers due to infant and child mortality. While there is much less immigration into the United States than there once was, it still averaged about 250,000 people per year in the 1950s. These immigrant families might easily have brought enough children to compensate for the death rate, but it is not likely that immigration accounted for the added 10-year-olds, since other young age groups, though increasing slightly during the decade, had a much smaller increase.

Quite a number of additional population features can be observed by carefully examining Figure 2. Beginning at the bottom of the pyramid, it is possible to detect the baby boom of 1946-1947 and its influence on the base of the United States population. Next there is the constriction of the shape of the pyramid near the middle which reflects the diminished birth rate of the 1930s. This may be seen by looking at the 10- to 20-year ages for 1950, or the 20- to 30-year age bracket for 1960 (be careful not to include the 1950 excess over 1960). A reflection of the greater longevity of females can be seen in the upper ages where the male side of the pyramid diminishes faster than the female side.

While the United States losses in World War II were not so great that there is any noticeable reflection of them in the age-sex pyramid, there are many countries where war losses are clearly identifiable. For example, 1959 data from the Soviet Union showed a considerable sex imbalance in the population over 40 years of age. The losses of males during World War II and the earlier revolutionary period account for this imbalance. In 1959, it was estimated that in the Soviet population over 32 years of age the women outnumbered men by 20 million.[9]

RACIAL COMPOSITION

There may be many societies where the factor of race can be ignored in demographic analysis, either because the racial composition of the population is homogeneous, or because race is not an important social fact. However, in the United States all of the major racial groupings are represented and the racial characteristics of people or groups are deemed to be important in social affairs.

The United States has been called a "racist" society, and while the label may be partly rhetorical it also contains much truth. Racism has been defined as

any set of beliefs that organic, genetically transmitted differences (whether real or imagined) between human groups are intrinsically associated with the presence or the absence of certain socially relevant abilities or characteristics, hence that such differences are a legitimate basis of invidious distinctions between groups socially defined as races.[10]

This definition emphasizes that racism exists when there are negative social attitudes (roughly, prejudice) and corresponding discriminatory behavior against racial groups in the population. There is ample evidence that racism in America is both pervasive and powerful. Some effects of racism can be seen in the demographic processes that will be considered in subsequent chapters, but for the moment the discussion will be limited to race as a feature of population composition.

Defining and Classifying Race

While racism is a social phenomenon, race is technically a biological concept, at least insofar as it has been used by physical anthropologists and geneticists. Nevertheless, one of the basic sources of demographic data, the census, treats race nonbiologically. Not even minimal scientific standards for classification in racial groups are met when the Census Bureau classifies individuals. For the census of 1950, the race of a person was determined by the census taker on the basis of his own observations. The enumerator or census taker was to ask questions about the race of a person only when in doubt. Under this method, for example, a person with a very small fraction of Negro ancestry, the major proportion being Caucasian, would probably have been classified as Negro if he lived in a Negro community with Negro neighbors. By some objective standard (skin color, hair texture, and the like), the person might as well have been classified as white, but the census taker followed the social custom by determining his race according to his social environment. This example also illustrates the illogical social practice of considering a person a Negro if it is known that he has some Negro ancestry, no matter how small the percentage, or how negligible the manifestation in his physical features.

Beginning in 1960, the United States census method of determining race was changed. Instead of the enumerator making the decision, the individual being enumerated was asked to designate his race. The census question asked, "Is the person—White, Negro, American Indian, Japanese, Chinese, Filipino,

Hawaiian, Part Hawaiian, Aleut, Eskimo, etc." The justification for this practice was discussed in an introductory statement to the census report. About the matter of race it said:

The concept of race, as it has been used by the Bureau of Census, is derived from that which is commonly accepted by the general public. It does not reflect clear-cut definitions of biological stock, and several categories obviously refer to national origin.[11]

In the 1970 United States Census, self-designation of race was again used. But by that time a new element had entered the racial picture, for among many Americans the term "Negro" had taken on negative connotations. The word Negro was viewed as one that had been imposed on Black Americans by Whites. The Census Bureau responded to this issue by offering a dual choice on the Census form: "Negro or Black." It is not known if this combination was acceptable to many Black Americans, or how it might have influenced their responses. In general, the effects of the change to self-designation of race in the 1960 census and the change in wording of the 1970 census are not known, but such changes illustrate again how the demographer must be alert to any factors that may affect the accuracy and comparability of population data.

The Non-White Population

Often the census reports racial data in a simple two-fold classification system: White and non-White. Since Negroes made up about 92 percent of the non-White population in 1960, the two categories, Negro and non-White, are almost equivalent, and are often used as if they were interchangeable. But demographers do so with the recognition that it is simply an expedient that must be employed when more refined data are not available. Generally, if one is dealing with the entire United States population there is no particular problem in equating non-White with Negro, but in particular states and regions a large error may be introduced by this assumption. For example, in some states with sizeable Indian or Oriental populations, or both, the percentage of non-Whites who are Negroes may be much less than 92 percent. Extreme cases are North Dakota and South Dakota where in 1960 only 6 percent and 4 percent of the non-Whites were Negroes (the bulk of the remainder being American Indian). In California, with a non-White population of more than a million, the percentage of non-Whites in 1960 who were Negro was only about 70 percent. In that state there is a sizeable Oriental population, and some American Indians, and both groups were included in the non-White racial category.

Increasingly, the concept of non-White, as employed by the Census Bureau, has been criticized by those who use population data. Clearly, it is not a scientific concept, so in this regard it is similar to the census usage of the concept of Negro. But unlike the concept of Negro, non-White cannot be defended as a socially meaningful concept. In the social life of the United States distinctions are made between Negroes and American Indians, between Chinese and American Indians, and so on. In social as well as economic and geographic contexts distinctions are made between the groups who are lumped together as non-White. Increasingly non-White is a concept that is recognized as having very little meaning, and to many people it reflects the ethnocentrism of a White-dominated culture.

With these objections in mind, it must be admitted that the non-White category will be dealt with in the following discussion, even though the primary interest is in the Negro population. But it is only because refined data are unavailable that such usage is required.

The Negro Population

Probably the most noteworthy feature of the racial composition of the United States is the percentage of the total population that has been and is now Negro. The census of 1790 is often used as a baseline; at that time Negroes made up 19.3 percent of the total population. From 1790 on, the Negro proportion of the total population declined until 1920, when it was 10.3 percent. This percentage remained virtually unchanged through the census of 1960, when it was 10.5 percent. The percent of the population classified as Negro through the years has been influenced primarily by birth and death rates, since migration of Negroes to this country essentially ended by the middle of the nineteenth century. Just what percentage of the United States population will be Negro in the future also depends greatly on the rate of fertility that will prevail during the next couple of decades. While the percentage of Negroes in the United States has increased somewhat between 1960 and 1970 (to about 11.5 percent), there is no reason to expect, in the long run, any pronounced change in the proportion. This point merits attention only because some racist groups have occasionally promoted the false notion that high Negro fertility will soon have Negroes outnumbering Whites in the United States. Such ideas are simply racist fantasy.

RELIGIOUS COMPOSITION

The religious composition of a society is often of considerable importance because religions tend to be the institutional embodiment of values, and values often influence demographic processes. A common connection between religious values and population is the view that religions take toward life and procreation. In the most familiar case, the Roman Catholic Church continues to be specifically opposed to certain methods of conception control (mechanical and chemical methods), and opposed to the use of abortion as a birth-control measure. While the position of the Catholic Church regarding fertility control is well known, it is less often recognized that most Protestant denominations had similar objections until only a short time ago. In both England and the United States the major Protestant denominations opposed contraceptive practices until about 1930, and it was not until the 1950s that there was open and widespread Protestant support for contraception.[12]

Religion and the Census

Unlike the other important population characteristics, religious classification is not counted and reported by the United States Census or the vital-registration system. No question on religion is included in the census questionnaire, principally because such a question might be perceived by some people as a threat to religious freedom, or as a violation of the principle of the separation between church and state. There seems to be little validity to the further argument that people would refuse to give information to the census taker about their religious affiliation. In a sample survey conducted by the Census Bureau in 1957, a question on religion was asked in 35,000 households across the country. When census takers followed up on this inquiry, asking the reactions of the people to the religion question, less than three percent indicated a mild resentment; and less than one percent expressed strong resentment.[13] It should be added that questions on religion are very common in public-opinion polls and social surveys and there is rarely any objection to such questions. This is true even when the questions asked go far beyond simple matters of affiliation, and ask about the intensity of religious feeling.

Even though most people in the general public would probably not object to a question on religion in the census, it is likely that if such a question were to be included, some individuals would object. It would take only a few people to create a *cause célèbre* from a religion question. Since there are people who feel that the census already goes too far in asking about personal matters, they would see this as just one more intrusion into personal privacy. This controversy would add to the apprehension of people who are already concerned about the possibility of the government establishing an enormous computerized data bank that would allow the population to be controlled.

Religious Composition of the United States

Since there are no census data on the subject, information about the religious composition of the United States must come from other sources. One such source is the data gathered and published by the individual religious denominations, but these data are incomplete and far from consistent. Different denominations employ a variety of standards for counting their membership, and at least one denomination refuses to allow the number of its membership to be published (Church of Christ Scientist).[14]

A frequently cited source of information on church membership in the United States is the *Yearbook of American Churches,* published by the National Council of Churches. According to this source, nearly two-thirds of the United States population (64 percent) held church membership in 1967. This percentage is in distinct contrast to the reported church membership of the United States in the last half of the nineteenth and early part of the twentieth centuries. In 1850 about 16 percent of the population was reported to hold church membership. By 1900 the percentage was up to 36 percent. In 1940 it was 49 percent, and in 1950 it was 57 percent. But these figures cannot be taken as clear-cut evidence of a long-term increase in religiosity in America. Lipset has argued that religious involvement was as widespread in the United States in the nineteenth century as it was during the middle of the twentieth century.[15] He found that other indicators of national religiosity did not reveal dramatic increases from the nineteenth to the twentieth centuries. For example, the ratio of clergymen to population did not increase between 1900 and 1950, while ratios for other professions did. Also, comparable public-opinion polls have not revealed an increase in religiosity in the twentieth century. It should also be noted that the statistical evidence on church membership is misleading because in many denominations the process of becoming a member used to be more time consuming and arduous than it is today. Apparently many people participated in the church in the nineteenth century without becoming formal members.

Lipset concluded that there have been no dramatic shifts in the religious tendencies of Americans. He did note, however, as have many others, that among the countries of the Christian world the people of the United States have consistently been the most religious, both in terms of church attendance and expressed denominational affiliation. In the 1957 Bureau of the Census survey, less than 4 percent of the population 14 years of age and over did not report a religious affiliation. The percentage of Americans attending church on a given Sunday has for the past thirty years ranged to nearly 50 percent.[16] Both figures are much higher than those typically found in Europe, especially the Protestant countries.[17]

RESIDENCE

To a demographer residence means the type of community, ranging from the rural to the urban, in which people live. The phenomenon of urban living is more than just living in a densely settled population. There is a difference in the ways of life in rural and urban places—a difference in the culture—which has important implications for almost every aspect of human behavior, not the least of which is demographic behavior. Birth rates, death rates, and migration patterns are all related to the rural-urban dimension. Thus, the variable of residence, like race and religion, is an important structural feature of any population.

Perhaps the most striking demographic difference between rural and urban people is the difference in their fertility. John Graunt, the English political arithmetician of the seventeenth century, was among the first to note that the rate of population growth in rural areas was greater than in urban areas. This tendency was very likely attributable to higher fertility in rural places, because a general migration from rural to urban areas was also observed. This general pattern of higher fertility in rural places has been regularly observed in Western society, as has migration from rural to urban places.

Mortality rates have also been related to rural-urban residence. Historically, at least, it is true that the rate of mortality was higher in the urban place than in the rural. This generalization may not hold under existing rural-urban conditions. This issue will be discussed in more detail in Chapter 5.

The Rural-Urban Composition of the United States

The shift in the United States' from an essentially rural population to a predominantly urban one has been the biggest structural change in American history. When the census of 1790 was taken, about 5 percent of the population lived in urban places. By the year 1900, about 40 percent of the population lived in urban places, and by 1960, the percentage had risen to 70 percent. The exact percentage of the population that is considered urban is, of course, dependent upon the definition used. The 70-percent figure is based on the Census Bureau definition, which classifies all people who live in communities of 2500 or more as urban. In recent years, the problem of classifying people who live in suburban or rural-urban fringe areas has caused the Census Bureau to develop the concept of "urbanized" areas. An urbanized area may lie outside of the legal boundaries of a city, but it is characterized by urban residential density, and is concerned primarily with the business, commerce, or communication activity of the central city.

Population in the Central City

One of the population phenomena connected with urban life is the movement of people into and out of the central core of major cities. It has long been true that the newest migrants to the cities of the United States come directly to the central core of the city. (This pattern does not seem to hold true universally, since, for example, in Latin America, the new migrants often tend to settle first on the fringes of the city.) In recent years, in United States cities, the new migrants have been predominantly Negroes, although New York and other Eastern seaboard cities have received a considerable number of Puerto Ricans. Thus, one of the features of recent urbanization is that the racial composition of the central core of American cities is changing. In New

York City between 1950 and 1960, there was an actual loss in the number of inhabitants. New York City had 110,000 fewer people in 1960 than it had in 1950, primarily because over a million more White persons moved out than moved in. However during that same decade, 162,845 more non-Whites and 273,677 more Puerto Ricans moved into New York than moved out.[18] (The reason that the decrease in New York's population was not more than 110,000 is that there were more births than deaths.)

If these new migrants also move out of the central city and into the suburban areas as they make economic gains, they will be following a well-established pattern in American migration. This is essentially what the migrants from Ireland, Germany, Italy, and the Eastern European countries did in earlier years. As new migrants, they lived in the congested center of the city, but many individual families moved into the outlying areas when they made economic gains. Negroes, however, face the problem of discrimination in the sale and rental of housing and in employment, so that it is much more difficult for them to escape the central city, even when it is economically possible for them to do so. The future of the central cities in the United States depends upon the way in which Americans are able to cope with the continuing problem of occupational and residential discrimination.

SUMMARY

The composition of a population is important for several reasons. Demographically it may be of interest to know how the structure of a population changes. For example, the sex composition of a population may be shaped by migration patterns or some other cultural practice. Female infanticide may lead to fewer girls than boys in a population, while hazardous occupations and wars may lead to a relative shortage of males. The age composition of a population may be influenced in an unexpected way by improvements in mortality. If the reductions in mortality occur at the younger ages, particularly in the first year of life, the effect of such an improvement could be a younger population than would otherwise prevail.

Very often the composition of populations, especially the age and sex composition, must be considered when social or vital rates are being compared. Many social and vital rates (crime, suicide, fertility, mortality) are related to age and sex, so unless populations have the same composition these factors must be taken into account when comparisons are being made.

The composition characteristics that have been given special consideration in this chapter are age, sex, race, religion, and residence, but the interest in population composition will not end here. As each of the dynamic elements of population is considered, the influence of structural characteristics becomes important. One characteristic that was not introduced in this chapter, but one which will prove to be very important, is the social-class or socioeconomic structure of the society. The notion of social class or socioeconomic position is a complex concept; it is abstracted from many concrete characteristics such as occupation, education, income, and the like. As such, it differs from age, sex, race, religion, and residence. It is a truly sociological concept and one that is very important for understanding demographic events. Discussions of population composition often present some of the most commonly employed indicators of social class,—for example, income distribution, educational composition, occupational structure. These factors have not been discussed in this chapter, but several of them will be considered in those contexts where they are important as determinants of demographic behavior.

: : SELECTED READINGS AND MATERIALS

Blau, Peter M., and Otis Dudley Duncan. *The American Occupational Structure.* New York, John Wiley and Sons, 1967.

Bogue, Donald J. *Principles of Demography.* New York, John Wiley and Sons, 1969. Chapters 7 through 15 provide detailed descriptions and extensive analyses of the population composition of the United States and countries around the world.

Gaustad, Edwin Scott. *Historical Atlas of Religion in America.* New York, Harper and Row, 1962. A geographic and descriptive presentation of the religious composition of the United States, both historically and at the present time.

Glazer, Nathan, and Daniel P. Moynihan. *Beyond the Melting Pot: The Negroes, Puerto Ricans, Jews, Italians and Irish of New York City.* Cambridge, Mass., M.I.T. and Harvard Press, 1963.

Kiser, Clyde V., editor. *Demographic Aspects of the Black Community, The Milbank Memorial Fund Quarterly,* Vol. 48, No. 2 (1970), Part 2.

Nam, Charles B., editor. *Population and Society: A Textbook of Selected Readings.* Boston, Houghton Mifflin, 1968. Chapter 8, "Population Composition," and Chapter 9, "Population Distribution."

Taeuber, Karl E., and Alma F. Taeuber. *Negroes in Cities: Residential Segregation and Neighborhood Change.* Chicago, Aldine, 1965.

: : NOTES

1. Judith Blake, "Family Size in the 1960's—A Baffling Fad?" *Eugenics Quarterly,* 14: 61 (March 1967); and Pascal K. Whelpton, "Why Did the United States' Crude Birth Rate Decline during 1957–1962?" *Population Index,* 29: 120–125 (April).

2. Ansley Coale, "How a Population Ages or Grows Younger," in *Population: The Vital Revolution,* edited by Ronald Freedman (Garden City, New York: Anchor Books, 1964), pp. 49–50.

3. Emile Durkheim, *Suicide*, translated by John A. Spaulding and George Simpson (Glencoe, Illinois: The Free Press, 1951). The analysis described is on pp. 171–197.

4. C. A. McMahan, "An Empirical Test of Three Hypotheses Concerning the Human Sex Ratio at Birth in the United States, 1915–1948," *The Milbank Memorial Fund Quarterly*, 29: 286 (1951).

5. Paul G. Glick, David M. Heer, and John C. Beresford, "Family Formation and Family Composition: Trends and Prospects," in *Sourcebook in Marriage and the Family*, Marvin B. Sussman, ed. (New York: Houghton Mifflin, 1963), p. 38; and Donald S. Akers, "On Measuring the Marriage Squeeze," *Demography*, 4: 907–924 (1967).

6. Akers, pp. 920–921.

7. Conrad Taeuber and Morris H. Hansen, "A Preliminary Evaluation of the 1960 Censuses of Population and Housing," *Demography*, 1: 9–11 (1964). By means of an index designed to measure age heaping, Taeuber and Hansen have shown that the extent of this error in the 1950 United States census was only about one-fifth as great as in the 1880 census.

8. Hugh H. Wolfenden, *Population Statistics and their Compilation* (Chicago: University of Chicago Press), 1954, pp. 33–36.

9. *Population Reference Bureau*, "Population Trends in the U.S.S.R.," 17: 114 (1961).

10. Pierre L. van de Berghe, *Race and Racism: A Comparative Perspective*, (New York: John Wiley and Sons, 1967), p. 11.

11. U.S. Bureau of the Census, *U.S. Census of Population, 1960. Detailed Characteristics. United States Summary*. Final Report PC (1)—1D. (Washington, D.C.: U.S. Government Printing Office, 1963), Part 1, Vol. I, p. xiii.

12. Flann Campbell, "Birth Control and the Christian Churches," *Population Studies*, 14: 135 (1960).

13. Dorothy Good, "Questions on Religion in the United States Census," *Population Index*, 25: 5 (1959).

14. William Petersen, *Population* (New York: Macmillan, 1961), p. 119.

15. Seymour Martin Lipset, *The First New Nation* (New York: Basic Books, 1963), pp. 140–150.

16. W. Seward Salisbury, *Religion in American Culture* (Homewood, Illinois: The Dorsey Press, 1964), p. 83.

17. Lipset, p. 150.

18. William Dobriner, *Class in Suburbia* (Englewood Cliffs, N.J.: Prentice-Hall, 1963), p. 158.

Chapter 4 Migration

There are three important issues in the study of migration:

1. *The Nature of Migration*. Several important distinctions can be made between the different types of migration. If these differences are clarified it is easier to analyze and assess the causes and the effects of migration.

2. *The Causes of Migration*. Why do people migrate? What are the important factors determining whether or not people will migrate? The principal task of a theory of migration must be to explain why migratory behavior occurs.

3. *The Effects of Migration*. When people migrate it will affect the social systems they leave and the social systems they enter. Migration is also likely to affect the personal and psychological lives of the migrants. The effects of migration on the person, the community, and the society will be considered after a discussion of the types and theories of migration.

THE NATURE OF MIGRATION

The word *migration*, and the related words *migrant* and *immigrant*, tend to produce an oversimplified and erroneous picture in the minds of most people. While the words suggest a unitary phenomenon, migration is both varied and complex.

Let the reader try a little self-experiment in order to see this point clearly. Take the word *immigrant*. Construct a mental picture of an immigrant, or better yet, of a group of immigrants. What image comes to mind? For most Americans the word evokes a stereotyped picture of a cluster of people who have just arrived at some port of entry. The group is often a family in which the wife is wearing a kerchief, the husband is wearing a flat, European-style cap or broad-brimmed hat. Both are dressed in nondescript, rumpled clothing and they have slightly dazed or bewildered expressions. Huddled around them are several small children with equally puzzled or frightened expressions. This stereotypic image of the late-nineteenth- and early-twentieth-century immigrant to the United States probably still shapes the thinking of most Americans when they hear the word immigrant.

The same experiment may be tried with the word *migrant*. Americans are likely to think of a migrant as a migratory farm worker, or for some people

54

migrant may suggest the "Okies" leaving the Midwest for California. For others perhaps the word brings to mind Negroes leaving the rural South for some Northern urban ghetto.

The images evoked by the words immigration and migration are not totally erroneous, but they are far from accurate descriptions of present-day immigration and migration. As a case in point, the characterization of the immigrant family above may have been accurate for many Southern European immigrants at the turn of the century, but it is not a realistic portrayal of recent immigration to the United States. Since 1945, immigrants to the United States have *not* typically been unskilled and semiskilled workers. In recent migration, partly because of the needs of the American economy and partly because of the preferences given by American immigration laws, many of the immigrants have been in higher level occupational categories.[1] More than one-third of the immigrants who have come to the United States since 1945 have been in professional or skilled occupations. Twenty-five percent more have been in managerial, clerical, or sales occupations. Thus, about 60 percent of the recent immigrants to the United States were *not* unskilled or semiskilled workers. The new immigrants are no longer the "weary and down-trodden" coming to American shores for refuge.

Similarly, while the word migrant suggests to most people a migrant farm worker, such a characterization does not describe most of the internal migrants in the United States today. Each year about one person in five in the United States changes residences. About 7 percent of the people move to a house in a different county every year.[2] If moving to a different county is taken as the criterion for being a migrant, then about 15 million Americans are migrants each year. By comparison, the number of people in the migrant-farm-labor force, while difficult to determine with any exactness, is very likely under 500,000 persons.[3] Only a small fraction of American migrants can possibly be characterized as migrant farm workers.

If popular conceptions about migration are more misleading than helpful, then careful attention must be given to the essential elements of the concept, and to the dimensions that characterize different types of migration.

A Definition

A migrant is a person who makes a permanent change in his regular place of residence. Migration is the movement of individuals or groups from one place of residence to another who have the intention of remaining in the new place for some substantial period of time. Some definitions include the provision that the move must be from one political or geographical unit to another. This provision makes it possible to distinguish between a mover and a migrant. The mover changes his residence but remains in the same community, city, or county.

The United States census provides a convenient and often-used measure of migration. The census determines for persons over five years of age where they were living five years prior to the time of enumeration. Four categories of people are thus distinguished: (1) those living in the same house as they were five years earlier; (2) those living in a different house, but in the same county (movers); (3) those living in a different county, but in the same state; and (4) those living in a different state. Researchers usually classify the people in categories 1 and 2 as nonmigrants, and those in categories 3 and 4 as migrants.

Types of Migration

One starting point for developing a theory of migration is to think in terms of types of migration. The most commonly used typology of migration is the distinction between internal and international migration—that is, between the movement of people within the boundaries of some nation-state and movement from one nation-state to another. While the explanations for these two types of migration are likely to be very different, the distinction is more important for administrative and political purposes than it is for any theoretical development.

A much more elaborate classification system was developed by Petersen, in which the basic distinction was between *conservative migration* and *innovative migration*.[4] Conservative migration occurs when a person moves from one place to another in order to retain his existing way of life. The move is necessitated by some changes that have occurred, or are occurring, in his current place of residence. In this case, if the person were to stay he would have to change his mode of living, so migration is an effort to conserve important parts of the existing way of life. Innovative migration, on the other hand, is the movement of a person in order to obtain a new way of life.

Petersen's typology of migration has the following classes:

Primitive Migration. This type of migration occurs when people are unable to cope with natural or ecological forces and move in order to survive. Primitive migration may be either conservative, as when people try to find a new place that is like their home under earlier conditions, or innovative, as when people seek out a new way of life. For example, people who move to the city after their agricultural land fails to provide an adequate livelihood are engaged in innovative primitive migration. In primitive migration the emphasis is on survival in a physical sense. If the people do not move, they will not survive.

Forced, or Impelled, Migration. This type of migration is characterized by population movement which is forced by the state, or some other political or economic power. Slave trade, flight from the government, oppression, and expulsion by the government are all variants of forced, or impelled, migration.

Free Migration. This type is distinguished by individual choice: the will of the migrant is the crucial factor causing the migration. While primitive migration occurs because people cannot meet their needs in their old place of residence, and forced migration occurs in response to some political (or other) power, free migration occurs when individuals on their own initiative actively seek out new homes. The people who best characterize free migration are the pioneers, the trail-blazers, and the adventurers, but free migration is a useful concept for describing the movement of many individuals in an open society.

Mass Migration. Finally, there are the migrants who move because of social forces or social patterns. In discussing mass migration, Petersen says, "Migration becomes a style, an established pattern, an example of collective behavior." In mass migration the movement is more a group pattern than a matter of individual choice. When mass migration occurs, the individual almost has to make the conscious decision *not to move*, instead of the decision *to move*.

Each of the four types of migration is associated with a particular set of forces:

Type of Migration	Pre-eminent Forces
Primitive migration	Ecological, geographic, or natural
Forced, or impelled, migration	Political, economic, or physical
Free migration	Personal or psychological
Mass migration	Social

In any actual migration there may be some elements or traces of all four types. As an illustration, the type of internal migration occurring in the United States today is probably closest to free migration. This does not mean that migration is of the pioneer or trail-blazer type; it simply means that many of the internal migrants in the United States today are individuals or nuclear families who are acting independently. Usually the move is made for their own personal needs or to reduce some felt deprivation. It is often the aspiration for higher status that acts as the most potent personal factor producing free migration.

The type of migration least likely to be found in the United States today is primitive migration, and yet it might be argued that when the soil, or a mineral deposit, or a forest becomes depleted there is some movement of people because their basic physical needs will no longer be met if they remain where they are. Perhaps equally rare in American society is forced, or impelled, migration. Occasionally individuals are forced to move, as when criminals are deported, when members of a racial or ethnic group are harassed and intimidated, or when young men leave the country to avoid the draft, but these instances contribute little to the total volume of migration.

A more difficult question is whether much of the migration occurring in the United States may properly be called "mass migration." Is there a kind of collective behavior or a social momentum which acts as a prime force in the movement of Americans? Do many Americans move to some region, city, or state simply because others from their social group have moved there before them? There is some evidence in the migration literature that this has been the case, at least for some family groups from certain regions.[5] This pattern has been described as "chain migration" and will be discussed more fully in the following section.

THEORIES OF MIGRATION

Ravenstein's Theory

The most long-standing and oft-cited theory of migration is that advanced by Ravenstein under the title "The Laws of Migration."[6] These "laws" were statements in the form of propositions about the nature of migration trends, streams of migration, and migration differentials. For example, Ravenstein noted that migration tended to flow from the rural place toward the urban place (an empirical observation that was also made in the seventeenth century by John Graunt). He also observed that migration occurred in streams; that is, in distinct flows of people from a particular place of origin to some specific destination. These streams tended to be made up of more females than males if the distance of migration was short. When migration occurred in a stream, there was also a counterstream of migrants moving in the opposite direction. Among the variety of factors producing migration, Ravenstein held that the "desire of most men to 'better' themselves in material respects" was the most influential.[7]

Ravenstein's theory of migration offered a number of important propositions, most of which were fairly well grounded in fact at the time he made his observations. It suggested that the economic motive was the primary cause of migration, and in this regard it set the tone for almost all subsequent migration theories.

Theory of Intervening Opportunities

Another well-known theory of migration is Stouffer's theory of intervening opportunities.[8] Stouffer started with one of Ravenstein's observations that most people migrate short distances and few people migrate long distances. He attempted to develop a mathematical formulation that would accurately represent the differential movement of people over physical distances. Stouffer asserted that "the number of persons going a given distance is directly proportional to the number of intervening opportunities."[9] The key assumption of the theory was that, in moving from one place to another, a person would not pass over opportunities, but would move only far enough to realize the objectives being sought. The opportunities would include such things as housing or employment openings. That most people migrated short distances and fewer people migrated long distances was attributed to the fact that a person would have to pass over many opportunities to migrate the longer distance. The theory was transformed into a mathematical formula, which was tested in 1940 by examining the population movement within a single city. The model proved to be a fairly good predictor of movement within the city, but it had no facility for taking the direction of movement into account. The result was that the model tended to overestimate the movement of people toward the center of the city, for the prevailing movement was actually from the center outward.

Stouffer modified his model in 1960, and and while the changes made it possible for him to achieve fairly good agreement between the expected and observed movement from one metropolitan area of the United States to another, there were a number of notable cases where the model failed to coincide with reality. Since 1940, there have been numerous attempts, with some success, to apply Stouffer's model or some variation of it to population migration data.[10]

Theories like the intervening-opportunities model are often labeled *gravitational theories*. They are generally formulated as mathematical models in which the primary elements are factors such as population size, population density, and geographic distance. While human aspirations or motives may be the basic assumptions underlying gravitational theories, the movement of people is usually conceptualized in terms of the physical world. People are often viewed as physical objects responding largely to external forces. In addition to Stouffer, various other sociologists have developed gravitational models to explain the general movement and distribution of people,[11] but at present the bulk of this work is being done by population geographers and demographic ecologists. This pattern is quite appropriate, since the principal variables of gravitational theories are population size and distance, and these fall quite naturally into the geographical-ecological domain.[12]

Lee's Theory

The recent publication of several theories of migration make up for the scarcity of sociological theories. One such theory is that advanced by Lee, which posits four very general factors to serve as the basis for a series of migration hypotheses.[13] For every decision to migrate there will be (1) positive and negative factors associated with the place of origin, (2) positive and negative factors associated with the place of destination, (3) intervening obstacles, and (4) personal factors. The concept of *personal factors* has two different meanings. First, personal factors are simply characteristics of a person or a family, such as age, family size, or stage of the family life cycle. But, the term also refers to "personal sensitivities, intelligence, and awareness of conditions elsewhere." This second meaning adds a substantial new dimension to the theory, for if personal factors are to include the knowledge, perceptions, and awareness of the individual, then the first three factors in Lee's scheme must always be filtered through this fourth factor. The positive and negative values attached to the origin and destination, as well as the perception of intervening obstacles, can only have meaning as they exist in the mind of the potential migrant. The core of the theory identifies three general sets of factors—*origin values, destination values,* and *intervening obstacles*—that enter into the decision making of the individual through his perceptions and knowledge. Lee states, "Clearly the set of +'s and −'s at both the origin and destination is differently defined for every migrant or prospective migrant."[14]

Working from these four factors, Lee went on to advance hypotheses related to the volume of migration, streams and counterstreams of migration, and the characteristics of migrants.

1. *Migration volume.* If people move because of differences between their area of origin and the potential area of destination, then migration will be greatest in those areas with the most diversity. If the areas of a territory are different, in terms of social or economic conditions or the characteristics of the people, then the volume of migration should be high among them. On the other hand, if an area is the same throughout, if it is completely homogenous, then the amount of migration should be small since there would be little reason for people to move from one place to another.

2. *Streams and Counterstreams.* Hypotheses about streams and counterstreams of migration rest in part on the influence that knowledge plays in reducing obstacles to migration. For example, the hypothesis "For every major migration stream a counterstream develops" was based on the idea that the people moving from an origin to a destination would increase the level of knowledge at both ends of the stream about the origin, the destination, and the intervening obstacles. With this increase in knowledge, migration should increase in both directions. This particular hypothesis also gains support from the fact that some migrants will eventually migrate back to their place of origin.

3. *Migration-Stream Efficiency.* The efficiency of migration streams may be thought of as the ratio of stream to counterstream, or the net amount of migration in one direction or the other. For example, a migration stream would have 100 percent efficiency if all the migration between place A and

place B was in a single direction. The efficiency of the migration stream would be zero if exactly as many people moved from A to B as moved from B to A. The efficiency of a migration stream should be high whenever the major factor causing the migration is a negative evaluation of the features at the place of origin. People will not be likely to go back to a place of origin if they have left it because of its negative features. Also, they will not promote migration back to their original home by describing it to the people in their new place of residence. Illustrative of this are the Irish, who migrated because of the famine in their home country, and the many American Negroes who have left the South because of unfavorable living conditions there.

The efficiency, or *net migration*, of a migration stream should also be high whenever the intervening obstacles between the area of origin and the area of destination are great. Migrants are not likely to make an arduous or otherwise difficult move unless they have a good reason to migrate in the first place, and once having made the move they are not likely to move back again.

4. *The Characteristics of Migrants.* In terms of social characteristics, migrants are almost always found to be selective, and not simply representative of the population at the place of origin. Often migrants are in the extremes in the population they are leaving; that is, some migrants will have the most valued characteristics, such as intelligence, industry, and health, but at the same time many migrants will have the less valued characteristics.

However, in their over-all social characteristics, migrants *as a group* tend to be intermediate for both origin and destination populations. Both the fertility and educational levels of rural-urban migrants have manifested this pattern, falling midway between those of the nonmigrants at origin and the population at destination. Lee has noted that "one of the paradoxes of migration is that the movement of people may tend to lower the quality of population, as expressed in terms of some particular characteristic, at both origin and destination."[15]

This feature of migration has been observed in the intelligence levels and occupational characteristics of rural-to-urban migrants. Studies by sociologists in the 1940s and 1950s revealed that the rural communities in the Midwest lost disproportionately more of their most intelligent youngsters through out-migration to the urban places. A higher proportion of those rural youngsters who were going into higher-status occupations were migrating from their home communities. However, from the perspective of the urban place, the in-migration of rural youth appeared quite different. While on a percentage basis the rural place lost a higher proportion of its most talented youngsters, in *absolute* numbers the urban place received many more migrants with lower grades and intelligence-test scores who were going into lower-status occupations.[16] The result was that the occupational-intellectual quality of both the sending and the receiving communities was lowered.

Beshers' Theory

Beshers' theory focuses largely on the individual or familial decision-making process that leads to migration.[17] In Beshers' words:

> We shall assume that migration is a result of a decision process within the family, and that the decision process is constrained on one hand by characteristics of the family and its constituent individuals, and on the other by labor markets, commuting patterns, and housing markets.[18]

Beshers introduced the concept *modes of orientation* as the basis for understanding the decision-making process. A mode of orientation reflects the fundamental principles that an individual uses when he takes some action.[19] One mode of orientation is called *the purposive-rational mode* and is characterized by the "extensive calculations of consequences of alternatives, including consequences far in the future, and the capacity to adhere to a plan of action that will attain these future goals." In contrast is the *traditional mode*, in which the decision making is largely determined by custom and habit. Finally there is a *short-run hedonistic mode*, in which the individual looks only a very short distance into the future and makes his decision on the basis of his immediate needs and feelings.

When migration decisions are governed by the purposive-rational mode of orientation it is possible to single out some of the elements of family life that will shape the decision. In the nuclear family the customary sex roles will give the husband a special knowledge and authority in certain areas, while the wife will have areas where she is particularly competent. The husband specifies the job-related constraints, such as the degree to which his job is linked to a particular locality and how migration will affect his career and future income. On the other hand, the wife will specify the family-related constraints, such as the effect that migration will have on the social, emotional, and educational needs of the children. The wife will also have a considerable voice in how migration will affect the housing needs of the family.

The major contribution of this theory by Beshers is its focus on the rational-purposive mode of personal orientation and thus its emphasis on the importance of individual and family decision making in the process of migration. In an urban-industrial society, decisions to migrate do not often result from what Beshers calls the traditional mode of decision making. While the short-run hedonistic mode may apply to some of the migration decisions, probably only a small proportion of the people migrate in response to immediate situational factors. Urban-industrial migration is probably governed most by the rational-purposive mode of orientation.

A Comparison of Migration Theories

A comparison of the migration theories discussed here points up some basic similarities. The theories of Lee and Beshers, for example, both seek primarily to explain free migration. The emphasis of each is on the rational decision making process that leads to migration, although, as Lee notes, "the decision to migrate . . . is never completely rational, and for some persons the rational component is much less than the irrational."[20]

One persistent theme in these theories of migration is that the decision to migrate and migration itself, as long as it is not forced or impelled migration, is largely motivated by the migrant's desire to improve his condition. One may go back to Ravenstein's theory, which emphasized the economic motivations of migrants. He did suggest several other motivating factors, including bad or "oppressive laws, heavy taxation, an unattractive climate, uncongenial social surroundings. But, he continued, "none of these currents can compare in volume with that which arises from the desire in most men to 'better' themselves."[21] In Stouffer's intervening-opportunities theory the maximization of well-being, particularly the economic well-being of the migrant is stressed. And in Beshers' theory, the economic aspects of migration appear as job and career constraints affecting the decision to migrate.[22]

The emphasis on the relationship between migration and economic betterment, then, is an important element in most theories of migration, and a large amount of research supports the existence of this relationship. A second major factor shared by migration theories—and, again, borne out by research —is the influence of family and kin groups. Family characteristics have a potential influence on when people migrate, where they migrate, and how they adjust to their new place of residence after they migrate.

Thus, two institutions, the economy and the family, have prime roles in the process of migration. The economic institution is reflected in such factors as jobs, careers, and economic opportunities. The family exerts an influence through kinship and nuclear-family relations and the stages in the family life cycle. Some of the empirical evidence in these areas is summarized in the sections that follow.

ECONOMIC FACTORS

At the societal level, there is a well-established relationship between the level of migration in a society and the condition of the economy. Migration increases during times of economic prosperity and decreases during periods of economic decline. This proposition has been supported by many studies[23] and has been explained theoretically by Lee. This relationship between migration and the state of the economy can be attributed to the expansion or stability of industries and businesses during different parts of the economic cycle.

When economic growth and expansion occur, they are likely to occur in varying degrees in different parts of the society. For the person living in an area where there is little economic growth, the attractiveness of moving to a place of opportunity is heightened by the relative unattractiveness of his present residence. On the other hand,

during depressions . . . some of the newly created businesses fail and others cease to expand. A leveling of opportunities occurs, and sheer familiarity with the place of residence . . . militates against moving to places where positive factors no longer so heavily outweigh those at home.[24]

One of the important mechanisms in the relationship between migration and the economy is the flow of information from one part of the society to another. If migration is to occur between segments of the economic system which are thriving and those that are not growing, there must be some flow of information from the former to the latter. Generally, the greater the distance between two areas the smaller this information flow will be. This information flow is an implicit operative factor in Stouffer's theory of intervening opportunities, and it is probably a strong determinant of streams and counterstreams of migration.

Once some people have migrated from a given origin to a specific destination, a greater amount of information will flow between the two places. Visits, return visits, letters, and telephone calls all serve to inform the members of the home community about the opportunities in the new community or region.[25] This flow of communication may be one of the important roles that the family plays in the migration process. It will be discussed in more detail below.

A striking example of the way migration responds to economic conditions was found in a study of the relationship between the net migration from Puerto Rico to the United States and the yearly national-income figures for the United States.[26] The relationship is shown graphically in Figure 3, where it may be seen that almost every decline in the United States national income over a fifty-year period was followed by a decrease in net migration from Puerto Rico.

Migration is often directly related to the improved economic status of the migrant. It may often be stimulated by job and career mobility. Although research findings on economic advancement and geographic mobility have not been conclusive, one study of urban dwellers demonstrated a strong relationship between residential-mobility *intentions* and the potential for upward mobility.[27] Several factors were found to be predictive of residential mobility, but the two most important were expectations about social mobility and the respondent's estimates of his social-class position as compared to that of his neighbors. Age of the household head and family size, while related, were

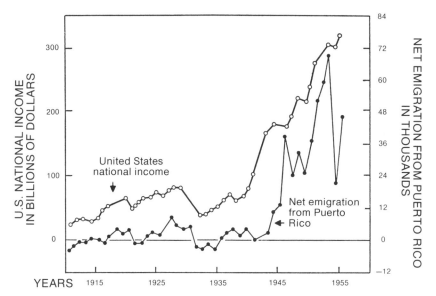

FIGURE 3. RELATION BETWEEN PUERTO RICAN MIGRATION AND ECONOMIC CONDITIONS IN THE UNITED STATES. Source: Reuben Hill, J. Mayone Stycos, and Kurt W. Back, *The Family and Population Control* (Chapel Hill, North Carolina: The University of North Carolina Press, 1959), p. 22. (Reprinted by permission.)

much less predictive of mobility intentions. These findings are somewhat at odds with those of some other studies of urban mobility, which have found family life cycle and familism variables much more highly related to residential mobility.[28] However, Leslie and Richardson conclude that migration decisions are best understood as being subject to the combined forces of familial factors (stage of family life cycle, family size, attitudes toward the families of orientation and procreation) and economic factors (business cycles, careers, and job contingencies).

THE FAMILY

The family is involved in migration in a number of significant ways, but there is less research literature on the nature of this relationship than on the relationship between migration and economic factors. What is known is that residential mobility is associated with the life cycle of the family. One study found that the mobility rate for families where the head of the household was under 35 was twice as high as the rate for those families where the head was between 35 and 44, and five times greater than where the head of the household had reached 65.[29] One way to interpret this pattern is to see residential mobility as an adjustment to expanding family size, since the period of greatest movement is also the time when children are being born and are growing up. The demand for more residential space is almost surely an important factor in intraurban and urban-suburban movement.[30]

For long-distance migration, however, the family is more likely to be a deterrent rather than a stimulus to moving. First, if a long-distance move is a move away from the parental families (or kin groups) of the nuclear family, and it often is, then the move will be more difficult to make because it involves the rending of family ties. In addition, the composition of the nuclear family itself may deter movement. The presence of children in the family can lower the probability of moving because while the children are young they add to the burden of moving, and as they grow older they form attachments to their community that must be severed if migration occurs. As these children mature and leave the parental home to establish neolocal residences, their parental ties will once again act as an attraction causing them to settle nearby. The parents, now left in their "empty nest," are free to move, but in addition to long-established community ties, they may now prefer to live near their children and grandchildren. All of the considerations suggest that the family is a deterrent to long-range migration.

However, the chain described above does get broken and migration does occur. Then, paradoxically, the same features of the family can stimulate migration. One of the most common manifestations of this process is found in *chains* of migration. In chain migration, one member of a kin group moves and others follow until most of the family is relocated. Perhaps the first migrant is a son who is later followed by his younger brothers or other siblings. Eventually most of the members of the kin group may migrate to the new place.

Emigration to the United States from Southern Italy as it occurred in the late nineteenth and early twentieth century illustrates chain migration.[31] One kind of chain was initiated by the *Padroni*, or bosses, who were already established in the United States and sponsored and supported new immigrants from their home towns in Italy. Though the *Padroni* were not generally blood relatives, they were often godfathers to the immigrants they assisted. But while the *Padroni* system did account for some chain migration, it was more common among Italian immigrants for a male family member to come to the United States alone and later send for his wife and children. The new arrival usually went directly to the relatives and friends who had financed his passage. These guardians either housed the newcomer in their own quarters or found a room in the neighborhood. Work was usually found close by, since the "Little Italies" were located conveniently near the principal markets for unskilled labor. Often these immigrants intended to return to their home communities in Italy after accumulating some capital, but generally it became economically more feasible for a man to bring his wife and children to the United States and remain permanently.

Another example of chain migration has been documented in a twenty-year study of the migration patterns of families coming from several communities in Eastern Kentucky.[32] The migration of these Kentucky families to urban places was not random, but followed consistent patterns along family lines. The most common pattern was for members of a given family to settle in the same city.

The relative strengths or influences of family and economic factors upon migration patterns are not yet well-documented, but one indication is found in a study by Berardo, who reported on the migrants working in the aerospace industry at Cape Kennedy, Florida.[33] By their own evaluations, these migrants moved primarily for economic reasons. In this sample of predominantly white middle-class migrants, more than half (62 percent) indicated they had moved to Cape Kennedy for economic reasons, while only 5.3 percent moved to Cape Kennedy to be near relatives. Berardo interpreted this result as a refutation of the notion that "the location of kin influences the directional pattern of migration." However, he did note that fully one-fourth of his sample indicated that they "were reluctant to leave their former community specifically because they had family and relatives living there."[34]

A FRAMEWORK FOR THE STUDY OF MIGRATION

There is a great need for a better understanding of the relative influence of economic and family factors on the migration of individuals and families. It is likely that most migration can be explained by their often competing, but sometimes complementary, forces. At the moment, only the major outlines and dimensions of their influence can be suggested, but any minimally adequate explanation of migration will give a prominent place to economic and family factors.

There are at least three different levels at which the influence of the economy and the family on migration can be conceptualized and hypotheses of relationships can be formulated: the *societal level*, the *personal-structural level*, and the *personal-psychological level.* The following outline summarizes some of what is known about the influences on migration, and speculates on other possible relationships between migration and the family-economic factors.

I. The Societal Level

A. *Economic factors:* The direction and volume of migration will be influenced by changing economic conditions, such as economic growth or decline, expanding or contracting economies, recessions and depressions. If the economic structure of a society is characterized by bureaucratic and large-scale organizations, instead of being organized around the family group, there is likely to be more migration. In a society where the basic economic unit is the extended family, a person's economic livelihood is partially dependent upon his remaining close to his kin group. The more a person's economic position is based on ability and skill rather than family ties, the more it is possible, and perhaps even imperative, to move.

B. *Familial factors:* Migration may be influenced by structural or technological changes in the society which influence the relationships between the nuclear family and the parental families of the husband and wife. For example, new laws may produce changes in the social-security or medical-care systems and thus affect the responsibilities of the grown child toward his aged parents. The over-all result of an increase in such services would be to allow greater freedom of movement for the children, because the obligations and responsibilities toward their parents would be reduced.

Technological changes, such as improved methods of communication and transportation, would allow families to retain close family ties even though they may be living far apart geographically.[35]

II. The Personal-Structural Level

A. *Economic factors:* Migration is related to career contingencies, such as promotions, transfers, and dismissals. Migration occurs when individuals seek new jobs or change professions. Other personal economic considerations that may be related to migration include the liquidity of economic assets, the stage and nature of home ownership, the costs of moving, and the relative costs of living at the new place as compared to the old. In short, there are many economic constraints that may keep a family from moving, as well as economic motivations that impel them to move. Measuring and sorting the effects of these economic factors at the personal level is a task that remains to be done.

B. *Familial factors:* Migration is known to be related to stages of the individual and family life cycles. Young adulthood is a time of decision about whether to stay at or near one's parental home or to move away. The decision to move from the parental home may be contingent upon the ages and needs of an individual's parents. For a woman, whether or not she migrates will often be determined by whether or not she marries, or, if she does, where her husband's occupation or career take him. In the procreating family, migration may be greatly influenced by the number and needs of the children in the family.

III. The Personal-Psychological Level

A. *Economic factors:* Migration may be determined by the attitudes that individuals have about their economic circumstances and opportunities. Especially important at this level are the aspirations that people have toward economic success and upward social mobility. In general, positive attitudes about upward mobility should lead to increased mobility.

B. *Familial factors:* Migration may be related to attitudes and values about family life and kinship groups. The most salient attitudes in this realm include obligations and responsibilities toward parental families and other kin (for example, siblings, grandparents, and the like), and respect for the needs and wishes of the children in the procreating family.

The factors listed under each of the three headings are those that have either been shown to be or are likely to be related to migration patterns. Obviously, much research is needed, even to sort out the differential effects of these factors. Any given researcher will have to select the level (societal, personal-structural, or personal-psychological) that seems most relevant to him. There has been a tendency in demography to move from the societal forces to the psychological factors. As migration becomes more and more dependent upon the decision making of individuals, the attitudes and orientations of individuals become an increasingly relevant focus for understanding the movement of people.

THE EFFECTS OF MIGRATION

When people make a permanent change in their place of residence, their lives will be affected. The communities they leave and the communities they enter will also be affected. And when there is extensive mobility in a society, it is going to have some effect on the nature of the society. In this final section the effects of migration are considered.

Migration and American Character

The character and distribution of the United States population has been greatly influenced by migration, first by the migration from other countries, and second by the continuous movement of people across the continent toward the frontier. It has been argued that this continuing movement of the American people was a factor of the utmost importance in shaping American society and American character. Lee has argued that migration "has been a force of greatest moment in American civilization, and that from the magnitude and character of migration within this country certain consequences logically follow." While migration cannot totally explain everything about Americans, "it was and is a major force in the development of American civilization and the shaping of American character. . . ."[36] And American historian George Pierson has stressed that the most prevalent characteristic of Americans is their migration and "excessive mobility."[37]

The hypothesis that migration has shaped American character has been offered in lieu of the frontier hypothesis, which bears the name of the historian Turner. The Turner thesis emphasized that American institutions and character became distinct because of the existence of a Western frontier available for settlement. The migration hypothesis is not a rejection of the frontier thesis, but is instead an elaboration of it.

What, then, does the migratory nature of Americans explain? The list of items that has been suggested is fairly long and varied, and most are hypotheses rather than fully substantiated facts. For example, the migration of Americans may make them more individualistic and self-sufficient, since the American who moves from his home community cannot so easily rely on his family or kin group for support. Paradoxically, the lack of familial support may cause the migrant to exhibit an outward conformity as he makes his adjustments to new places, situations, and people. Migration may be an important factor in producing a social conformist whose radar is always picking up and adjusting to signals from his new milieu. Also, migration may be an important component in the American penchant for change, and migration can act as an "equalizer" or "democratizer" producing a less rigid social structure.

The list of American characteristics possibly attributable to migration can be extended to include the pragmatism and nationalism of Americans as well as their tolerance for disorder and corruptness. It has also been suggested that migration has been the great producer of American optimism.

These ideas and hypotheses about the effects of migration are cast in broad terms. In essence, they argue that migration has shaped the social structure and culture of the society. Such hypotheses are difficult to test because they are difficult to state with any specificity, empirical evidence is hard to collect, and the criteria for rejecting or accepting them are nearly impossible to establish. But through these macroscopic hypotheses, one is alerted to the possibility of more limited and specific hypotheses that are much more amenable to testing and thus might in the long run be more fruitful. For example, on the basis of his own research, Lee concluded that hospitalization for mental illness was related to migration. Migrants were found more frequently among the hospitalized than nonmigrants. While the exact mechanism that produced this relationship is not known, Lee suggested that the "struggle with the changing environment may play an important part."[38]

The Social Adjustment of Migrants

The factor last mentioned, the struggle with or the adjustment to the new community environment, is one of considerable importance in the study of population migration. It may be offered as a general proposition that when migration occurs there will be some disruptive effects, both for the migrating individuals and families and the receiving community.

The studies of the adjustment process of migrants have focused most closely on the adjustments of rural migrants to urban places.[39] Research findings have shown consistently that the rural migrant living in the urban place has a low economic status relative to the person who has lived in the urban place all his life. Several studies of rural-to-urban migrants have paid particular attention to the social participation of the migrants in the social and political life of the community. Generally, the migrants have a lower participation rate in the voluntary organizations of a city than do the nonmigrants. Both the economic status of migrants and their voluntary-association memberships suggest that problems of adjustment do arise when there is movement to the urban place. However, further research has indicated that the longer a migrant spends in the city the more he becomes indistinguishable from the life-long urban dweller.

Adjustment and the Family

The family or kin group appears to play a role in the adjustment of migrants to their new environment. Studies of migrants coming from the Kentucky Appalachian area showed that having family members already living in the urban place reduced some of the problems of moving. However, other studies have failed to find the presence of family or kin-group members to be of special significance in the adjustment of migrants. The determinant in this regard appears to be the status of the migrant group. If the migrants have a relatively low social status, then the presence of kin or family in the new community probably takes on special significance. Examples of such low-status migrant groups are the European immigrants in the nineteenth and early twentieth centuries, the rural migrants from Appalachia, South-ern rural Negroes, Americans of Mexican descent, and Puerto Ricans. On the other hand, if the migrant is not a member of a lower-status ethnic or racial group, the presence of family members probably will have much less influence upon his adjustment. One illustration of this point is found in Berardo's study of migrants to the Cape Kennedy area. The migrants to this Florida aerospace center were largely middle-class skilled or profes-sional workers, and Berardo found that their psychological adjustment to the new community was unrelated to the amount of contact they had with their kin. Indeed, there was a slight relationship in the opposite direc-tion: The migrants with the least kin contact were more likely to be satisfied with their new community than those with a high degree of kin contact.[40] This tendency suggests that adjustment to a new place is considerably in-fluenced by the status position of the new migrant. The higher his status, the easier and quicker the adjustment will be, and the less it will be contingent upon the presence of extended family members in the receiving community.[41]

SUMMARY

Migration occurs when individuals, families, or groups make a permanent change in their place of residence. Increasingly, in most societies, but especially in those that are urban and industrialized, migration is the result of decision making by individuals in the nuclear family.

The decision to move, or not to move, can be influenced by many different factors, but casual observation, research findings, and theoretical writings all point to the dual importance of family and economic considerations. Elements of both of these institutional factors can act to promote, as well as inhibit, migration. Under certain economic conditions migration will increase, while under others it will decline. Career and occupational considerations may keep people from migrating or force them to move. Family and kin-group factors, while most commonly inhibitors of migration, can on occasion stimulate or cause migration. Often family and economic factors are counterforces affecting migration, but occasionally they can be consonant with one another. There is a general consensus among students of population that the economic influences far outweigh the familial, but much research is still required before the effects of these interrelated forces can be sorted out. Perhaps there are other sets of factors that influence migration behavior, but in present-day societies the significance of economic and familial influences is not likely to be supplanted.

Of equal importance are the effects of migration on the social systems the migrants leave and enter, and on the migrants themselves. Families, neighborhoods, communities, and societies are all influenced by the movement of people. It is certain that both the demographic and social character of American society have been greatly influenced by the migration into and within the country. At the community level, great changes have been produced in towns, villages, and country neighborhoods that have lost people through migration. In these rural communities, the loss of young people, many of whom have migrated to the cities, has been especially significant. The cities were able to grow and thrive in part because of the talents and the energies of these migrants. But at the same time, the migrants created a variety of social and environmental problems for the urban place. These problems of urban life—problems that have been very much shaped by migration—remain to be solved in American cities as well as many other cities of the world.[42]

: : SELECTED READINGS AND MATERIALS

General

Beshers, James M. *Population Processes in Social Systems.* New York, The Free Press, 1967. Chapter 5, "Migration."

Kammeyer, Kenneth C. W., editor. *Population Studies: Selected Essays and Research.* Chicago, Rand-McNally, 1969. Section III, "Migration."

Nam, Charles B., editor. *Population and Society: A Textbook of Selected Readings.* Boston, Houghton Mifflin, 1968. Chapter 6, "International Migration Patterns"; and Chapter 7, "Internal Migration Patterns."

Scott, Franklin D., editor. *World Migration in Modern Times.* Englewood Cliffs, New Jersey, Prentice-Hall, 1968.

Shryock, Henry S., Jr. *Population Mobility within the United States.* Chicago, Community and Family Study Center, University of Chicago, 1964.

Periodicals and Journals

International Migration Review. Published quarterly by the Center for Migration Studies, 209 Flagg Place, Staten Island, New York 10304.

: : NOTES

1. Thomas J. Mills, "Scientific Personnel and the Professions," in *The Annals of the American Academy of Political and Social Science: The New Immigration,* Thorsten Sellin, ed. (Philadelphia: The American Academy of Political and Social Science, 1966), Vol. 367, pp. 35–41.

2. U.S. Bureau of the Census, *Statistical Abstract of the United States, 1969,* 90th edition (Washington, D.C.: U.S. Government Printing Office, 1969), Table No. 38, p. 33.

3. *Statistical Abstract,* Table 340, p. 233.

4. William Petersen, "A General Typology of Migration," *American Sociological Review,* 23: 264 (1958).

5. James S. Brown, Harry K. Schwarzweller, and Joseph J. Mangalam, "Kentucky Mountain Migration and Stem Family: An American Variation on a Theme by Le Play," *Rural Sociology,* 28: 48–69 (1963).

6. E. G. Ravenstein, "The Laws of Migration," *Journal of the Royal Statistical Society,* 48 Part II: 61–235 (June 1885); and "The Laws of Migration," *Journal of the Royal Statistical Society,* 52: 241–305 (June 1889).

7. Ravenstein, 1889, p. 286.

8. Samuel A. Stouffer, "Intervening Opportunities: A Theory Relating Mobility and Distance," *American Sociological Review,* 5: 845–867 (1940). Also reprinted in Samuel Stouffer, *Social Research to Test Ideas* (New York: The Free Press, 1962), pp. 68–91.

9. Stouffer, *Social Research,* p. 71.

10. In his 1960 paper, Stouffer cited the applications of the intervening-opportunities theory that had been made to that date. A few of these tests and some more recent ones include: Margaret Bright and Dorothy S. Thomas, "Interstate Migration and Intervening Opportunities," *American Sociological Review,* 6: 773–783 (1941); Fred Strodtbeck, "Population, Distance, and Migration form Kentucky," *Sociometry,* 13: 123–130 (1950); Theodore Anderson, "Intermet-

ropolitan Migration: A Comparison of the Hypotheses of Zipf and Stouffer," *American Sociological Review*, 20: 287–291 (1955); Omer R. Galle and Karl E. Taeuber, "Metropolitan Migration and Intervening Opportunities," *American Sociological Review* 3: 5–13 (1966).

11. See John W. Stewart, "Demographic Gravitation: Evidence and Application," *Sociometry*, 11: 31–57 (1948); Stuart C. Dodd, "The Interactance Hypothesis: A Gravity Model Fitting Physical Masses and Human Groups," *American Sociological Review;* 15: 245–256 (1950).

12. For the reader who may be interested in pursuing this approach to population distribution and movement, the following publication surveys much of the research and theory: Richard L. Morrill, "Relevant Migration Theory," in *Migration and the Spread and Growth of Urban Settlement* (Lund, Sweden: Lund Studies in Geography, Series B. No. 26, 1965), especially Chapter 5, pp. 33–43.

13. Everett S. Lee, "A Theory of Migration," *Demography*, 3: 47–59 (1966).

14. Lee, p. 50.

15. Lee, p. 57.

16. C. T. Pihlblad and C. L. Gregory, "Occupations and Patterns of Migration," *Social Forces*, 36: 56–64 (October 1957); Noel P. Gist and C. D. Clark, "Intelligence as a Selective Factor in Rural-Urban Migrations," *American Journal of Sociology*, 44: 36–58 (July 1938); Noel P. Gist, C. T. Pihlblad and C. L. Gregory, "Selective Aspects of Rural Migrations," *Rural Sociology* 6: 3–15 (March 1941).

17. James M. Beshers, *Population Processes in Social Systems* (New York: The Free Press, 1967), pp. 131–151.

18. Beshers, p. 133.

19. The modes of orientation come from the work of Max Weber, *Economy and Society*, Guenther Roth and Claus Wittich, eds. (New York: Bedminster Press, 1968), pp. 24–26.

20. Lee, p. 51.

21. Lee, p. 48.

22. Beshers, pp. 136–138.

23. Harry Jerome, *Migration and Business Cycles* (New York: National Bureau of Economic Research, 1926); Dorothy Swaine Thomas, *Social Aspects of the Business Cycle* (New York: Dutton, 1925); Walter Willcox, *International Migrations*, Vol. 1 (New York: National Bureau of Economic Research, 1929); Carter Goodrich, *et al.*, *Migration and Economic Opportunity: The Report of the Study of Population Redistribution* (Philadelphia: University of Pennsylvania Press, 1935), Chapter IX.

24. This explanation and the quotation are drawn from Lee, p. 53.

25. J. J. Mangalam, *Human Migration: A Guide to Migration Literature in English: 1955–1962* (Lexington, Ky.: University of Kentucky Press, 1968), p. 15.

26. Reuben Hill, J. Mayone Stycos, Kurt Back, *The Family and Population Control* (Chapel Hill: University of North Carolina Press, 1959), p. 22.

27. Gerald Leslie and Arthur H. Richardson, "Life Cycle, Career Pattern and the Decision to Move," *American Sociological Review*, 26: 894–902 (1961).

28. Peter Rossi, *Why Families Move* (Glencoe, Ill.: The Free Press, 1955); Wendell Bell, "Social Choice, Life Styles and Suburban Residence" in *The Suburban Community*, William Dobriner, ed. (New York: G. P. Putnam and Sons, 1958), p. 255.

29. Leslie and Richardson, p. 894.

30. Rossi, pp. 139–151, 177–180; Bell, p. 235.

31. John S. MacDonald, and Leatrice D. MacDonald, "Chain Migration, Ethnic Neighborhood Formation, and Social Networks," *The Milbank Memorial Fund Quarterly*, 42: 82–97 (1964).

32. Brown, Schwarzweller, and Mangalam, "Kentucky Mountain Migration."

33. Felix Berardo, "Kinship Interaction and Communications Among Space Age Migrants," *Journal of Marriage and the Family*, 29: 541–554 (1967).

34. Berardo, p. 544.

35. Eugene Litwak, "Geographic Mobility and Extended Family Cohesion," *American Sociological Review*, 25: 385–394 (1960); and Berardo, p. 552.

36. Everett S. Lee, "The Turner Thesis Re-examined," *American Quarterly*, XIII: 77–83 (1961).

37. George W. Pierson, "The Migration Factor in American History," *American Quarterly*, XIV (1962), Supplement, pp. 275–289. The following discussion reflects the combined arguments of Lee and Pierson.

38. Lee, "The Turner Thesis," p. 82.

39. Lee Burchinal and Ward Bauder, "Adjustments to the New Institutional Environment," in *Family Mobility in Our Dynamic Society*, Iowa State University Center for Agricultural and Economic Development, (Ames, Iowa: Iowa State University Press, 1965).

40. Felix Berardo, "Kinship Interaction and Migrant Adaptation in an Aerospace-Related Community," *Journal of Marriage and the Family*, 28: 296–304 (1966).

41. Burchinal and Bauder reach a similar conclusion, but go on to suggest that "continuous and near exclusive interaction with relatives, especially under conditions of insulated community life, can only accentuate inferior social status and probably retard the assimilation of migrants." (p. 222).

42. See Kingsley Davis, "The Urbanization of the Human Population," *Scientific American*, 213: 40–53 (1965), pp. 40–53; and Hans Blumenthal, "The Modern Metropolis," *Scientific American*, 213: 64–74 (1965).

Chapter 5 Mortality

The high rate of population growth in the world today is commonly called the "population explosion." In the minds of most people, the "cause" of the population explosion is the high fertility that prevails in many countries and regions of the world. In a certain sense it is true that excessive fertility is the cause, but it is equally valid to say that declining death rates have caused the high rate of population growth, for the world population can only grow when there is an excess of births over deaths. In the past half century it has been the drop in death rates that has caused the number of births to so much exceed the number of deaths. The death rate has dropped in almost every country of the world—in many of them, precipitously—while the birth rate has often remained relatively constant at a high level. Viewed from this perspective, the declining death rate is the cause of the population explosion.

The almost universal decline in death rates has resulted largely from the application of modern medicine, science, and technology. These technological innovations were often applied in populations where individual members of society had little or no knowledge of them. Yet the resultant effect upon the death rate may have been quite dramatic. For example, by action of the government, the water supply can be made purer, disease-carrying organisms can be eliminated, or transportation systems can be improved (thus reducing the possibilities of famine in outlying parts of the country). All of these actions may produce a decline in the mortality rate of the society, yet the people who benefit may be unaware, or only vaguely aware, that they have been performed. Many death-control measures can be instituted without any significant change in the values of the population.

There are other innovations that have decreased mortality, but these have required some awareness or knowledge on the part of the populace. Vaccinations and inoculations are examples of this type of innovation. Similarly, in order for them to reduce mortality, personal-hygiene practices and many sanitation procedures must be accepted by the people who use them. As a general rule, it appears that in most societies mortality-control measures have been more readily accepted than have the techniques of fertility control. In the long history of the world, almost all cultures have had to cope with the basic demographic fact of a high death rate. Under these conditions, societies invariably came to place a high positive value on life and a negative value on death.

76

But while death-control measures have been generally consonant with prevailing cultural beliefs, and have usually been readily accepted, it is also true that there have been notable instances when such innovations have been resisted. Many people resisted inoculation and vaccination when these measures were first introduced. Even though these medical innovations provided immunity from some of the most dreaded diseases in pre-industrial Europe, they were feared by many people and resisted by the leaders of the organized church.[1]

In recent years, other examples of resistance to medical and hygienic practices have been documented in connection with efforts to introduce changes into underdeveloped societies. An innovation is often based on some principle of modern science that runs directly counter to a prevailing cultural belief. One case study reported that strong resistance appeared when efforts were made to encourage the citizens in a rural Peruvian village to boil their drinking and cooking water before using it.[2] A public-health worker tried to introduce this hygienic procedure, but after two years only eleven out of the two hundred families were boiling their water. The failure was largely attributed to the fact that the practice was not consonant with the customs and beliefs of the village residents. In their culture, if water was to be boiled, it had to be done in the morning. If a woman was too busy during the morning to boil the water, she was reluctant to do so at other times of the day. The Peruvian villagers also believed that foods and drinks were inherently "hot" or "cold." This included water, which was "cold" before it was boiled, but once having been boiled it was always thereafter a "hot" substance. This belief in "hot" and "cold" substances led to a negative feeling about boiled water, since "hot" water was associated with illness. When a person was sick, it was considered better to give him "hot" substances to eat and drink. Therefore, water was boiled before giving it to a member of the family who was ill. Most of the Peruvian villagers were reluctant to boil their water when no one was ill, and they could not easily be convinced that such a practice might actually prevent illness, since a germ theory of illness was not a part of their culture.

This example shows that social and cultural practices can and do have an effect upon health and death. It is the principal aim of this chapter to demonstrate further how selected social and cultural factors influence the health and the mortality of human populations. The social factors to be considered include marital status, place of residence, social class, and racial discrimination.

MARITAL STATUS AND MORTALITY

The relationship between marital status and mortality is one of the most consistently found patterns in the analysis of mortality. In every adult age group, married persons have lower mortality rates than single persons, and the single, in turn, have lower rates than the widowed and divorced. As a general rule, the widowed persons in a population have higher mortality rates than the divorced at younger ages, but the situation is reversed when rates for later ages are measured.[3] Thompson and Lewis have shown that these mortality differentials by marital status are found in France (1945 data), Sweden (1960 data), West Germany (1960 data), and the United States (1959 data).[4] In all cases, the differences between the mortality of the married persons and the single, widowed, or divorced is greater for males than females. The single males have a death rate that is about 1.5 times as high as the married men at the same ages. The greatest single difference occurs between the married men aged 25 to 45 and those in the same age bracket who are widowed or divorced: the death rate for the widowed or divorced men is about 4.5 times as high as it is for the married men. At other age levels the difference between married men and widowed and divorced men is not quite as great, but it is, on the average, about twice as high. The pattern for the females is similar: the single women have a death rate about twice as great in the 25 to 45 age category, and about 1.5 times as great at the remaining adult ages as married women in the same age brackets. The widowed or divorced status does not seem to produce the mortality differential for women that it does for men, since widowed and divorced women have a death rate that is generally only about twice as high as it is for married women.

The reasons for these differences in mortality between the married and the unmarried have not been firmly established. Speculations have been advanced, but their validity is based mostly on their plausibility. Two general factors are most frequently offered as explanations: (1) the selection process that occurs when people choose marriage partners; and (2) the differences in living patterns, particularly those related to health and well being, between married and unmarried persons.

The first of these two explanations rests upon the assumption that in the process of mate selection those persons who are in poor health or have physical and mental disabilities will be less likely to find marriage mates. These persons thus remain in the single category and contribute disproportionately to the higher mortality of that group.

The second explanation of the mortality difference between the married and the unmarried rests on the idea that married people live healthier lives. The married person has a more regular life, eats more nutritious food, and has someone to care for him in case of sickness. Presumably all of these factors contribute to better health and, thus, to lowered mortality. This set of factors would account for the differences not only between the married and the single, but also between the married and those who have been widowed or divorced. But still other factors may be advanced to help explain the higher mortality of widowed and divorced persons. With respect to those who have been widowed, it may be noted that the same environmental and social conditions that led to the death of the person's mate may also contribute to his own death. Further, the increased incidence of suicide among the widowed and divorced is both indicative of psychological instability and a direct contributor to a higher death rate. Another significant factor is that both divorce and widowhood are not randomly distributed in the population, but are found disproportionately among the lower socioeconomic classes. Since there are more divorces and separations, and more younger deaths among the lower social classes, a part of the mortality differential between the married and the widowed/divorced can be accounted for in terms of their social-class position in the society.

RURAL-URBAN DIFFERENCES

In 1622 John Graunt of London analyzed rural and urban burial records and concluded

that the Country is more healthfull, then the city . . . so as the Fumes, Steams, and Stenches above-mentioned, although they make the Air of *London* more equal, yet not more *Healthfull.* [5]

Graunt's assertion that the country was a more healthful place to live than the city was derived from a comparison of the number of burials in a rural parish with the number in the city of London. While in the past demographers have generally agreed with Graunt's observation, today they are much less sure of its validity than they once were. The evidence about differential rural-urban mortality is sometimes conflicting, and there is often the possibility that some uncontrolled factor is intruding to make the over-all relationship a spurious one. The plausible or logical arguments for expecting higher mortality in either the urban or the rural place are of limited value because they can be made with equal strength on both sides of the case. The argument for lower mortality in the rural place is built around a premise expressed in the statement of Graunt quoted above. It is usually accepted without question that the country affords a more healthful environment for living than does the "crowded and dirty" city. Graunt, for example, explained the increased mortality of London in the seventeenth century by the smoke produced from burning the "Newcastle Sea-Coals"; a practice that had increased in the sixty years prior to his writing.[6]

There is a consensus that the urban place is crowded, dirty, unsanitary, smoky, a breeding ground for infectious diseases, and a place where life is beset by high tensions and anxieties. All of these unpleasant conditions have been, and are now, found in cities, and they do presumably contribute to ill health and death, but the extent to which they still produce a rural-urban death differential (which favors the rural place) is not absolutely clear. There is, for example, the counterargument emphasizing the superior medical and health care to be found in the urban place. This positive feature of city life would contribute to better mortality conditions in the city and favor the alternative hypothesis that mortality rates should be higher in the country.

The issue of rural-urban mortality differences is further confounded by the possibility that data quality may be contributing to the observed differences. It is possible that rural places keep poorer records on deaths, and thus the lower death rates that have often been found in rural areas may be due to low-quality data. One study has shown that the lower rural mortality rates found in three developing countries (India, Mexico, and Taiwan) were the result of underregistration of deaths in rural areas. Arriaga, the researcher who conducted this study, has said flatly that the "underdeveloped countries have a higher rural mortality than urban at the present time."[7]

Another possibility is that the differences in rural-urban mortality have been gradually changing over time. Before the conquest of infectious diseases, perhaps the city did have a distinctly poorer health environment than the country. But with a better understanding of disease transmission and the application of sanitation measures, cities may have erased the major rural-urban differences in environmental quality. The irony of this observation is that modern-day urban-industrial places may be moving again toward a less healthful environment: It appears that the by-products of industry and transportation in the cities are once again threatening the health and lives of urban dwellers.

On the basis of empirical evidence, Glass has reported that there is still a small advantage for the rural over the urban place.[8] But Thompson and Lewis have shown that the pattern is now related to age. Their conclusion, based on data from the United States, England, and Sweden was:

It would appear probable that city populations now possess certain advantages over rural populations in controlling deaths up to about 30–35 years of age, while at older ages living conditions in rural communities are better suited to retarding the onset of the chronic and organic diseases which develop later in life.[9]

SOCIAL CLASS AND MORTALITY

In all major societies, historical and modern, there have been, and are still, differentiations and inequalities that distinguish groups or categories of people. These groups and categories have been described as the social classes, or the socioeconomic strata of society. Social classes have been identified in a variety of ways, but sociologists generally agree that the different classes in a society share economic characteristics (differential access to material goods), possess different levels of political power, and have different styles of life for which they receive varying amounts of honor or prestige.[10]

Through their control of the economic resources and the political power of the society, those social classes that stand higher in the hierarchical structure have better and more "life chances" than those that are lower. Life chances include all of the valued and desired objects in the society, such as personal comfort, freedom of movement, entertainment, education, good health, and, of course, the greatest of all life chances, life itself. There is much evidence to support the proposition that people in different social classes do have different life chances, including the chance to live longer lives. In fact, insofar as the evidence exists, this proposition appears to be almost universally true.

The task of identifying, differentiating, and measuring social classes in a society has engaged many sociologists. While the theoretical concept of social class is multidimensional and complex, there is general agreement among sociologists that a number of different indicators can be used to measure social-class levels. Among the indicators that have been used to differentiate social classes in modern societies are income, occupation, education, and place of residence. The following discussion of the relationship between social class and mortality will accept the assumption that any of these indicators may be used legitimately to index social-class levels.

Antonovsky has provided the best and most complete review and assessment of the research literature on social class and mortality.[11] He examined and summarized literally dozens of studies, ranging from the life expectancy of the "legitimate offspring of British kings, queens, dukes and duchesses" between 1330 and 1954, to the most recent studies of age-specific mortality of different occupational categories in the United States. The studies he reviewed cover wide-ranging historical periods and a variety of western countries. One can best summarize Antonovsky's conclusions by quoting his overall evaluation directly:

Despite the multiplicity of methods and indices used in the 30-odd studies cited, and despite the variegated populations surveyed, the inescapable conclusion is that class influences one's chance of staying alive. Almost without exception, the evidence shows that classes differ on mortality rates.[12]

Among the few exceptions to the general rule is a study of employed males in the 15–64 age bracket in Amsterdam between 1947 and 1952. In this study the five occupational groups studied did not have the mortality differences typically found in other studies. For example, the mortality rate of the skilled workers did not differ from that of the unskilled workers; and the clerical-worker group had a mortality rate slightly higher than both the skilled and unskilled workers. This deviant case, reported by Antonovsky, occurred in a time and place that had "just about the lowest death rate ever recorded," and thus supported the further hypothesis "that as the overall death rate of a population is lowered, class differentials may similarly decline."[13]

In the earliest studies of class and mortality, the lowest class had a mortality rate about twice as high as the highest class, but in the later studies (since 1940) the ratio has more typically been about 1.3 or 1.4 to 1. This decline in the ratio coincided with an over-all decline in mortality and suggests that when the mortality rate is going down rather precipitously the differential between classes is more pronounced. Antonovsky summarized this point by saying,

> . . . when mortality rates are extremely high or extremely low, class differences will tend to be small. In other words, when men are quite helpless before the threat of death, or when men have made great achievements in dealing with this threat, life chances will tend to be equally distributed. On the other hand, when moderate progress is being made in dealing with this threat, differential consequences are to be expected.[14]

The relationship between class and mortality also varies by age. In study after study, the mortality differences between the classes has been greatest in the middle adult years, reaching a peak in the years between 30 and 44. After that, the social class differences in mortality start to diminish, and beyond age 65 they tend to disappear completely.[15]

The Chicago Studies

An excellent series of studies on mortality and social class was conducted by a group of demographers at the University of Chicago.[16] By combining mortality data and census-tract data on median rent or median income (used as indicators of socioeconomic status), these researchers provided a convincing demonstration of the effects of social class (and also race) on the life expectancy of Chicago residents. The data for this research cover a time period between 1920 and 1950 and reveal a mortality pattern that probably prevailed in American society generally during those years.

These studies made use of a demographic tool known as the *life table*, a method of analysis that goes back to the seventeenth-century political arithmeticians. Essentially, the life table is produced by applying known age-specific mortality rates to a hypothetical population numbering 100,000. The mortality rates, when applied on a yearly basis to this hypothetical cohort of people, determine the number of people who would remain at the end of each year. These figures can be used to calculate the number of people of any given age surviving to any later age. Since it is possible to determine the total number of years the entire cohort will live before the last one dies, the total number of years can be divided by the number of people in the hypothetical cohort (100,000) to determine the average length of life, or what is called *life expectancy*.[17]

In the Chicago studies of mortality the life table was used as a tool to measure the life expectancy for males and females and for Whites and non-Whites at five socioeconomic levels for the years 1920, 1930, 1935, 1940, and 1950. The socioeconomic status of individuals was determined, not by their individual characteristics, but by the median rental value or median income of the census tract in which they lived. While this is neither the most direct nor the most desirable measure of an individual's social-class position, the findings of the research are strong enough and consistent enough for one to feel reasonably confident about their general importance.

The analyses of Chicago mortality revealed that for males and females and Whites and non-Whites, those people with higher socioeconomic statuses had a greater average life expectancy than those with lower socioeconomic statuses. The extent of class differences was revealed by the number of years of life expectancy that separated people in different classes. Among the White males and females in 1930, the highest-status group lived on the average about 11 years longer than the lowest-status White group. Between 1930 and 1950 this difference in average life expectancy for Whites diminished, so that by the latter date it was about 7 years (about 6 years for females, 8 years for males). For the non-Whites in the population the difference between those in the highest- and lowest-status groups was about 9 years in 1930 and between 6 and 7 years in 1950.

While these differences by social class are quite large, the differentials were even greater when socioeconomic status and race were considered simultaneously. One such analysis revealed that in 1950 one-third of all the deaths among the residents of Chicago would not have occurred if the death rates of the highest status White group had prevailed for the entire population.[18]

Even more shocking is the fact that the non-Whites in Chicago, as late as 1950, might have reduced their deaths by one-half if they had had the same mortality as the highest status White group. In the year 1930 more than two-thirds of all non-White deaths in Chicago would not have occurred if they had enjoyed the same survival chances as the highest-status White group.

One could perhaps react to these facts by attributing them to an earlier historical period when the society was much less concerned with its disadvantaged citizens and racial minorities. However, such a sanguine position does not yet appear to be justified, for some recent research has again revealed pronounced class differences in mortality.[19]

Educational Level

There have always been severe methodological problems in studies of the type reported above. The major problem has been that the data on deaths generally come from the vital-statistics registration system, usually the death certificate, but such a source provides very little reliable data on the social and economic characteristics of the deceased. The result is that most studies, except for relatively small, specialized inquiries, have had to resort to indirect measures of social-status characteristics. Such was the case with the Chicago studies, in which social class had to be based on an economic characteristic of the census tract in which the deceased person lived. To overcome these difficulties, the Population Research and Training Center of the University of Chicago, with the cooperation of the National Center for Health Statistics and the Bureau of the Census, carried out a special study of deaths that occurred in the United States shortly after the data of the 1960 census were gathered. By a process of matching the death certificates and census data on individuals who died in 1960, much more detailed and more reliable information was obtained. These data allow for a detailed analysis of differential mortality by social-class level.

The researchers designated four levels of educational attainment: (1) less than 8 years of school; (2) elementary school, 8 years; (3) high school, 1 to 4 years; and (4) college, 1 or more years. Using these levels as indicators of the socioeconomic-status level, they found that "there was a strong inverse relationship between mortality and level of education attainment in the white population of the United States in 1960, with consistent declines in mortality as years of schooling increased."[20] The mortality differences by educational level were found to be greater for females than for males. For White women between the ages of 25 and 64 years, the mortality rate for the least-educated group (less than 8 years of school) was 61 percent higher than for college-educated women. Among the White males between 25 and 64 years, the mortality rate of the least-educated group was 48 percent higher than that of the college educated. Over age 65, there was little difference in mortality for the males with different educational levels, but for the females the death rate was still 59 percent higher for the least educated group.

Principal Causes of Death

The mortality differences by educational level were based on all causes of death combined, but this study also provided interesting data on the specific causes of death for the two sexes at different ages.

The three major causes of death in the United States ranked in the same order for both males and females. The principal cause of death was the category labeled *major cardiovascular-renal diseases*, which includes heart disease, hardening of the arteries, vascular lesions affecting the central nervous system, hypertensive disease, rheumatic fever, and chronic rheumatic heart disease. About 60 percent of the male deaths and 61 percent of the female deaths were caused by these cardiovascular-renal diseases. Next in importance were the *malignant neoplasms* (cancers), which accounted for about 16 percent of male deaths and 19 percent of the female deaths. The third major cause of death, though much smaller than the previous two, was the general category *Accidents*, which accounted for about 5 percent of male deaths and 3 percent of female deaths. The remaining causes of death—the most important being, roughly in order, influenza, pneumonia, cirrhosis of the liver, diabetes mellitus, suicide, and tuberculosis—accounted for less than 20 percent of the total, and no single one contributed as much as 4 percent.[21]

Among the three leading causes (cardiovascular-renal diseases, malignant neoplasms, and accidents), there were some distinct variations by age and sex. These variations are shown in Table 4.

TABLE 4. MAIN CAUSES OF DEATH AMONG WHITE MALES AND FEMALES BY
       SEX AND AGE, PERCENTAGE OF TOTAL

Causes of death	Males			Females		
	Total	25–64	65+	Total	25–64	65+
Cardiovascular-renal	60.4%	50.7%	66.0%	61.9%	38.8%	69.9%
Malignant neoplasms	16.2%	18.2%	15.0%	18.6%	32.8%	13.7%
Accidents	4.8%	8.8%	2.4%	3.2%	4.8%	2.6%
Other causes	18.6%	22.3%	16.6%	16.3%	23.6%	13.7%
Total	100.0%	100.0%	100.0%	100.0%	100.0%	100.0%

Source: Kitagawa and Hauser, "Educational Differentials in Mortality by Cause of Death: United States, 1960," *Demography*, 5: 328–332 (1968), Table 7. (Reprinted by permission.)

This table shows that for both sexes the cardiovascular-renal diseases were more likely to be the cause of death at later ages than at younger ages. However, the difference was most pronounced for the females where the increase went from 38.8 percent for the younger females to 69.9 percent for the older females. With regard to the malignant neoplasms, the males and females again showed similar patterns: cancer caused a higher percentage of deaths before age 65 than after. However, for females cancer was much more frequently the cause of death at the earlier ages than it was at the later ages (32.8 percent compared to 13.7 percent). As might be expected, accidents caused a higher percentage of deaths at the younger ages than at the later ages. This was true for both men and women, but the difference by age was particularly great for men, where accidents were almost four times as likely to be the cause of death below 65 years as they were above 65 years (8.8 percent of all deaths compared to 2.4 percent).

One further note about accidents as a cause of death should be added. One hears a great deal about automobile accidents as a cause of death in the

United States, so it is of some interest to know how much they contribute to mortality. First, for all males 25 years and over, motor-vehicle deaths accounted for 2 percent of the total, while for females they accounted for 1 percent. This cause of death was again highly age related, accounting for a much higher percentage of the deaths under age 65. For males 25 to 64 years, motor-vehicle deaths accounted for 4.1 percent of the deaths, while they accounted for only .7 percent of the deaths after age 65. For females in the younger and older age groups, the comparable percentages were 2.7 percent and .4 percent respectively.

Educational Level and Specific Causes of Death

The relationship between educational level and specific causes of death has also been examined. It should first be recalled that between the ages of 25 and 64 years the effect of education on mortality was quite pronounced for both sexes, but at age 65 and over only the female mortality rate showed differences by educational level. One might take this fact to mean that for males over 65 the effects of social class are no longer important, but this is not the case. For males over 65, certain specific causes of death were related differently to educational level. In this age group of men, deaths due to some diseases were found more often among those who were more highly educated, while deaths due to other diseases were found less often. These opposing relationships with education had the effect of canceling each other out, so that for men aged 65 and over there appeared to be no relationship between educational level and over-all mortality. The canceling effect can be demonstrated by considering the concrete case that is most responsible for it. Among males 65 years and older those with a high educational level were less likely to die of cardiovascular disease than those with less education. On the other hand, those with higher education had a greater likelihood of dying from cancer than the less educated group. One form of cancer—cancer of the prostate—was much more likely to appear among the more highly educated men than among those who had less education. While this effect occurred among the men 65 years and over, among the men between 25 and 64 *every* major cause of death was more prevalent among the less educated than the more educated, so there was no canceling effect.

Among younger men some specific causes of death had a very strong relationship to educational level. For example, the mortality rate as a result of tuberculosis was more than eight times higher for the less educated men than for those with the most education. Influenza and pneumonia, accidents (motor-vehicle and all others), and certain kinds of cancer (stomach, lung, bronchus, and trachea) were also found much more often as the cause of death among the less educated younger men than among those with more education.

Among the females, both below and above 65, there was only one major exception to the general pattern of higher mortality rates for the less educated. Cancer of the breast was the exception, since it was found to be the cause of death more frequently in the high-status group than in the low-status group. It was also noted that for women aged 65 and over cancer of the uterus and other female organs had about the same prevalence at all social-class levels.[22]

The general pattern of an inverse relationship between education and causes of death (the higher the educational level the lower the death rate) was clearly demonstrated by the data of this study. Kitagawa and Hauser noted that this inverse relationship held for the eight causes of death which accounted for 83 percent of all deaths of White adult males and females.[23] In commenting on the apparent "social causes" of death in American society, these researchers call attention to the possibility of reducing the currently static mortality rate by changing certain economic and social conditions. One might, for example, consider what percent of the White adult deaths in 1960 *would not have occurred* if the people in the three lowest educational levels had had the same mortality as those persons who had at least one year of college. The estimate from this study is that 9.4 percent of White-male deaths and 29.3 percent of the White-female deaths would not have occurred if people at all four levels of education had experienced the same mortality.[24]

RACE AND MORTALITY

The foregoing analysis of 1960 data covered only the White portion of the American population, but as the earlier Chicago studies revealed clearly, the effect of social class on mortality was evident for the non-White as well as the White population. Further, the combined effect of social class and race proved in the Chicago studies to be at least partially additive, that is, a person's race and his social-class position both influenced the length of his life.

Non-Whites in the United States have higher death rates than Whites at every age from birth onward. During the first three years of life the non-White death rate is approximately twice as high as the White rate. During the childhood and teenage years the differences are not as great, but the death rate for non-Whites always exceeds that for the Whites. Beginning at age 20 the death rate for non-White females moves to about double the White female rate, while the male differential does not double until about age 25. From the young-adult years until about age 45 the non-White rate for both males and females is always twice as high as for the White rate, and sometimes, especially for the females, the death rate for non-Whites is nearly triple that of the Whites. The mortality rate for non-White females during the middle-adult years is apparently increased by their greater maternal mortality (deaths related to pregnancy and childbirth). During these childbearing years the non-White maternal-mortality rate is about 3.5 times as high as White maternal mortality. After the age of 45 the non-White mortality rate continues to be about one and one-half times as high for the non-White males and about twice as high for the non-White females as for Whites in the same categories.[25]

The persistently higher mortality of non-Whites in the United States is explained by a number of factors, most of which reflect the patterns of discrimination and segregation imposed upon Black Americans. In addition to the corrosive effects of intense poverty experienced by many Negroes, there are also well-documented patterns of discrimination that prevail with regard to medical and hospital services. Throughout the country, including northern cities, Negroes are often not allowed to use the available hospital and medical facilities freely. Often they are limited to using the public hospitals and medical centers even though they are economically able and willing to pay for the services of private facilities.[26]

INFANT MORTALITY

The human infant is a very defenseless and dependent organism at birth. Without considerable care over an extended period of time, its chances of survival are very small. For this reason characteristics of social organization may have a most dramatic effect upon infant mortality (death during the first year of life.) Social disorganization in a society or community is likely to have a noticeable effect on the infant-mortality rate. Newsholme wrote in 1910, "Infant mortality is the most sensitive index we possess of social welfare and sanitary administration, especially among urban conditions."[27]

In American society the infant-mortality rate remains surprisingly high compared with those of many other countries. In the decade of the 1960s at least twelve countries had infant-mortality rates lower than the United States (see Figure 4).[28] As might be expected from the previous discussion, the most pronounced difference in infant-mortality rates within American society is the difference between the rates for Whites and non-Whites. In the United States the non-White rate continues to run nearly twice as high as the White rate. In 1967 the White rate was 19.7 deaths per 1000 live births compared with the non-White rate of 35.9 per 1000.[29]

The Chicago studies of mortality and socioeconomic status found that between 1930 and 1950 the infant-mortality differential among social classes was dramatically reduced for the White population. The infant-mortality rate in 1930 for the White population in Chicago with the lowest socioeconomic status was 125 percent higher than the rate for the highest-status White group. In 1950 the average was about 40 percent higher. However among the non-Whites the differences between the highest-status and the lowest-status groups were much less pronounced, and it was more difficult to discern a trend

INFANT DEATHS PER 1,000 LIVE BIRTHS

FIGURE 4. INFANT MORTALITY IN COMPARABLE NATIONS AS REPORTED TO THE UNITED
NATIONS IN 1968. Source: *United Nations Demographic Year Book, 1968.* The rates
represented are for 1967, except those for the following countries: Finland, New
Zealand, United Kingdom, France, Eastern Germany, and the United States, which
are for 1968; and the rate for Norway, which is for 1966. Reprinted here from *Children,*
17:84 (May-June 1970).

between 1930 and 1950. In part, this finding may be accounted for by the fact
that among non-Whites the status differentials were also much less pronounced, but there may be yet another reason why the non-White population
had a less clear class-related pattern; that is, the residential segregation of
Negroes in urban America.

In 1950, Yankauer reported a study of infant mortality in New York City,
and while his evidence is not conclusive, it does suggest that racial segregation
(residential) may well have been implicated in high infant-mortality rates.[30]
Yankauer, a former District Health Officer of New York City, divided the city
into areas according to the degrees of racial segregation, from those areas with
the highest percentage of non-White residents to those areas with the lowest
percentages. Yankauer found, as expected, that both non-White and White
infant-mortality rates increased as one went from the areas with the lowest
percentage of non-White residents to those with the highest percentage. But
the important finding of the study was that *he did not find significant economic
differences* among the non-Whites who lived in differently segregated areas

of the city. The non-Whites who lived in the nearly all-White areas and those who lived in the nearly all-non-White areas did not differ much in their occupational and educational characteristics. This finding suggests that the differences in non-White infant mortality between those non-Whites living in the most segregated ghetto areas of the city and non-Whites living in the nearly all-White areas must be explained on some other basis than simply socioeconomic status. What, then, was the answer? Why did the non-Whites who lived in the urban ghettos have higher rates of infant mortality than those non-Whites who lived in more integrated or nearly all-White areas? The answer to this question may be found by examining some of the features of the urban ghetto. One characteristic of urban slums and ghettos is fairly well known; namely, that people who live in them pay *more* money for *poorer housing*. Due to discrimination practices in the renting and sale of housing outside the ghetto, Black citizens as well as other ethnic or racial minorities subjected to discrimination must often pay artificially high prices for inferior slum housing. This inequity in housing costs means that the ghetto resident must use a higher proportion of his total income for housing; thus he has less money available for other things required for healthful living—including medical care. It is hardly necessary to add that the poor quality of the housing itself is detrimental to the health and well-being of the inhabitants.

An additional characteristic of the ghetto is that retail shopping outlets are limited. There is an inadequate supply of food and merchandise, and that which is available is often of poor quality and over-priced. This additional strain on the ghetto dweller's budget is likely to have at least an indirect effect on his health.

Another characteristic of the ghetto is its extreme overcrowding. The dense residential population creates a generally unhealthy environment, and is particularly likely to produce unsanitary conditions. This factor also leads to an overcrowding of neighborhood medical facilities. The relatively few hospitals and clinics that are accessible for ghetto residents are typically overcrowded and understaffed.

While the exact impact of these various ghetto conditions on non-White infant mortality is not known, there can be little doubt that the sum total of these adverse conditions must contribute to the observed relationship between urban residential segregation and infant mortality.[31]

SUMMARY

There is substantial evidence to suggest that the nature of a social system directly influences the life chances of members of the society. One significant feature of social life that has a pronounced effect upon mortality is the social-class system. While the effect of socioeconomic status is greatest when the death rate is undergoing a change from a high to a low level, the studies by Kitagawa and Hauser indicate that as late as 1960 in the United States (although the death rate had been around 10 per 1000 for a number of years), the social-class level of a person was still clearly related to cause of death.

Further, the Black citizens of the United States, who have existed and still do exist in a social system that is shaped by racism, clearly have a mortality pattern—by any of several measures—that reflects their position in the social structure. The data on non-White mortality should alert Americans to the price that the society has paid, and continues to pay, for official and de facto policies of racial segregation.

: : SELECTED READINGS AND MATERIALS

General

Iskrant, Albert P., and Paul V. Joliet. *Accidents and Homicide.* Cambridge, Mass., Harvard University Press, 1968.

Kammeyer, Kenneth C. W., editor. *Population Studies: Selected Essays and Research.* Chicago, Rand-McNally, 1969. Section IV, "Mortality and Morbidity."

Nam, Charles B. *Population and Society: A Textbook of Readings.* Boston, Houghton-Mifflin, 1968. Chapter 6, "Mortality Trends and Differentials."

Shapiro, Sam, Edward R. Schlesinger, and Robert E. L. Nesbitt, Jr. *Infant, Perinatal, Maternal, and Childhood Mortality in the United States.* Cambridge, Mass. Harvard University Press, 1968.

Periodicals and Journals

Milbank Memorial Fund Quarterly. Published by the Milbank Memorial Fund, 40 Wall Street, New York, New York, 10005. The *Quarterly* contains articles on a variety of population topics, but often on mortality and morbidity.

Statistical Bulletin of the Metropolitan Life Insurance Co. Published by Metropolitan Life, One Madison Avenue, New York, New York, 10010. The Bulletin is frequently devoted to specific issues of mortality and morbidity.

: : NOTES

1. Bernhard J. Stern, *Social Factors in Medical Progress* (New York: Columbia University Press, 1927), pp. 53–65.

2. Edward Wellin, "Water Boiling in a Peruvian Village," in Benjamin D. Paul, ed., *Health, Culture and Community* (New York: Russell Sage Foundation, 1955), pp. 71–103.

3. Donald Bogue, *The Principles of Demography* (New York: John Wiley & Sons, 1969), p. 605.

4. Warren S. Thompson and David T. Lewis, *Population Problems*, 5th edition (New York: McGraw-Hill, 1965), pp. 365–366.

5. John Graunt, *Natural and Political Observations Mentioned in a Following Index and made upon the Bills of Mortality* (London: 1662. Reprinted by the Johns Hopkins Press, Baltimore, 1939), p. 76.

6. Graunt, p. 76.

7. Eduardo E. Arriaga, "Rural-Urban Mortality in Developing Countries: An Index for Detecting Rural Underregistration," *Demography*, 4: 98–107 (1967).

8. David V. Glass, "Some Indicators of Differences Between Urban and Rural Mortality in England, Wales and Scotland," *Population Studies*, 17: 263–267 (1964).

9. Warren S. Thompson and David T. Lewis, *Population Problems*, 5th edition (New York: McGraw-Hill, 1965), p. 364.

10. This conceptualization, in its essentials, follows the ideas of German sociologist Max Weber, who wrote in the early years of the twentieth century. See Weber's *Economy and Society*, Guenther Roth and Claus Wittich, eds. (New York: Bedminster Press, 1968), Vol. 2, pp. 926–939.

11. Aaron Antonovsky, "Social Class Life Expectancy and Overall Mortality," *Milbank Memorial Fund Quarterly*, 45: 31–73 (1967).

12. Antonovsky, p. 66.

13. Antonovsky, p. 66.

14. Antonovsky, p. 68. In the following chapter we will see that a nearly parallel pattern appears in the relationship between social class and fertility. Class differences in fertility are greatest during the period when fertility is declining most rapidly.

15. Antonovsky, p. 67.

16. The studies of differential mortality in Chicago which serve as the basis for the following discussion are: Albert J. Mayer and Philip Hauser, "Class Differentials in Expectation of Life at Birth," originally published in *La Revue de L'Institut International de Statistique*, 18: 97–200 (1950), and reprinted in *Class Status and Power*, edited by Reinhard Bendix and Seymour Martin Lipset (Glencoe, Illinois: The Free Press, 1953), pp. 281–284; and Evelyn M. Kitagawa and Philip M. Hauser, "Trends in Differential Fertility and Mortality in a Metropolis—Chicago," in *Contributions to Urban Sociology*, edited by Ernest W. Burgess and Donald J. Bogue (Chicago: University of Chicago Press, 1964), pp. 59–85.

17. For a detailed, yet simplified, description of the life table, see William Petersen, *Population*, 2nd edition (New York: Macmillan, 1969), pp. 209–213. For much more extensive discussions see George W. Barclay, *Techniques of Population Analysis*, (New York: John Wiley & Sons, 1958), pp. 93–134; and Hugh H. Wolfenden, *Population Statistics and Their Compilation* (Chicago: University of Chicago Press, 1954), pp. 81–136.

18. Kitagawa and Hauser, in *Contributions*, p. 81.

19. Evelyn M. Kitagawa and Philip M. Hauser, "Educational Differentials in Mortality by Cause of Death: United States 1960," *Demography*, 5: 318–353 (1968).

20. Kitagawa and Hauser, "Educational Differentials," p. 333.

21. Kitagawa and Hauser, "Educational Differentials," pp. 347–348.

22. For a further discussion of the differential incidence of cancer (not necessarily fatal) among social classes, ethnic groups, and nationalities see Graham Saxon, "New Clues to the Causes of Cancer," *Trans-action*, 5: 43–48 (1968).

23. Kitagawa and Hauser, "Educational Differentials," p. 348.

24. Kitagawa and Hauser, "Educational Differentials," p. 350.

25. U.S. Bureau of the Census, *Statistical Abstract of the United States: 1969*, 90th ed. (Washington, D.C.: U.S. Government Printing Office, 1969), p. 54.

26. St. Clair Drake, "The Social and Economic Status of the Negro in the United States," *Daedalus*, 94: 771–846 (1965). See also Thomas F. Pettigrew, with Ann Pettigrew, *A Profile of the Negro American* (Princeton, N.J.: Van Nostrand, 1964).

27. Sir Arthur Newsholme, *Report by the Medical Officer on Infant and Child Mortality*, Supplement to the 39th Annual Report of the Socal Government Board (London, 1910).

28. Frank Falkner, "Infant Mortality: An Urgent National Problem," *Children*, 17: 83–87; Helen C. Chase, "Registration Completeness and International Comparisons of Infant Mortality," *Demography*, 6: 426–427 (1969).

29. U.S. Bureau of the Census, *Statistical Abstract of the United States, 1969*, p. 55.

30. Alfred Yankauer, "The Relationship of Fetal and Infant Mortality to Residential Segregation," *American Sociological Review*, 15: 644–648 (1950).

31. Yankauer, p. 648.

Chapter **6** Fertility

Since, as was discussed in the last chapter, the rapid growth of the world's population has actually resulted from a decline in mortality, it follows that population growth could be slowed down by increasing the death rate. Indeed, it is possible that in the next several decades the death rate may increase greatly in certain regions of the world. But no one is seriously suggesting that rapid population growth *should* be reduced by raising the death rate. Therefore, the world is left with only one humane solution to its population problem: Fertility must be reduced. A unanimity is developing in support of this position, a unanimity that did not exist a decade ago. At that time people either were unaware of rapid population growth or were offering a variety of pseudo solutions—migration to other planets, living on or under the sea, and the like. The general issue of world-population growth will be discussed in the next chapter, but it is mentioned here because an understanding of fertility behavior will be a crucial factor in the solution to the population problem. This chapter considers various issues related to fertility. Some will ultimately bear directly on the possible solutions to the population problem; others are presented for their intrinsic interest.

FERTILITY AS SOCIAL BEHAVIOR

Much of the material in this chapter will illustrate the proposition that fertility behavior is eminently social behavior—behavior that is shaped by the social contexts and the decision making of individuals and couples. Most of the variations and changes in fertility behavior, whether they occur within a society or between societies, cannot be accounted for by biological or physiological factors. Of the three dynamic features of population, fertility falls between migration and mortality in the degree to which it is biologically or physiologically determined. And although there is no convenient metric for quantifying this assertion, it appears that fertility behavior is close to migration at the social end of the continuum.

There is a need at this point to distinguish between the terms *fertility* and *fecundity*. When American demographers use the term *fertility*, they invariably mean the actual fertility behavior of some person or group. To the demographer the word fertility does not indicate the fertileness of a person or group, as it usually does to the layman—and apparently also to the medical

94

profession.[1] Instead, the word *fecundity* is used to refer to the biological capacity for reproduction. Referring back to the distinction between the social and the biological character of fertility, the argument is that variations in the level of fertility are *not* the result of differences in fecundity, but are more often produced by the responses of individuals and couples to the social systems in which they live.

BIOLOGICAL THEORIES OF FERTILITY

Historically there have been a number of population theories that argued for declining fecundity as the primary causal factor in declining fertility. Theories of this sort, labeled biological theories, often focused upon some societal characteristic, and argued that it affected fecundity, which in turn resulted in reduced fertility. Illustrative of this genre of theory is Sadler's principle that as a population grows more dense, fecundity declines. Conversely, Sadler argued, if the population is sparse, the fecundity of the population increases.[2] Sadler was writing in the early part of the nineteenth century, and was specifically arguing against the Malthusian theory of population growth. His theory ran counter to Malthusian theory because, according to Sadler, populations have a built-in mechanism that will keep them from growing too large. As density reaches a certain—unspecified—level, fecundity will decline and the population will stabilize at an optimum number.

Another of the well-known biological theories is that of the nineteenth-century English scholar Herbert Spencer. Spencer argued that as societies develop and become more complex, there is a natural decline in the fecundity of the population. The reduced capacity for reproduction, according to Spencer, was directly attributable to the amount of energy expended upon "mental labour carried to excess."[3] Spencer was particularly sensitive to the women of modern society, about whom he wrote scoldingly, "the deficiency of reproduction power among them may be reasonably attributed to the overtaxing of their brains—an overtaxing which produces a serious reaction of the physique."[4] So for Spencer, the working woman, especially one who did mental work, was diminishing her capacity to reproduce children. Interestingly, it is true that there is a distinct tendency for women who are employed, particularly in managerial or professional occupations, to bear fewer children than women who are not employed, but this is likely to be due much more to personal choice than to infecundity.

At least two major biological theories have emphasized a dietary factor as the cause of reduced fecundity. The first was a theory advanced by Doubleday, who argued that whenever a species or genus is threatened by adverse conditions, nature compensates for this danger by increasing its fecundity. Since a shortage of proper food may be such a threat to a population, the fecundity of its women will tend to increase under conditions of food scarcity. Conversely, according to this theory, whenever the food supply is abundant, the capacity for reproduction will tend to decline.[5]

In the 1950s Josué de Castro, a Brazilian nutritionist, advanced a theory in which he argued that the amount of protein in the diet is *inversely* related to reproductive capacity. Thus, when the proportion of protein in the daily diet is high (as it generally is in modern, industrial countries) the fecundity will be low. Alternatively, when the amount of protein in the diet is low, fecundity will be high. The evidence de Castro provided to support his theory was generally correlational; that is, data correlating the protein levels in the diet with birth rate. He showed that countries with a high amount of protein in the daily diet had the lowest birth rates and vice versa. Such evidence only proves that two factors covary in some fashion, and does not prove any causal connection. De Castro did describe some experimental evidence produced by studies of rats, but the results were not conclusive enough to allow inferences about human populations to be made.[6]

It is not the intention in this brief discussion to debunk the biological theories of fertility. The interested reader is invited to examine these authors, particularly de Castro since his theory is most current and most adequate by present-day scientific standards. In this way the validity of the theories can be evaluated more fairly. The position taken here is simply that if there are physical or biological factors affecting fecundity, and thus fertility, it must be left to the physiologists and biologists to conduct the research, for they possess the necessary technical skills to make the tests. Simultaneously, it is the task of the social scientist to investigate the influence of his particular system of variables on the phenomenon of human fertility. That will be the goal of this chapter, for as stated at the outset, the basic premise is that social and human motivational factors will have a great influence on fertility.

CHILDLESSNESS

Our point of departure for demonstrating the importance of social factors is an analysis of childlessness. Childlessness is generally attributed to fecundity, or as the case has it, infecundity. If a woman bears no children during the years when she would normally be capable of reproduction, the cause can be either physiological or social. If a woman does not have a child because she is physiologically incapable (or her mate is), then the cause is infecundity or sterility. If there are other factors involved, the cause may be broadly considered social. Bogue recently analyzed childlessness in detail and produced evidence suggesting that even this extreme form of childbearing (or nonchildbearing) is much influenced by social factors.[7]

The first and rather obvious social factor influencing childlessness in a total population is the proportion of the population entering into marriage. If some number of women in the society do not marry and do not bear children while unmarried, then the proportion of childless women in the society will thereby be increased. Most European countries, and to a lesser extent the United States, have higher percentages of never-marrying people in the population than other countries of the world, so they also have a higher proportion of childless adult women. But this factor alone does not account for all childlessness. The rest must be attributed to either involuntary or voluntary sterility. Judging from the nations of the world in which nearly everyone enters marriage and very little fertility control has been achieved, it has been estimated "that not less than 5 percent of all couples around the world are physiologically unable to bear children and will remain sterile throughout their lives as a result."[8]

Some countries have reported as many as twenty-five and thirty percent of their women aged 40 and over to be childless, but the countries with the highest percentages where the statistics were reliable are the United States and Hungary. These two countries reported approximately 18 percent of their women aged 45 to 49 years to be childless. (This figure for the United States is somewhat high because it refers to the women who had completed their fecund years in the early 1960s, and thus includes women who went through their prime childbearing years during the 1930s. During the depression years there was a general reduction in fertility that was produced in part by some women who chose to remain childless. It appears that cohorts of United States women who are now completing their childbearing years will have a smaller percentage of childless women.) Following Bogue's estimate, the fact that 18 percent of the women in Hungary and the United States were childless means that approximately 10 to 12 percent of the women in these two countries apparently chose not to have children.

Bogue also analyzed childlessness among all United States women over 15 years of age who had been married at least once. The analysis of this more restricted category eliminated the factor of childlessness due to spinsterhood. Comparing the percentages of the women who were childless at various educational-attainment levels, Bogue found that being childless was highly related to education. For every age group, among Whites and non-Whites, those women with the most education had a much higher rate of childlessness than those at the lower educational levels. While not conclusive evidence, this consistent relationship between education and childlessness suggested that not bearing children is often a matter of choice, not infecundity.

It has frequently been observed that non-White women are more often childless than White women. This higher percentage of childlessness among non-Whites has usually been attributed to the higher incidence of venereal disease among non-Whites. Especially before the end of World War II, the venereal-disease rate was high for non-Whites, and doubtless contributed to sterility. Yet venereal disease was found more frequently among the less educated than the more educated, so that if this factor accounted for childlessness among the non-Whites, there should have been more childless women among the less educated. This was not the case; rather, the opposite condition prevailed, with the most highly educated non-White women having decidedly higher percentages of childlessness than the less educated.

These facts do not preclude the possibility that much of the *total* non-White childlessness has been due to infecundity. Since the number of non-White women with low educations greatly exceeded those with high educations, it is still possible that childlessness among non-Whites could have been caused by infecundity. Finally, as Bogue observed, since non-Whites with high education are more often childless than non-Whites with low education, the same relationship as prevailed for Whites, "the nonwhite population seems to be responding to the same forces that promote childlessness as is the white population. . . ."[9]

Differential Fertility

An elementary way of demonstrating the effects of social and cultural systems on fertility is to examine differential fertility. The analysis of differential fertility among societal groups or categories has been one of the most enduring tools of social demography. It has doubtless been so because of the availability of data for major social groupings (or census categories)—for example, White-non-White populations, rural-urban residence, and occupational and educational levels. A major category that has traditionally produced fertility differences is religion, but this is a social characteristic for which United States census data have not been available. The result is that special surveys have been needed to reveal religious differences in fertility.

An examination of differential fertility will accomplish several tasks. In addition to sensitizing the reader to the general relevance of social factors, this analysis serves to identify the causal mechanisms producing fertility differences. By locating the groups or categories in the society that have different levels of fertility, it is possible to make some inferences about the operative mechanisms that will eventually be isolated as the determinants of fertility. General explanatory theories of fertility must, as a minimum requirement, explain variations in fertility that have been observed between such segments of the population as rural and urban residents, racial groups, or social classes. Therefore, an analysis of differential fertility is both a search for theoretical understanding and, as theories emerge, a partial test of their validity.

There is also an intrinsic reason for examining differential fertility. It is of interest to know which groups and categories in American society have been, and are at present, demonstrating high levels and low levels of fertility. One would also like to know, whenever possible, what the expectations for the future are. Will the now existing differences between religious, socioeconomic, and racial groups grow larger or diminish? These are some of the questions that will be considered in the following discussion.

Racial Differentials

It is hardly an overstatement to say that most people in the United States discovered race in the 1960s. It is probably not necessary to recount the stages and events in the Black Revolution, but recent developments include the emergence of Black pride and Black identity, accompanied by dramatic exposures of a backlashing White racism. All of these things have increased the awareness of race in American society. At a time when many Americans, perhaps a majority, were at least sensing that a racially integrated society might be the route to a more stable, less threatening society, the vanguard of the Black Revolution turned toward "separatism." The success of this effort will be determined by the response of the "middle" of the Negro population, and this response in turn will shape much of the behavior, including the fertility behavior, of Black Americans. The theoretical rationale behind this statement will be developed more fully below; it is sufficient to say here that the position of Black Americans in the social structure of the society—whether integrated or separated—will be of prime importance to their demographic future. Before developing this point, it may be helpful to review some of the demographic experiences of Negroes in America, and to present some facts about recent Negro-White fertility differences.

The best estimates of Negro fertility during the nineteenth century are found in the work of Farley.[10] Using census data, he estimated that between 1830 and 1880 the crude birth rate of American Negroes was over 50 per 1000 population. For the years between 1830 and 1850 he set the Negro birth rate at 53.9. For 1850 to 1880 his estimate was 54.5. During the same five decades, the crude birth rate for the White population dropped from 51.4 to 35.2.[11] A birth rate of over 50, such as prevailed among both Whites and Negroes in 1830, is a rate that approaches the highest found in the world today, and probably represents a near maximum under conditions of inadequate nutrition and poor medical care.

While non-White fertility has always been higher than White fertility, the degree to which it has exceeded White fertility in this century has not been as great as is often supposed. Generally, since 1920 the non-White fertility rate has been about 30 percent higher than the White rate, although in 1965, the year of greatest difference, it was 46 percent higher (see Figure 5).[12]

Except for the period between 1947 and 1950, the trends of non-White fertility, the increases and decreases, have always paralleled those of White fertility. Figure 5 shows the trend lines for White and non-White fertility since 1920. Similarities in the up and down trends are quite striking, although it does appear in several instances that the trend was more pronounced for one or the other of the two racial groups. Perhaps the most striking example of this tendency occurred between 1950 and 1957, when the increase in fertility rate was more pronounced for the non-White population. While the trend lines vary somewhat, their general similarity again supports the proposition that the forces influencing fertility have been the same for the White and non-White populations.

Several special features of non-White fertility trends have engaged the interests of demographers in recent years. One is a paradoxical feature of non-White fertility, described by Farley in the following manner:

Crude birth rates for the Negro population of the United States indicate that fertility declined while Negroes remained in the South and then climbed in the last twenty-five years as Negroes became urbanized. . . . Negro fertility has risen despite the urbanization of Negroes and improvements in their socio-economic characteristics.[13]

The particular aspect of this phenomenon that is most in need of explanation is the dramatic increase in non-White fertility during the decade between 1947 and 1957. During the first three years of that decade, White fertility actually declined; then it turned and went up until 1957, but not as dramatically as non-White fertility. One reason for this racial difference was suggested in the discussion of childlessness above: The fecundity of Negroes in the United States doubtless increased during the years after World War II due to the decline of venereal disease as well as other fertility-impairing diseases. Also during the years after World War II, many Negroes moved to urban places where general health conditions were better than those in the rural South. Medical care, through private and public health facilities, was likely to be more available to Negroes in the cities than it had been at their former places of residence.[14]

The second factor accounting for the paradox of increasing Negro fertility at a time of increasing urbanization lies in the distinction between a statistical and cultural definition of the word "urban." Farley hinted at this idea when he said, "Much evidence suggests that despite urban residence Negroes are not being assimilated as previous in-migrants were."[15]

Petersen presented a much stronger case. He argued that the Negroes migrating from the rural South to the urban North "have not been a self-selected group especially well equipped for urban jobs and modes of life. Their migration has been primarily *out* of the rural South, and thus to cities even when there were no urban jobs available."[16] Petersen noted that similar

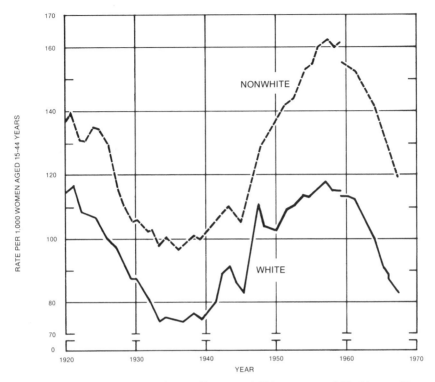

FIGURE 5. FERTILITY RATES BY COLOR. (Rates per 1,000 women aged 15–44 years. For 1959–64 based on registered live births; for 1920–59, on live births adjusted for underregistration.) Sources: *Natality Statistics Analyses, United States 1964* (Washington D.C.: National Center for Health Statistics, 1967), Series 21, No. 11, p. 12; and *Statistical Abstract of the United States 1969*, 90th edition (Washington, D.C.: U.S. Government Printing Office, 1969), Table 57, p. 48.

patterns of urbanization have recently occurred in underdeveloped countries. He also pointed up some historical instances:

In England of c. 1800 . . . many of the declassed peasants who swarmed into the rising industrial centers found jobs in the new factories, but over several decades the not yet established urban working class could hardly be distinguished from the lumpen-proletariat of paupers and casual workers. And the present massive shift of American Negroes to the centers of American civilization has been stimulated less by the attraction of urban jobs than by the rejection of the rural South.[17]

In short, a great many nominally urban Negroes in the 1950s were more rural than urban in their orientation, experience, and outlook. They left the rural place because economic, political, and social pressures forced them out. They entered an urban social structure that discriminated on the basis of race. The Negroes found discrimination in housing, education, and employment such that they, even more than previous in-migrants, were kept from being truly assimilated into the urban culture. They came to the cities as disadvantaged rural people, and as a result of discrimination they remained disadvantaged in many ways. Their fertility patterns in this circumstance remained more rural than urban, except that improved medical care may have increased the general level of their fecundity.

The Future Fertility of Black Americans

Since 1957 both the White and non-White fertility rates have been dropping, with the non-White rate dropping more rapidly. But what can be expected for the future, particularly for the non-White segment of the population? Part of the answer lies in the analysis of non-White fertility broken down by social classes.[18] One study in the 1950s revealed that non-White women with at least a high-school education, particularly if they lived in urban areas, had lower fertility than Whites with a comparable educational status. The data implied that if non-Whites continued to improve their general socioeconomic position in the society, particularly if economic, educational, and residential discrimination could be reduced in urban places, their over-all fertility level would be equal to that of Whites.

More recently, fertility data from the 1960 census, plus information from some special social surveys, were offered in support of a different theoretical interpretation of the fertility of Negroes, as well as other societal minorities.[19] The theory treated the minority status of a group in a society as an important factor influencing the fertility of that group. All data point in the same direction: Negroes in American society, Jews in the United States and Canada, and Japanese Americans in the United States have had *lower* fertility in the *upper and middle socioeconomic levels* than Whites of similar status. This observation suggests that the minority status of a group will act to reduce the group's fertility level below that of the dominant group. The primary operative mechanism of such a theory is the "insecurity" associated with minority-group status. If the minority group identifies with the goals and objectives of the majority, and if it is segregated from the majority group, then reduced fertility can be expected. (At least this prediction will be valid for minority groups that do not have strong norms and values favoring reproduction—as do Roman Catholics, for example.) Goldscheider and Uhlenberg, the formulators of this theory, say, "As minority group persons enter more generally into competition with the majority community, they tend to counteract some of their disadvantages by deferring or limiting childbearing."[20]

On the converse side, "If the desire for acculturation is not an integral part of the social situation of the minority group, members of minority groups often become concerned with group preservation and quantitative strength."[21] It is for this reason that the direction of the Black Revolution in

America is a factor of some relevance to the future demographic patterns of American Negroes. Perhaps the separatist tendencies of the current movement will not move the majority of American Negroes away from a long-standing integrationist movement. If structural barriers to integration are broken down, separatism should be less and less attractive as a solution to problems. Should integration be achieved, there would be reason to expect that the differences between White and Negro fertility will gradually diminish during the decade of the 1970s. If, however, separatism is accepted by the majority of Black Americans, then their fertility may remain substantially higher than that of Whites.

Differences among Religions

In the United States, Catholics, Jews, and Protestants are the broad religious groupings that have typically been studied for signs of differential fertility. At this level, the pattern of differential fertility is fairly clear and the findings are consistent. Catholics have had, and continue to have, higher fertility rates than Protestants and Jews.[22] Further, people who do not have a religion generally have the lowest fertility. While the religious differentials are clear, it is nevertheless difficult to establish that it is religion per se that influences fertility. The problem of interpretation is difficult because religion is related to other variables, which are themselves related to fertility. For example, religion is related to race (Negroes tend to be Protestant), residence (Catholics and Jews are more often urban dwellers than Protestants), and socioeconomic status (Jews are generally of a higher status than Catholics). Thus, several confounding factors have to be held constant if the effect of religion alone is to be established. In one study, in which the religious factor was successfully isolated, the researchers matched the 66 Jewish subjects in a national sample with Catholics and Protestants having the same social and economic characteristics. They concluded from this analysis:

Comparisons between the matched groups can be summarized as indicating that the fertility complex for Protestants is very much like that for Jews when they have similar social and economic characteristics, but that this is not true for Catholics. On almost all of the comparisons, the difference between Jews and Catholics is as great or greater when the social and economic characteristics are controlled as when they are not.[23]

Differences within Religions

Jews

Among Jews the major factors that have been found to influence fertility are generational differences and socioeconomic status.[24] First-generation (immigrant) Jews had larger families than did second-generation Jews, but third-generation Jews increased their fertility over their parents. With regard to socioeconomic status the evidence is somewhat tentative. Among first-generation Jews the highest fertility occurred among those who were low in the socioeconomic structure. For second- and third-generation Jews the opposite has prevailed: The higher the social class, the larger the family size.

Protestants

Among Protestants there are denominational differences in fertility,[25] but since the various denominations have such great variability in their social and economic makeup, it is difficult to assess the effects of denominationalism alone.

Both the Indianapolis study of "Social and Psychological Factors Affecting Fertility," and the Princeton study of "Family Growth in Metropolitan America" examined the effects of denominationalism on fertility, and in each instance the final judgment was that denomination was of little importance after other related variables such as social class had been controlled.[26]

An interesting case in which a dimension of religiosity was found to be related to fertility *attitudes* appeared in a study of the Southern Appalachian region.[27] Among the people in this region (metropolitan and urban residents as well as rural), the more fundamentalistic a person's religious beliefs were, the more likely he was to favor large families and oppose birth-control practices. Particularly in the metropolitan areas, the religious fundamentalists favored high fertility values more than their less fundamentalistic neighbors.

Catholics

Among Catholics in the United States the influence of a Catholic education on fertility is quite pronounced. Catholic women who have been educated in Catholic schools tend to be less successful in planning family size as their educational level is increased. However, if a Catholic woman has been educated in non-Catholic schools, then the success of her family planning increases with more education.[28] The same pattern appears with regard to desired family size. Women with Catholic educations desire more children as their educational level goes up, but among Catholic women who have not gone to Catholic schools there is no relationship between educational level and family-size desires. The same patterns hold true for Catholic husbands, although the tendencies are not as strong as for the wives.[29]

One recent international study of fertility and the Catholic religion produced new understandings of both religion and minority-group status.[30] In countries where the population was predominantly Catholic, the fertility of Catholics was almost always lower than in those countries where the Catholics were in the minority. Some populations were exceptions to the rule, but even they could be considered supportive when examined carefully. For example, a majority of the people in Ireland were Catholic, and yet the Irish Catholics had a high fertility rate. Day noted this exception to the general trend, and suggested that in historical perspective Ireland "is probably not really an exception at all, but rather, an instance of a sovereign people still thinking of themselves as a beleaguered minority vis-à-vis a recently dominant majority (the English)."[31] This explanation highlights the operative mechanism that seems to result in Catholic minorities having higher fertility rates than Catholic majorities. According to Day, "where Catholics are a majority there is no need to feel threatened or at bay *as a Catholic*, and hence, no particular incentive either to seek out co-religionists for support and example, or to attach oneself more closely to the Church and its teachings on account of the slights (or worse) one feels oneself to have suffered on its behalf."[32]

This analysis of Catholic-minority fertility has some convergences with the discussion of Negro fertility in the United States. While unique historical events may produce a different outcome for any particular minority group, there are in these two analyses some elements that suggest a minority-group theory of fertility. In the case of Catholic minorities, it was suggested that minority-group status plus ethnocentrism may explain their high fertility. This same set of concepts, only slightly modified, may explain or predict some features of Negro fertility in the United States. As suggested above, if Negroes in the United States increasingly see themselves as a minority group attempting to maintain their racial identity rather than lose it in an integrated society, new patterns in Black fertility may emerge. The well-known separatist policies of the Nation of Islam (popularly known as the Black Muslims), a religious-social organization, may be an example of the degree to which Black separatism will favor high fertility. Edwards has reported that the Black Muslim couples in his study had families which could be characterized as a "stair-step succession of births." And "the Muslim subjects expressed indignation and disgust at the queries on birth control methods. Not a single Muslim respondent [fourteen families] reported that any methods of birth control 'natural,' or otherwise, had been used by either spouse since they became serious adherents to the ideology of the Nation of Islam."[33]

Both the Catholic-minority fertility and Black Muslim fertility values are consistent with the notion that a minority group will attempt to retain its integrity in a dominant and alien society by increasing its fertility. This explanation can also be employed, with some adjustments, to explain the high fertility of other groups, such as religious groups like the Canadian Doukhobors and American Mormons, or nationalist groups like the Jews in Israel (surrounded as they are by the Arab majority).[34]

Socioeconomic Status

The relationship between socioeconomic status and fertility has been noted so frequently in both the writings of demographers and the discussions of laymen, it hardly seems possible that there could be any further discussion of the issue. "As socioeconomic status increases the level of fertility decreases," is simply the scientist's way of expressing the old chiche that ends, "and the poor get children." The scientific and the popular statements are partially valid, but they must be qualified. One kind of qualification is historical, for the evidence is that the relationship between high fertility and low social class in Western society has been stronger during some periods of history than others. There are certain social, economic, and technological conditions under which the relationship holds, while under others the relationship is weakened, modified, or even reversed.

Traditional Societies

It has been argued that an exception to the usual inverse relationship between fertility and status may be found in the traditional peasant society, where "numerous progeny are seen as good." Under these conditions, "the classes with the greatest control over their destiny ordinarily live longer and also have larger families."[35] Supporting this position is a study of twenty Polish villages where, in two generations of peasant families, the wealthier, land-owning couples had more children than those couples less well off. Additional support for the proposition may be found in India. Davis reported in his analysis of the Indian population that a study was conducted among an exclusively rural sample of 275 Punjab villages, and there was some tendency for the higher-status villagers *in agriculture* to have higher fertility. However, the fertility of school teachers, priests, clerks and menials did not conform to this pattern, but showed the more familiar relationship between high status and low fertility.[36] Several scholars have found that in agricultural areas of China there was also a positive association between socioeconomic status and fertility.[37]

While a positive association between economic status and fertility may prevail in some traditional peasant societies, there is also evidence that the opposite occurs. There are instances where fertility control is practiced among the wealthier classes in order to maintain their favored position. This is likely to occur when some valued resource is in limited supply and a large progeny threatens to exhaust it. For example, the Nambudiri Brahmins, a rich, land-owning caste in Southern India, have exercised great control over the number of their offspring.[38] Large numbers of children would force them to divide their estates, causing them to lose some of their economic and social advantage. To avoid this result they restrict fertility severely, and when necessary resort to infanticide.

The over-all validity of the proposition that fertility and economic status are positively related in peasant societies remains to be demonstrated by additional evidence.

Socioeconomic Status in Western Society

It is possible to discern some changes and trends in the relationship between social class and fertility in Western society during the last century. Wrong reviewed the experiences of several Western European countries, plus Australia, Canada, and the United States, and concluded that the year 1910 was a significant historical turning point in the relationship between social class and fertility.[39] While there had been a long-term tendency for the lower social classes to have higher fertility than the higher social classes, it was not until the beginning of a rapid decline in fertility in about the years 1870 to 1880 that the relationship became pronounced. "The inverse correlation of fertility and socioeconomic status [higher class-lower fertility] was probably more marked in the period . . . [between 1870–1910] than it has ever been before or since in Western civilization."[40]

This inverse relationship between status and fertility, particularly during the period between 1870 and 1910, must be attributed in great measure to the differential practice of birth control in the different strata of the society. The upper-middle classes started using the available methods of family limitation first, while it was later and only gradually that the lower classes began to use them. These class differences in fertility control have been documented best in a study by Banks,[41] and by the Indianapolis study of fertility in the United States.[42] While there are still some differences in the effective use of birth-control techniques by the several social classes, this factor was probably most influential in producing class differences in fertility around the turn of the century.

After 1910 there was a much less uniform pattern in the relationship between class and fertility. There was, first of all, a general contraction of fertility differences among the various socioeconomic groups. Furthermore, while the upper classes led the way in declining fertility before 1910, certain intermediate classes began to do so after that date. According to Wrong, "It can be concluded, then, that leadership in rate of decline tended to pass in this period to the low-status non-manual workers, urban wage-workers, and the middle-income groups."[43]

During the thirty years between 1910 and 1940 there was a general tendency for the lower classes to have more children, but by the end of that period there were many more exceptions to the trend than at earlier times. Some of these exceptions were in the form of reduced relationships between fertility and socioeconomic status, and others showed varying degrees of positive associations. The exceptions to the inverse relationship have manifested themselves in three basic patterns. These patterns, plus the inverse relationship, are shown schematically in Figure 6.

The relationship shown in A is the familiar inverse relationship between socioeconomic status and fertility found most prominently in the period 1870

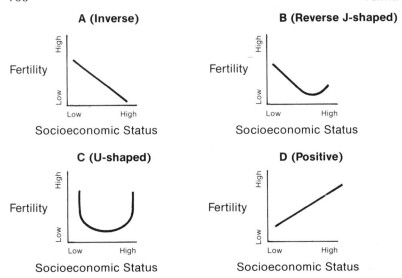

FIGURE 6. SCHEMATIC FORMS OF THE RELATIONSHIP BETWEEN SOCIOECONOMIC STATUS AND FERTILITY

to 1910, as described above. The relationship shown in *B* is one of the variants that appeared in some populations after 1910, and it too shows a general inverse relationship, but the pattern is changed because the very highest socioeconomic classes have fertility that is somewhat higher than the middle class. This "reverse J-shaped pattern" was observed among French public-service employees in 1906, in numerous United States cities in 1930, and in the entire urban population of the United States in 1940. "Most of the American studies showed that only the highest of the two or three highest income groups, amounting to a relatively small percentage of the total population, deviated from the usual inverse pattern."[44]

The pattern shown in *C* is a "U-shaped curve." It depicts the lowest and the highest social classes as having the highest fertility, and the middle classes as having the lowest. In terms of actual fertility, the U-shaped pattern was found in Oslo, Norway in 1930, and in a modified form in Sweden for a short period in the 1930s, where the smallest families tended to be found in the middle of the income range.[45]

Ideal family size (the number of children parents *think* would be the ideal) has also been related to status. Samples of adults from several European countries between 1939 and 1958 show both the U-shaped pattern and a positive association between socioeconomic status and fertility ideals.[46] In Great Britain and Germany fertility ideals often had a U-shaped relationship with socioeconomic status, with the lowest and highest social classes indicating a preference for more children than the middle classes. By contrast, and illustrative of the positive relationship, in both Sweden and France the lowest economic groups often had the lowest average ideal family size and the highest status group had the highest ideal family size.[47]

Finally, the positive association between *actual* fertility and socioeconomic status has been observed in several highly delimited populations. The most frequently cited case is that found in the Indianapolis study in 1941. The sample of this study was intentionally restricted to native White urban Protestants who had been married between 1927 and 1929. In the final sample, slightly more than one thousand families were interviewed and they provided the data for one of the most elaborate and extended fertility studies ever conducted.[48]

The couples in the sample of the Indianapolis study were classified according to their success in having the number of children they wanted. Four general categories were defined: (1) "Number and spacing planned," (2) "Number planned," (3) "Quasi-planned," and (4) "Excess fertility." These labels are relatively self-explanatory, but since category 1 is the most relevant for the present discussion a few words may be said about it. The couples in this category were those who indicated that they had been completely successful in planning their fertility in the sense that "they had no pregnancies that were not deliberately planned by stopping contraception in order to conceive."[49] Among these particular couples, the ones with the highest socioeconomic status had the highest fertility. Fertility was measured by the number of children ever born per 100 couples; and socioeconomic status was measured by twelve different indicators of status, plus a summary index based on a combination of eight. Some measures of status showed the positive relationship between socioeconomic status and fertility more clearly than others. Those showing the strongest associations were "husband's annual earnings since marriage," and "educational attainment of the husband."[50] It must be reemphasized, however, that the positive relationship was found only among those couples who planned both the number and spacing of their children. It did not even hold for those couples who were successful in planning the *number* of their children.

In addition to this oft-cited positive relationship found in the Indianapolis study, some positive associations have been found in studies of select segments of the Swedish and American populations. In studies of Swedish populations in the 1920s and 1930s, positive relationships were found between income and fertility. Other American studies that revealed positive associations were limited to particular elite groups, such as graduates of Ivy league schools.[51]

While these few instances of positive relationships between social status and fertility have been noted in modern societies, they have not completely replaced the inverse relationship. However, the differences that are found between classes (if inverse) do tend to be much smaller than they were previously. In the 1960 "Growth of American Families Study," for example, husband's income did have a slight negative relationship with fertility (and fertility expectations) for the Protestants in the sample, but for the Catholics the relationship tended to be U-shaped, with higher fertility in the lowest and highest income groups.[52] When husband's occupation was taken as the indicator of status, the same relationships occurred. However, when farm families were excluded, the differences between occupational-status groups were very small.

These observations relate to the point recently made by Goldberg, who argued that much of the inverse relationship between economic status and fertility (at least in the United States) is due to the interaction effects of farm background.[53] His analysis of the Indianapolis data and other recent studies revealed that the "traditional inverse relationship between fertility and economic status in the total population may be largely attributed to the negative relationship between those variables among farm reared elements of the population."[54]

The total effect of what has been learned about the relationship between socioeconomic position and fertility may be summed up in a few brief statements. The inverse relationship was most pronounced in Western society when the birth rate started to fall rapidly in the last part of the nineteenth and the first part of the twentieth century. It resulted primarily from the different responses of social classes to family-limitation and birth-control practices. As birth-control practices became available and were accepted throughout the social structure, new patterns of fertility emerged. The relationship between status and fertility has sometimes been found to be U-shaped and, on occasion, positive. This information has led to a certain amount of speculation and theorizing about the pattern of this relationship that might be expected in the future. One possibility is that the "three different types of relation between fertility and income represent different stages in a process of transition from the inverse pattern."[55] In line with this idea, the final stage of the process could be a positive relationship between status and fertility, or no relationship at all. Some writers have expressed the belief that differences in the fertility rates of social classes are likely to disappear completely; that is, there will be no relationship, either positive or negative. Yet the isolated instances of a positive relationship between status and fertility are seen by others as a sign of the future.

An Economic Theory of Fertility

One writer who believes that the higher economic classes will have more children than the lower classes is the economist Becker.[56] His theory has provoked a great deal of interest and stimulated much discussion among demographers. Becker employed the conceptual framework of the economist to theorize about the relationship between economic status and fertility. He based his theoretical scheme on the assumption that in modern societies there is widespread availability and acceptance of contraceptive techniques. He argued that when such a situation prevails family formation is largely controlled by the decision making of individual couples. Becker thus started by positing the ideal-typical situation, where "each family has perfect control over both the number and the spacing of its births." Under these conditions, parents who get some "psychic income or satisfaction" from their children will consider them as a "consumption good."[57] If children are equivalent to consumer durables (such as major appliances and automobiles), then the economic principles that apply to consumption should also operate in family formation. Specifically, as the real income of a couple is increased they will expend more on each child (increase the quality), but more importantly they will also have more children (an increase in quantity).[58] There is much evidence supporting the proposition that there will be greater expenditures on each child as a family's income increases. However, the important demographic proposition here is that *the number of children will increase as income increases.* About this hypothesis the facts are much less clear, for it assumes the same positive correlation between socioeconomic status and fertility that was just discussed, and except for some fragmentary evidence, the positive relationship has not often been observed.

Blake is the most outspoken critic of Becker's theory.[59] However, her research and analysis is important beyond the effect that it may have on Becker's theory, for it carefully explores the entire question of the motivations and constraints surrounding childbearing. In particular, she has developed a critique of Becker's economic explanation of fertility that seriously questions the direct analogy between having children and buying consumer durables. One of her first and most effective criticisms is concerned with the system of constraints surrounding the purchase of consumer durables on the one hand, and the bearing of children on the other. The "desire" or "demand" for economic goods is controlled and limited by the credit system of the economy. A person can generally get only as many goods as he can reasonably pay for. The credit system will act to keep the consumer generally within his economic means. Therefore, the acquisition of consumer durables *will* be commensurate with one's economic position, because an external institution sees to it that it is so. Is there an analogous constraint mechanism with regard to the acquisition of children? As Blake makes clear, there is not. Indeed, when it comes to having children, the social system *supports* people in their choice to have them, even in the face of their inability to "pay the price":

. . . not only are individuals under strong institutional pressure to marry and start a family, but the decision to do so, even in the face of financial difficulties, receives widespread moral (and, if necessary, tangible) encouragement. The "consumption" of a family by individuals who cannot "afford" one is regarded quite differently from their decision to purchase a consumer durable that they cannot afford.[60]

This matter of the social support for having children is of great significance for understanding fertility behavior. Societies do tend to give great moral support to the production of children, even to the extent of giving people the freedom to have more children than they can "reasonably" afford. It must be noted, however, that one researcher has found some evidence that the matter may not be as extreme as Blake suggests. Rainwater interviewed individuals coming from 257 American urban families, exploring their reasons and justifications for large and small families. While the people interviewed gave many different reasons for approving and disapproving of both large and small families, Rainwater concluded that there was one central norm operating: "One shouldn't have more children than one can support, *but one should have as many children as one can afford.*"[61] But Blake's assertion can still be valid in the face of this norm, for there is great tolerance in the range of "what people can afford" when it comes to children. And again it must be emphasized that there is no institutional structure comparable to a credit system that will act to control the acquisition of children. At best there is only the social opprobrium coming from friends and relatives, and it typically comes only *after* the family size is "too large."

In addition, there are social norms about family size that will keep the lower economic groups from having the few children that would be more in accord with their economic ability. A family with no children or one child runs counter to the norms of most societies. Rarely do people consider one child or no children the ideal-sized family. Less than one-half of 1 percent of a sample of American women thought that a family size of zero or one was ideal.[62] But the norm against the very small family goes beyond personal preferences. Rainwater found that feelings about the woman who wants only one child are very negative, while the woman who wants a larger number of children is evaluated much more favorably. Particularly among a sample of people from the lower economic strata, the "woman who wants only one child" is viewed as being selfish, sick, neurotic, and cold. In contrast, the "woman who wants three children" is viewed as an average, good, and loving person, while the "woman who wants seven children" is thought of as a good woman, patient, kindhearted, and sweet.[63]

Another consideration militating against the very small family (at any economic level) is that the only child is seen as an inferior product by most people. The only child is considered selfish, spoiled, and lonely, so the minimum "acceptable" number of children in a family is two, even for the least well-to-do people. This norm again detracts from the possibility of a positive association between socioeconomic status and fertility, since the lower ranges of fertility are effectively excluded for all families.

There are indirect costs and considerations associated with childrearing that may operate more for the wealthy than for the lower social classes, and which may discourage those people with the greatest economic resources from having the most children. For many lower-status people the chances for upward mobility are so remote that they may give little attention to the fact that having fewer children may enhance their chances, or their children's chances, for mobility. By contrast, the wealthier classes, even though they are already in advantaged positions, may limit their family size in order to give their children the greatest possible opportunity for still further mobility.

Furthermore, on the matter of costs, the higher classes may have more alternative opportunities—for example, travel, entertainment, civic activity, leadership—which make the *indirect costs* of having children higher for them than for the lower classes.

Finally, Blake examined the question of why children have utility in the first place. The answer is that the production of children provides more than just "psychic income or satisfaction." The more crucial sociological point is that through their familial and kinship systems societies produce a *social* need in individuals for "family statuses, family satisfactions and kinship affiliations" that can only be met by having children:

That one should desire these statuses is the final result of complex institutional control, but, *given this desire*, children and only children can satisfy it. It is the societal support for the family that provides the strong desire for children and that makes it highly unlikely that poorer people will be willing either to remain childless, or to curtail their family size to the extent required for producing a direct relation of family size and income.[64]

Becker's theory places all of its emphasis on the model of economic consumption, and in so doing it neglects the social factors that are equally influential. There is a need for an ordering of all the salient factors, both economic and social, in a complete theory of reproduction.

A FRAMEWORK FOR STUDY

This concluding section describes a framework for understanding the process of family formation in developed societies. These ideas cannot properly be called a theory of fertility because too many elements of a good theory are still missing. The objective is to present a way of looking at the process of family formation so that it is consonant with and illuminated by the existing evidence.

An elementary sociological proposition about fertility serves as the basic principle of this frame of reference: Every social system, if it is to survive, must have an institutional structure and value system that ensures the continuing production of new members. Without institutional and cultural forms supporting reproduction, a society would not replace the members lost by death, the population would decline, and eventually the society would disappear. An extension of this proposition is that the institutional structure and the cultural values that societies have developed to ensure reproduction have been developed under historical conditions of high mortality. The short average length of life that prevailed in earlier historical periods indicates that many people died before they reached reproductive maturity. Under these conditions, only reproductive norms that produced very high fertility could provide the replacements necessary for the society to maintain or increase its population size.

It is also necessary to note that people must not only be motivated to bear children, but, because of the helplessness of the human animal through the first years of life, they must also be motivated to care for and rear children. People must receive satisfactions from the parental role; thus, the social system provides such rewards.

From a sociological perspective, societal support for childbearing and childrearing is a fundamental fact that shapes fertility patterns. It provides the basis for both the theoretical and practical approaches to human fertility. The remainder of this chapter will be concerned primarily with the theoretical implications of societal support, while the next chapter will consider more fully its practical applications.

Fertility as the Result of Decision Making

It is a basic assumption of the framework being introduced that fertility behavior in present-day, urban-industrial society is the result of a decision-making process by individuals and couples. Through most of history and in all societies, demographic events have been largely determined by fate, or chance. To use the words of one writer, "fertility [was] the fateful concomitant of the expression of sexual desires."[65]

However, increasingly, particularly in modern societies, this submission to fate is no longer the most prominent feature of childbearing behavior. Individual couples are making the decisions about the children they have:

We find that fertility has become dependent on a conscious decision to have children, although, as in mortality, uncontrollable biological factors which cannot be controlled at the present time still play a large role.[66]

While fertility can be viewed as the outcome of decisions made by individual couples, one must also recognize that the actual decision will not always be on a conscious level, and it certainly will not always be a single, unitary act at a particular point in time. Back has pointed out that there is a "psychic cost" for the freedom to make decisions. Knowing that a decision can have important consequences for his life, the individual may avoid making it, or make it by default. For example, although two people may have contraceptive techniques available to them, they may not use them regularly. This behavior is not the same as the conscious decision to conceive a child, but the end results are often the same, and the decision not to take an action is still a decision.[67]

The second feature of the actual decision-making process is that rarely is there a single point in time when a decision to have a child is made. More commonly, the ultimate outcome is the result of a process or a series of minor decisions.

With these considerations in mind it is possible to suggest the following broad outline of how family formation occurs in modern society. When a couple marries, the two people may discuss very carefully and quite explicitly the number of children they want and when they want them. If they do, if they have a workable contraceptive technique available to them (in both physical and moral sense), and if there is no infecundity or no contraceptive accident, then they may well be able to plan the number and spacing of their children. This idealized version of fertility decision making is not likely to be the most common type, however. The more likely process can be conceptualized in a manner such as is shown schematically in Figure 7.

This figure represents, from left to right, the number of children that a couple may have. Ideally, the couple enters marriage in a childless state, and before a child has been conceived.[68] The movement of a couple from childlessness to having a child will be produced by various forces that might be conceived of as vectors. The total effect of these vectors on a married couple will determine if and how soon they have their first child. In the same way, moving from one child to a second will be determined by the relative force of the vectors. When the vectors moving in the direction of having an additional child are exceeded by the vectors going in the opposite direction, then childbearing for the couple, in general, will cease.

The vectors shown in Figure 7 are basically of three types. They include the general "cultural press" for having children, and two sets of "situationally specific factors." One set of situationally specific factors exerts pressure for having a child, while the second set pushes against having an additional child.

The Cultural Press toward Parenthood

The evidence from American studies of fertility conducted in the last decade and a half indicates that during the early period of marriage the most influential of these vectors in the *cultural press*. This single label covers all the institutional and cultural supports for childbearing. It is best understood as a set of values which holds that *it is good and proper to have children:* or,

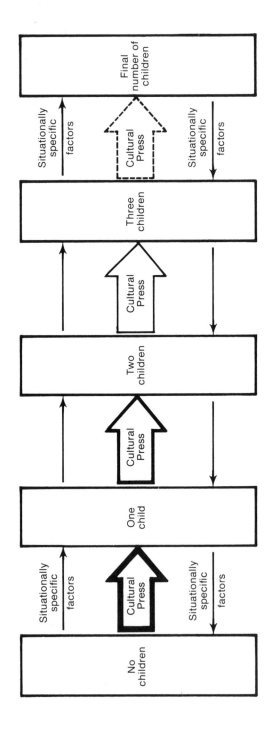

FIGURE 7. THE PROCESS OF FAMILY FORMATION

stated negatively, to have a marriage without children is to be unfulfilled.

The socialization process that occurs in the life of an individual is sufficiently effective to cause most couples to accept the virtues and values of having children without question. The most formidable evidence in support of this hypothesis is the typical pattern that has been found among many, perhaps most, young married couples. The pattern has been labeled the "casual approach to family planning."[69] The typical pattern has been described in the following manner:

> First of all, nearly two out of three newlyweds do not start using contraception before the first conception. In a majority of cases, this is because they want to have a baby as soon as they can. Those who do begin contraception stop and conceive only eight or nine months later than other couples. Usually their first child arrives less than two years after marriage.
> After their first birth, the typical couple wants to have another child soon. Although most begin to use contraception before the second child comes along, they still feel no strong pressure to avoid conception for more than a few months. As a result, many young couples are careless contraceptors, omitting contraception occasionally or failing to use it properly.
> This casual approach to family planning is fairly prevalent until the couple has all the children they want.[70]

For most young couples, during the first year or two of marriage, the process of family formation is governed more by the general cultural press for children than by any careful, considered, rational decision making. It is only after one or two or three children have been born that the more specific considerations come into play, and decision making in a more familiar sense begins to operate.

Rainwater has suggested that the pattern may differ slightly from the one described here, and also that it may vary according to the social-class level of the couple. In his study, couples were interviewed who had been married for about eight years and had an average of about two children. Husbands and wives were asked how many children they had wanted early in their married life and how many they now wanted. More than half of the couples, who ranged in social-class levels from lower-lower to upper-middle and included both Whites and Negroes, indicated that they *had* had an early preference for a specific number of children. However, it is difficult to say whether these retrospective reports reflected their true feelings at the time of marriage, or whether the views expressed were simply a reconstruction of how they *could have felt* at an earlier time. The fact that the lower social classes were generally less likely to indicate that they had had an early preference does lend credence to the data. Many of the couples did indicate, however, that they had changed their views about the preferred number of children since the time when they had first married. The direction of this change tended to be class-related also:

... when middle class men and women shift their family size preferences as time goes on they do so in the direction of smaller size; when lower class people shift it is in the direction of a larger size. The middle class shifts represent a scaling down of earlier desires in line with an appreciation of some of the realities of child rearing. . . . [71]

The description and analysis of what happens to family-size preferences over time among the middle-class respondents is consistent with the framework suggested above. Early family-size preferences (whether specific in number or not) are based largely on the idealistic, almost moralistic, value placed on children by the culture. Early "enthusiasms" and "aspirations" for having children characterized many of the middle-class respondents:

Most of the couples who have scaled down their ideas of how many children to have started off with rather high expectations; a few have come down from three to two, more from four to three, most from over four to three or four. This latter category includes about equal numbers of Catholics who started off with wishes for really big families of seven to ten children and quickly recognized the unreality of these enthusiasms, and Protestants who started off with wishes for four to six child families and found such numbers beyond their financial and psychic means. Apparently this sort of thing occurs most often in the lower-middle class. . . .[72]

Lower-class respondents had a tendency to *upgrade* their preferred family size, if it changed at all during their married years, but the character of the change was somewhat different than that described for the middle-class couples. Usually their expressed preference for a larger number of children than the number they had originally preferred was a passive or resigned acceptance of the number they were actually having. As they continued to have children over the desired number, they accepted them "with pleasure ('The more they come the sweeter they are.') or resignation ('It's God's will, I guess.')."[73]

Situationally Specific Factors

The discussion thus far has focused on the traditional cultural values labeled cultural press. Little has been said about the *situationally specific* factors that are also represented as vectors in Figure 7. Some of these factors move a couple toward more children, while others act to stop the couple from having more children than they already have. The term situationally specific refers to the conscious and explicit reasons that couples may have for wanting or not wanting a child at any particular point in their life cycle. These explicit and conscious motives are directly related to the specific goals or objectives of the individual couple. While these situationally specific factors may be infinite in their variety—dependent as they are on the particular circumstances of each couple—it is possible to suggest a few that are likely to be widespread.

First, some of the positive situationally specific factors (those moving a couple toward having a child) might include (1) the desire to have a child (or a male child) to please parents or other kin (possibly a particularly prominent factor pushing toward having the first child); (2) the desire to have a child in order to reduce the chances of the husband being drafted into the military service; (3) the explicit desire of a couple to have their children while they are young; (4) the desire to have a sibling mate for the already born child (most pronounced when the couple has one child and wishes to avoid the "only child syndrome"); (5) the desire to have a child later in the reproductive period so that the parents may forestall the time of the "empty nest," after their eldest child has left home.

Examples of the negative situationally specific factors include (1) the desire to complete the husband's or wife's education, or the husband's military service, before having a child (or another child); (2) the desire of a couple to have personal freedom to work, travel, and the like before having a child; (3) the desire to achieve some specific economic goal before having a child; (4) the desire to give a small number of children particular advantages that would not be possible should more children be born.

This list of both positive and negative factors could be expanded indefinitely and in ever-increasing detail, but it will really be empirical research that establishes which factors or sets of factors are most important in determining family size. The research results available now are limited, since few studies have been conducted longitudinally (following the same couples over time) to see just how the factors influencing fertility change in response to changing circumstances. The general theme reflected here is that the cultural press tends to be the most important force until some children are born and then the situationally specific factors (both positive and negative) become increasingly important. When the negative factors outweigh the positive, most couples will stop having children. In support of this position is the research showing that almost all married couples go through many years of fecundity without producing children. This period is estimated to be more than ten years for the average American couple.[74] Stopping fertility during the fecund years is, of course, accomplished by practicing birth control, but more precisely it is the improved use of contraception that keeps couples from having more children than they want.[75]

Interviews with 905 American women shortly after the birth of their second child, and again some three years later, revealed how successful they had been in avoiding unwanted pregnancies. It was learned that the risks of accidental pregnancy were reduced at least by a factor of five between their early marriage years and the period after desired family size had been reached. The reduction in pregnancy risk was the result of more regular use of contraceptives rather than infecundity, reduced coital frequency, or changes to more effective contraceptives.[76]

Another empirical study lends considerable support to the general framework described here.[77] Conducted in Aberdeen, Scotland, this was a longitudinal study of more than 1300 women at the time they had their first baby and again at the end of five years. About one-fourth of the women who were interviewed when they were pregnant with their first baby were undecided about the exact number of children they wanted. Others were able to give a specific number, but when they were reinterviewed five years later many had changed their preferences. "At the 5-year follow-up, after the experience of marriage and child-rearing, nearly all mothers had definite views and were able to discuss the economic, social and emotional reasons for choosing a particular number of children or for a modification in their original preference."[78] Apparently, at the time of the first interview, before the birth of the first child, most mothers were unable to offer concrete reasons for wanting children.

Thompson and Illsley, the researchers, concluded:

Many women did not have a precise idea about family size when they first embarked on childbearing, and preferences expressed at this time were not a good predictor of future behaviour. This was particularly true of those groups of the population whose education and cultural experience had not inculcated a habit of forward planning or of a rational linking of desired ends with appropriate means. Nevertheless, with experience of married life and of the satisfaction and strains of parenthood, attitudes on family size were decided or modified. Changes usually reduced the number of children preferred, but when it was increased this was often in order to accomodate reality.[79]

This conclusion suggests again that the early part of family formation is often the result of a general cultural press that places a positive value on the production of children. It is only after the cultural value has been satisfied by the birth of at least some children that more realistic considerations begin to play a greater role. When the negative value of having more children exceeds the positive value, most couples will stop having children even though fertility is still physiologically possible.

SUMMARY

In order for societies to continue over time they must have some mechanism for insuring that their populations will continue to be produced. The institutional structures and the cultural values of all societies provide both incentives and rewards for the bearing and rearing of children. Fertility behavior is a socially determined behavior. It is shaped and modified by the changing social systems in which people live.

Demographers have traditionally demonstrated the social nature of fertility by studying the variations in fertility found among the different economic classes, races, religions, and the residents of rural and urban places. While it is still possible to show differences in fertility between these various social categories, they are less and less useful for explaining the societal trends of fertility.

As fertility becomes more and more the result of a decision-making process by individual couples, new approaches to the study of fertility are required. To understand fertility behavior today there is a need for a frame of reference that has decision making as its central focus. The frame of reference introduced in this chapter has described fertility decision making as a process that changes in character through the life cycle of a married couple. During the early stages of family formation, the principal influence on the decision (or perhaps it is a nondecision) is the general cultural press for having children. In the later stages, more "situationally specific" factors emerge. Eventually the situationally specific factors determine the ultimate family size of a couple. This characterization of fertility decision making has emerged in broad outline from a variety of recent sociological studies of fertility. While many modifications and specifications have yet to be made to this frame of reference, it does promise to be a fruitful approach to the study of fertility.

: : SELECTED READINGS AND MATERIALS

General

Banks, J.A. *Prosperity and Parenthood: A Study of Family Planning among the Victorian Middle Classes.* London, Routledge and Kegan Paul, 1954.

Beshers, James M. *Population Processes in Social Systems.* New York, The Free Press, 1967. Chapter 4, "Fertility."

Hill, Reuben, J. Mayone Stycos, and Kurt W. Back. *The Family and Population Control.* Chapel Hill, North Carolina, The University of North Carolina Press, 1959.

Kammeyer, Kenneth C. W., editor. *Population Studies: Selected Essays and Research.* Chicago, Rand-McNally, 1969. Section V, "Fertility."

Kiser, Clyde V., Wilson H. Grabill, and Arthur A. Campbell. *Trends and Variations in Fertility in the United States.* Cambridge, Mass., Harvard University Press, 1969.

Rainwater, Lee, *Family Design, Marital Sexuality, Family Size and Contraception.* Chicago, Aldine Publishing Co., 1965.

Westoff, Charles F., Robert G. Potter, Jr., and Philip C. Sagi. *The Third Child.* Princeton, New Jersey: Princeton University Press, 1963.

Whelpton, Pascal K., and Clyde V. Kiser, editors. *Social and Psychological Factors Affecting Fertility.* Vol. I-V. New York, *Milbank Memorial Fund,* 1946–1958. A series of articles describing the results of the Indianapolis study. These articles were originally published in the *Milbank Memorial Fund Quarterly* between 1946 and 1958.

Whelpton, Pascal K., Arthur A. Campbell, and John E. Patterson. *Fertility and Family Planning in the United States.* Princeton, New Jersey, Princeton University Press, 1966.

: : NOTES

1. William Petersen, *Population,* 2nd edition (New York: Macmillan, 1969), p. 173.

2. Michael Thomas Sadler, *Ireland: Its Evils and Their Remedies,* 2nd edition (London: John Murray, 1829), pp. xviii–xix.

3. Herbert Spencer, *The Principles of Biology,* Vol. 2. (New York: D. Appleton, 1873), p. 485.

4. Spencer, p. 486.

5. Thomas Doubleday, *The True Law of Population, Shown to be Connected with the Food of the People,* 3rd edition (London: Smith, Elder, 1853), pp. 1–8.

6. Josué de Castro, *Geography of Hunger* (Boston: Little Brown, 1952), pp. 70–72.

7. Donald Bogue, *Principles of Demography* (New York: John Wiley & Sons, 1969), pp. 724–729. The following discussion reflects Bogue's analysis of childlessness.

8. Bogue, p. 725.

9. Bogue, pp. 726–727.

10. Reynolds Farley, "The Demographic Rates and Social Institutions of the Nineteenth-Century Negro Population: A Stable Population Analysis," *Demography,* 2: 386–398 (1965).

11. U. S. Bureau of the Census, *Historical Statistics of the United States, Colonial Times to 1957* (Washington, D.C.: U.S. Government Printing Office, 1960), Series B 19–30, p. 23.

12. U.S. Bureau of the Census, *Statistical Abstract of the United States, 1969,* 90th edition (Washington, D.C.: U.S. Government Printing Office, 1969), Table 57, p. 48.

13. Reynolds Farley, "Recent Changes in Negro Fertility," *Demography,* 3: 188 (1966).

14. Farley, "Recent Changes," pp. 200–202.

15. Farley, "Recent Changes," p. 202.

16. Petersen, p. 477.

17. Petersen, p. 472.

18. Anne Lee and Everett Lee, "The Future Fertility of the American Negro," *Social Forces,* 37: 228–231 (1959).

19. Calvin Goldscheider and Peter R. Uhlenberg, "Minority Group Status and Fertility," *The American Journal of Sociology,* 74: 361–372 (1969).

20. Goldscheider and Uhlenberg, p. 371.

21. Goldscheider and Uhlenberg, p. 371.

22. Ronald Freedman, Pascal K. Whelpton, and John W. Smit, "Socioeconomic Factors in Religious Differentials in Fertility," *American Sociological Review,* 26: 608–614 (1961); Calvin Goldscheider, "Fertility of the Jews," *Demography,* 4: 196–209 (1967); Basil Zimmer and Calvin Goldscheider, "A Further Look at Catholic Fertility," *Demography,* 3: 462–469 (1966). Zimmer and Goldscheider found that the Catholic-Protestant differences prevailed in metropolitan areas, but were much stronger in the central cities than in the suburbs.

23. Freedman, Whelpton, and Smit, p. 610.

24. Goldscheider, "Fertility of the Jews," p. 200.

25. U.S. Bureau of the Census, *Statistical Abstract of the United States, 1958* (Washington, D.C.: U.S. Government Printing Office, 1958), Table 40, p. 41.

26. Ronald Freedman and Pascal K. Whelpton, "Fertility Planning and Fertility Rates by Religious Interest and Denomination," *The Milbank Memorial Fund Quarterly,* 28: 294–343 (1950); reprinted in P. K. Whelpton and Clyde V. Kiser, eds., *Social and Psychological Factors*

Affecting Fertility, Vol. 2 (New York: Milbank Memorial Fund, 1950), pp. 417–466; and Charles F. Westoff, Robert G. Potter, Philip C. Sagi, and Elliot G. Mishler, *Family Growth in Metropolitan America* (Princeton, N.J.: Princeton University Press, 1961), pp. 217–218.

27. Gordon F. De Jong, "Religious Fundamentalism, Socioeconomic Status, and Fertility Attitudes in the Southern Appalachians," *Demography*, 2: 540–548 (1965).

28. Westoff, Potter, Sagi, and Mishler, pp. 217–218.

29. Charles F. Westoff, Robert G. Potter, Philip C. Sagi, *The Third Child* (Princeton, N.J.: Princeton University Press, 1963), p. 117.

30. Lincoln H. Day, "Natality and Ethnocentrism: Some Relationships Suggested by an Analysis of Catholic-Protestant Differentials," *Population Studies*, 22: 27–50 (1968).

31. Day, p. 46.

32. Day, p. 46.

33. Harry Edwards, "Black Muslim and Negro Christian Family Relationships," *Journal of Marriage and the Family*, 30: 605–607 (1968).

34. Day, p. 46.

35. Petersen, pp. 497–498. The following evidence was reported by Petersen.

36. Kingsley Davis, *The Population of India and Pakistan* (Princeton, N.J.: Princeton University Press, 1951), p. 78.

37. Dennis Wrong, "Trends in Class Fertility in Western Nations," *The Canadian Journal of Economics and Political Science*, 24 :216–229 (1958); reprinted in Reinhard Bendix and Seymour M. Lipset, *Class, Status, and Power*, 2nd edition (New York: The Free Press, 1966), p. 355.

38. Mary Douglas, "Population Control in Primitive Groups," *British Journal of Sociology*, 17: 271 (1966).

39. Wrong, pp. 355–356.

40. Wrong, p. 354

41. J. A. Banks, *Prosperity and Parenthood: A study of Family Planning among the Victorian Middle Classes* (London: Routledge and Kegan Paul, 1954).

42. Whelpton and Kiser, Vol. 2, p. 387.

43. Wrong, p. 356.

44. Wrong, p. 357.

45. Wrong, p. 357.

46. Judith Blake, "Demographic Science and the Redirection of Population Policy," *Journal of Chronic Diseases*, 18: 1191–1192 (1965).

47. Blake, pp. 1191–1192.

48. Whelpton and Kiser, Vols. 1–5.

49. Whelpton and Kiser, Vol. 2, p. 382.

50. Whelpton and Kiser, Vol. 2, pp. 393–414.

51. Wrong, p. 358.

52. Pascal Whelpton, Arthur Campbell, and John Patterson, *Fertility and Family Planning* (Princeton, New Jersey: Princeton University Press, 1966), pp. 103–104.

53. David Goldberg, "Fertility and Fertility Differentials: Some Observations of Recent Changes in the United States," in Mindel C. Sheps and Jean Clare Ridley, *Public Health and Population Change: Current Research Issues* (Pittsburgh: University of Pittsburgh Press, 1965), pp. 140–142.

54. Goldberg, p. 140.

55. Wrong, p. 358.

56. Gary Becker, "An Economic Analysis of Fertility," in National Bureau of Economic Research, *Demographic and Economic Change in Developed Countries* (Princeton University Press, 1960), pp. 209–231.

57. Becker, p. 210.

58. Becker, p. 217.

59. Judith Blake, "Are Babies Consumer Durables?" *Population Studies*, 22: 5–25 (1968). The following discussion follows Blake's critique closely.

60. Blake, p. 16.

61. Lee Rainwater, *Family Design, Marital Sexuality, Family Size and Contraception* (Chicago: Aldine, 1965), p. 15.

62. Whelpton, Campbell, and Patterson, p. 33.

63. Rainwater, p. 140.

64. Blake, p. 23.

65. Kurt Back, "New Frontiers in Demography and Social Psychology," *Demography*, 1: 90–97 (1967). Quotation p. 92.

66. Back, pp. 92–93.

67. Back, p. 95.

68. The latter assumption does not hold true for every couple, since there is evidence that at least fifteen or twenty percent of couples enter marriage after conception has occurred, but the general form of the model will apply to these couples also. For the evidence on premarital pregnancy see Samuel H. Lowrie, "Early Marriage: Premarital Pregnancy and Associated Factors," *Journal of Marriage and the Family*, 27: 48–56 (1965); Harold T. Christensen, "Studies in Child Spacing: I. Premarital Pregnancy as Measured by the Spacing of the First Birth After Marriage," *American Sociological Review*, 18: 53–59 (1953).

69. Whelpton, Campbell, and Patterson, p. 221.

70. Whelpton, Campbell, and Patterson, p. 221.

71. Rainwater, pp. 124–125

72. Rainwater, p. 126.

73. Rainwater, p. 130.

74. Robert G. Potter, Jr., "Some Comments on the Evidence Pertaining to Family Limitation in the United States," *Population Studies*, 14: 44–47 (1960).

75. Robert G. Potter, Jr., Philip C. Sagi, and Charles F. Westoff, "Improvement of Contraception During the Course of Marriage," *Population Studies*, 16: 160–174 (1962).

76. Potter, Sagi, and Westoff, "Improvement of Contraception," pp. 168–170.

77. Barbara Thompson and Raymond Illsley, "Family Growth in Aberdeen," *Journal of Bio-social Science*, 1: 23–39 (1969).

78. Thompson and Illsley, p. 29.

79. Thompson and Illsley, p. 36.

Chapter 7 World-Population Growth

The final questions about population must be concerned with the total human population—the world population. Several important questions may be asked about the population of the world: What has it been at various times in the past? How fast is it growing? How long will it continue to grow at its present rate? How large will the world population be in the future?

An answer to the question about population size in the past can be provided, because a consensus has developed among the specialists about broad trends in world-population growth. It is also possible to say, with considerable precision, something about the present rate of world-population growth. Looking toward the future, we can also estimate what the world population will be at some future time—*if the present rate of growth continues.* Since a continuation of present growth rates is unlikely—indeed, in the long run impossible—the question of the future world population becomes both more interesting and more difficult. This chapter will conclude with the question of the future world population, but first some attention will be given to population size in the past.

THE POPULATION OF THE PAST

In the long history of mankind—a history that may go back as much as two million years—the "population problem" has not been one of overpopulation. On the contrary, it may have been one of keeping the species alive. Man, in his relationship to nature and other species, had to struggle to survive for thousands of years, for he evolved as neither the strongest nor the fastest of the animals. Perhaps he was a more resourceful and intelligent animal, but these characteristics were not sufficient to *insure* survival. Only in the more recent history of man's existence has survival of the species became relatively assured. And only in very recent times has the growth rate of the human population been fast enough to create an overabundance of people. Now, many argue, the excessive number of people may actually be a threat to survival.

Only three hundred years ago there were about 500 million people on earth—a smaller number than the populations of either China or India today. Going back to the prehistory era, Washburn has estimated that during the hunting-and-gathering stage of culture there were probably only about

125

7,000,000 human beings in the world.[1] This is about the number of people presently being added to the population of the earth every five or six weeks.

The human population grew very slowly before the seventeenth century, but after that date the number of people began to increase rapidly.[2] From 6000 B.C. to 1650 A.D. the population of the earth doubled about every two thousand years. After 1650 the population doubled in less than two hundred years, or in only one-tenth of the time it had taken during the first seven thousand years of the historical period. In about 1830 the world population had reached one billion. By 1930 the second billion was recorded, so humankind had doubled again, and this time in only one hundred years. It only required thirty years, from 1930 to 1960, for the third billion to be added, and in the mid-1970s, when the world population reaches four billion, the population will be double the number it was in 1930. The 1930 to 1975 doubling will have required about forty-five years. Looking ahead further, if the current yearly growth rate of 2.0 percent continues unchanged, the next doubling—which would make the world population eight billion people—will require only thirty-five years.

It has become obvious to most people that if the earth's population continues to double every thirty-five years the world will become intolerable. If it does so, the population size will go from 8 billion, to 16 billion, to 32 billion, to 64 billion within the next one hundred and fifty years. As these figures are projected even further ahead, the size of the world's population becomes increasingly unrealistic and bizarre.

It is not the aim of this book to try to shock the reader into a realization of the disastrous consequences of rapid population growth. Such books have been written and are readily available for the interested reader. They make the case for population control forcefully and dramatically, and one hopes that their methods will alert and alarm those who are not yet concerned about the consequences and dangers of an overpopulated world.[3]

How Many People Have Lived on Earth?

It is often claimed that one-half of the people who *ever* lived are now alive. The source of this assertion is obscure, but it is repeated frequently enough so that it should be critically examined. There are two analyses that may be used as sources for a reliable answer to the question of how many people have ever lived on earth.

Keyfitz[4] has provided one answer by making a series of assumptions about when man originated, his average length of life during certain eras, and the numbers of people living at given times. He assumed that man's beginning was about 100,000 years before the birth of Christ, and that man's average length of life was about 25 years. By making assumptions about the size of the population at different points in time, Keyfitz calculated that by 1960 about 69 billion people had lived on earth. This total would mean that less than 5 percent of the people who ever lived are living now.

Different assumptions were employed in a paper written by Desmond.[5] She dated man's origin at 600,000 B.C. By assuming different birth rates for different time periods, and by estimating the size of the population at the beginning and end of each period, the calculations indicated that 77 billion people had been born by 1962.[6] This estimate is higher than the previous one, but considering the uncertainty of some of the assumptions, the two figures are remarkably close. In any case *the order of magnitude is such that the answer to the original question is once again that slightly less than 5 percent of the people who ever lived are now living.* Both figures clearly refute the claim that one-half of the people who have ever lived are living today.[7]

RECENT TRENDS IN WORLD POPULATION

While the long prehistoric period of population growth is of interest, the major concern of most demographers has been with the dramatic upturn in population growth since the seventeenth century. If the reasons for this rapid population increase in the last three hundred years could be clearly understood, it would be much easier to comprehend present and future population growth. It is especially important to understand the reasons for the dramatic increase in world population during the last fifty years.

Bogue calculated the rates of growth for various periods from 1650 onward, and found that the annual rate of growth between 1650 and 1750 averaged only 0.34 percent per year. From 1900 to 1920 the annual rate of growth averaged 0.65 percent, but in the decade of the 1950s the rate was up to 1.83 percent.[8] As indicated above, the present annual rate of growth is about 2.0 percent, so the rate continues to increase and *it is operating on an ever larger base population.*

Bogue also divided the countries of the world into two general categories —the "developed industrialized regions" and the "developing [pre-industrial] regions"—and examined their growth rates separately. He found that between 1650 and 1750 the growth rates for the industrialized and developing areas were virtually the same. After 1750 the growth rate for the industrialized regions began to exceed the growth rate of the developing regions. This trend continued until the third decade of the twentieth century. At that time the growth rate in the developing regions began to exceed that of the industrialized areas. Since the higher rate of growth in the nonindustrial, or developing, countries of the world has been more frequently commented on in recent years, it may be surprising that the most industrialized nations had higher growth rates in the two centuries before 1920. The higher growth rates in the industrialized countries during the eighteenth and nineteenth centuries can probably be attributed to the fact that death rates had gone down while the birth rates remained relatively high. In the nonindustrial countries at that time the birth rates were high, but the death rates were also high, so the result was a low rate of growth. This pattern of differences between birth and death rates in countries at different stages of economic development is a manifestation of what has been called *the theory of the modern demographic transition.* The idea of the demographic transition has been a prominent feature of demographic theory for the last twenty-five years. As a theory of population growth it has been highly praised and sharply criticized, but it is, in the words of one of its critics, "one of the best documented generalizations in the social sciences.[9] In its essentials, the theory of the demographic transition holds that as a society begins the process of modernization—particularly urbanization and industrialization—the population will grow rapidly for a time because the death rate for the population will have declined while the birth rate has remained high. After a time, according to the theory, the birth rate will also begin to decline and the rapid growth of the population will diminish.

The Emergence of Transition Theory

The theory of the modern demographic transition (sometimes called *the modern demographic cycle,* or *the demographic,* or *vital, revolution*) can be a very useful tool for understanding why the population of the world has grown as fast as it has in the last three hundred years, and especially during the last half century. The theory had its beginnings when Thompson published a paper in 1929 in which he presented the then available population data for various countries around the world.[10] The countries (or continents) of the world were divided into three groups according to analyses of data on their births and deaths. Group A was composed primarily of the countries of Northwestern Europe and North America; Group B countries included "Italy, Spain, and the Slavic peoples of Central Europe"; and the remaining countries and continents of the world were classified as Group C. The Group C countries were found primarily in Asia, Africa, and South America.

The Group A countries in Europe and North America had declining birth and death rates, but because their birth rates were declining faster than their death rates, the rate of population growth was declining. The Group B countries had death rates that were declining more rapidly than the birth rates, and were thus experiencing high rates of population growth. Both the birth and death rates in the Group C countries were high; therefore, the actual increase was relatively low at that time.

Thompson called attention to the link between the economic development of countries and the changing vital rates by noting that in "such lands as are developing modern industry and sanitation, there is likely to be a very

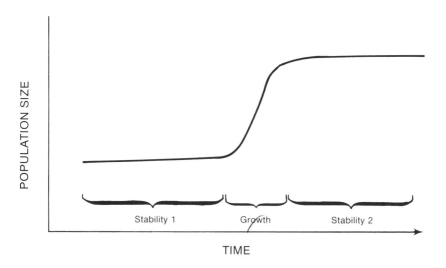

FIGURE 8. THE S-SHAPED CURVE OF POPULATION GROWTH

rapid increase in numbers during the next few decades." This statement contained an idea central to the theory of the demographic transition as it came to be developed during the next two decades. The transition referred to in the term "demographic transition" is that from a rural-agricultural economy to an urban-industrial economy. This transition had an effect upon the birth and death rates such that countries moving toward modernization had high rates of population growth.

After Thompson's first paper, many writers contributed to the development of transition theory. Cowgill has been particularly effective in delineating its key features and signaling its significance. The discussion of transition theory that follows draws heavily on his formulations.[11]

The Elements of Transition Theory

The key demographic fact that transition theory seeks to explain is population growth. Because the experience of mankind during the last three hundred years has been one of rapid population growth, it may give us pause to recognize the validity of an observation made by Cowgill about human populations. He said, "In spite of the insistent tendency toward population increase, the most common historical condition is not growth, but nongrowth, or seen at close range, short-term cycles of growth and decline which average out to stability . . . ."[12] This proposition, which has considerable empirical support, was implied by Malthus when he assumed that "the human species, like every other species, had the capacity to reproduce itself at a geometric rate and unless there were inhibiting factors, the rate of reproduction tended to approach the maximum capacity."[13]

If the nature of population growth is cyclical—that is, growth followed by nongrowth, followed by growth again—the pattern of population growth will show a more or less flattened S-shaped curve (see Figure 8). If migration is excluded, there are only two factors that can affect the rate of growth of a population: births and deaths. However, there are several different combinations of changes in the birth and death rates of a population which can produce the S-shaped growth cycle depicted in Figure 8.

The four most elementary possibilities are shown in Figure 9.

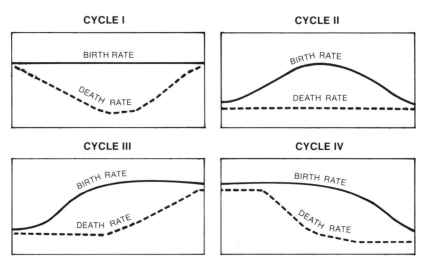

FIGURE 9. POPULATION GROWTH CYCLES PRODUCED BY CHANGING BIRTH AND DEATH RATES

Cycle I depicts a constant birth rate, while the death rate falls and then rises again. During any time period when the death rate is lower than the birth rate there will be a natural increase in the population. Cowgill called this "the primitive growth cycle" because it appears that before the Industrial Revolution this was the cyclical pattern most responsible for increases in population size.

It might be noted in passing that the constantly high birth rate of Cycle I, while high, is probably not at the biological or physiological maximum. Only rarely does a societal group approach the biological maximum in reproduction. The indications are that in almost all societies fertility is to some extent limited by the institutions and norms surrounding marriage and childbearing.

There may be various reasons for the declining death rate shown in Cycle

I, including improvements in the food supply, health conditions, or some other environmental factor. However, after some period of population growth the death rate is shown returning to its previously high level, perhaps because, as Malthus suggested, the increase in the number of people again strains the environmental resources.

Cycle II can normally occur only when both birth and death rates are already relatively low. Only under this condition can an increase in the birth rate produce a population increase. When this cycle occurs there will be a natural increase of the population as long as the death rate does not go up and the birth rate remains high. A rough approximation of Cycle II occurred in the United States after World War II, when there was an upsurge in births that made the fertility rate higher than it had been during the 1930s.

Cycle III has rarely been seen as an actual phenomenon, and stands primarily as a theoretical possibility. To occur it would require an increase in birth rates from some relatively low level, followed by an increase in the death rate (perhaps produced by overpopulation or overcrowding). If both rates were to stabilize at their new high levels, the population size would again be stable. Cowgill is very likely correct in saying, "There seems to be no precedent in the past for Cycle [III] and little prospect of its emergence in the future as a major cycle."[14]

Cycle IV is the schematic representation of what occurs during the modern demographic transition. It begins at a stable population stage that is produced by high birth rates and high death rates. Then some factor causes the death rate to drop, while the birth rate remains high—at least for a time. The resultant difference between a high birth rate and a lowering death rate causes population growth. According to transition theory, it is the process of modernization that produces the early decline in the death rate. As modernization begins—and modernization must stand as a shorthand symbol for many things—the death rate begins to fall while the birth rate continues at its high level. This is the transition stage. It is an economic transition, but it produces a demographic transition. During the transition stage there is a gap between the birth rate and the death rate that produces a high rate of natural increase. While there may be some exceptions, it appears that as most European countries started the modernization process, they exhibited a pattern of mortality decline, followed at some later time by birth-rate declines.[15]

The Criticisms of Transition Theory

While the transition model has received much support as a valid generalization describing the demographic concomitants of modernization, it has also been the object of criticism. It has been criticized for being "a crude, conceptually primitive model of population change that fails adequately to separate causal from descriptive propositions."[16]

It has been asserted that transition theory "continues to have the character of an empirical generalization, since the rationale presumably implicit in it has never been systematically stated."[17] The thrust of these criticisms is that the theory does not include in it an explanation of why modernization acts to change birth and death rates in the way it does. Why would modernization, especially in its beginning stages, produce a downturn in the mortality rate, and only later produce a similar decline in the fertility rate?

It should be made clear that the relationship is not inevitable—modernization may not lead inexorably to declining mortality. Van Nort has been critical of transition theory, or transition theorists, because they have overlooked the possibility that a government may possess the knowledge to reduce mortality and yet not utilize this knowledge.[18] One must agree that particular historical circumstances may produce a situation where modernization does not immediately depress the mortality rate. But whenever the demographic facts are known for societies that have undergone modernization, the pattern predicted by the theory has been observed.

Mortality Declines and Early Modernization

The explanation for the effect that modernization has on mortality and fertility grows out of the universal value that human societies have regarding life. As was discussed in Chapter 5, all societies place great positive value on producing life and being alive, while, on the other hand, death is almost always negatively valued. There have been, and are, societies which allow or encourage infanticide, suicide, ritual killing, war, and geriatricide, but these exceptions carry small weight against the overwhelming countervalue embodied in the institutions of all societies to promote and continue life. To put it simply, life is highly valued and death is abhorred in all societies. Historically, in the face of threatening environmental conditions, the human institutions could hardly have developed in any other way.

Given the nearly universal positive value placed on life, it is understandable that any features of modernization that would tend to promote or save life would be quickly accepted. Thus the first explanation for the early decline of mortality lies in the fact that the prevailing cultural values will not reject those aspects of modernization that improve life chances.

There is another important reason for the early decline of mortality as modernization begins. Hertzler stated the case well:

There can be considerable reduction of mortality without individual or family intelligence, knowledge, or inclination. The means can be applied with little or no interference in the daily ways of life of the people. . . . Deaths can be greatly reduced by governmental control of water supply and waste disposal, by the control of noxious and infectious insects, bacteria, germs, or animals which cause or transmit disease, and by governmental action in the improvement of transportation and the distribution of food to areas threatened with famine. Measures such as these do not require much cooperation on the part of individual or community beneficiaries.[19]

It should also be noted that modernization can affect mortality in many ways—ways that are just as likely to be gradual and undramatic as they are to be some startling new breakthrough. When thinking about the prolongation of life, one thinks most readily of important medical and scientific advances, but these may not always be the most important factors. Death rates can also be reduced by such prosaic things as a more abundant, nutritionally balanced food supply, or reductions in the unhealthy conditions and hazards of work.

As a case in point, McKeown and Brown, after examining the role of medicine and hospitals in the reduction of mortality in eighteenth- and early nineteenth-century England, concluded that it was not changes in medical practices that had produced the mortality decline. Rather, "Improvements in the environment are . . . regarded as intrinsically the most acceptable explanation of the decline of mortality in the late eighteenth and nineteenth centuries."[20]

Fertility Declines in Modern Societies

Another question about the mechanics of transition theory is, Why does fertility drop only after a society has moved some distance toward modernization? The answer is two-fold. First, fertility changes in the population are the result of the personal choices and decisions of individuals and couples about childbearing. Changes in the death rate can occur because an outside agency takes some action that improves the individual's chance for life. The cause of a change in the death rate can be external, but a change in the birth rate must come from changes in the thinking of individual members of the population. Such changes in attitudes and values usually come along after modernization has changed the objective circumstances of people.

The second element is the social fact, discussed before, that all societies have developed institutions and values that promote fertility. As Notestein stated in his early enunciation of transition theory, "All such societies [which in the past have had to face heavy mortality] are therefore ingeniously arranged to obtain the required births. Their religious doctrines, moral codes, laws, education, community customs, marriage habits, and family organizations are all focused toward maintaining high fertility."[21] Since the well-entrenched structural supports for having children are not likely to change quickly, the birth rate may remain high for a considerable period after the death rate has gone down.

There are several features of modernization that are likely to cause individual couples to eventually change their views about childbearing. The emergence of individualism and aspirations for economic mobility are two characteristics of urban-industrial life that have been suggested as causes of decreasing family size.[22] Hertzler emphasized the aspirations theme when he wrote:

With the increase in wealth and income, people develop desires for greater quantity and quality of material and social satisfactions . . . To compete successfully and to achieve higher levels put heavy economic penalties on the large family. Children contribute less and less to family income, and the cost of maintaining them and giving them the extending range of opportunities increases.[23]

Hertzler also mentioned the impact of "the general technological advance," which includes the "increasing diffusion of, knowledge of, and the increasing availability and use of, contraceptive techniques and materials. The social and cultural situation and individual and family motivations cause more people to resort to these."[24]

Contraception and Declining Fertility

The role of contraceptive technology and knowledge in the decline of fertility deserves special consideration because its influence is often overestimated. Modern contraceptive technology, particularly the chemical-pharmacological methods but also many of the mechanical means, are of relatively recent origin. Yet there is overwhelming evidence that some fertility declines occurred in some segments of European societies before most of these birth-control techniques had been invented and certainly before they were widely used. Petersen has noted that "the average family size in the United States began to fall at the beginning of the nineteenth century, and in France probably even earlier, in both cases presumably because of the more frequent practice of *coitus interruptus.*"[25]

On the same point, it is often alleged that recent declines in American fertility are attributable to the development of the oral contraceptive. Yet the recent fertility decline in the United States appears to have started as early as 1957–1958, while the "birth-control pill" did not come into widespread use until the middle of the 1960s. The relationship between the increasing use of "the pill" in the 1960s and the declining birth rate has been carefully examined by Ryder and Westoff, and they concluded their analysis by saying "that what has been happening to fertility in the 1960s would have happened in direction if not in degree even if the oral contraceptive had not appeared on the scene. . . ."[26]

Further evidence on the role of contraceptive technology may be found in the fact that the fertility rate in the United States in the year 1933 reached a level as low as that of 1970 (18 per 1000). This was long before the oral contraceptive, and before the widespread use of several of the most effective mechanical techniques of fertility control. From a sociological perspective it is difficult to accept the idea that technological factors are the prime causes of changes in fertility. There is too much evidence that fertility levels can be controlled even when advanced birth-control methods are not available.[27] Furthermore, it is also evident that fertility can be high even when contraceptive techniques are available. The sociological view, stated succinctly, is this: "The propaganda for family limitation and even increased efficacy of contraceptives are relevant mainly as catalysts, reinforcing motivations that derive from the social structure."[28]

Lowered Mortality and Declining Fertility

Returning to the issue of fertility declines during the final stages of the demographic transition, Davis has formulated the rationale for the differential decline of birth and death rates partially along the lines already suggested, but he sees the prior decline of mortality as an essential feature of the process:

. . . the decline of fertility lags behind that of mortality. This is because the struggle for survival has forced all societies to place a high value on both reproduction and the preservation of life. With the coming of a more deliberate, innovative control over human affairs, a movement to limit reproduction in unaccustomed ways meets strong opposition as being contrary to an established value; whereas an effort to preserve life, even in unaccustomed ways, generally receives approval as *favoring* an established value. Only after the successful preservation of life has resulted in larger families and these larger families have proved an embarrassment in the highly urbanized and mobile structure of modern society, does the individual seek a way around the practice of his high fertility mores. He leaves the public attitude intact but tends to violate it in his own private behavior. Thus the lag of birth control behind death control is implicit in the growing rationalism of modern life, which first attacks the negative value (death) and later the positive value (high fertility).[29]

More recently, Davis has elaborated this same theme and has shown that it is consistent with the demographic and economic experiences of a number of societies.[30] Discussing the dramatic adoption of population-control techniques by the Japanese in the 1950s, he noted, "Within a brief period they quickly postponed marriage, embraced contraception, began sterilization, utilized abortions, and migrated outward."[31] This response, called the "multiphasic response," was not caused by increasing poverty, for it occurred at a time of considerable economic growth in Japan. Similarly, the countries of Northwestern Europe have by many different methods decreased population growth after a sustained period of high natural increase. As in the case of Japan, poverty does not seem to be the explanation, for prosperity was rising in Northwestern Europe at the time fertility declined. It was the individual's response to prosperity that caused him to modify his reproductive behavior. As infant mortality declined, each child had more siblings with whom he had to share the family's resources. When the individual formed his own family, the greater "survivability" of his own children caused him to reduce fertility so that he—and they—would be more able to take advantage of the prosperity offered by the economy. Davis summarized the issue in the following manner:

My thesis is that, faced with a persistent high rate of natural increase resulting from past success in controlling mortality, families tended to use every demographic means possible to maximize their new opportunities and to avoid relative loss of status.[32]

The fertility declines in modern societies, a major feature of transition theory, seem to be explained by a common core of ideas. Fertility is the result of individual or family action. *Couples diminish their fertility when they feel that by doing so there is some likelihood of improving or holding their position in the social structure.* This can only occur in an economic system where children are not economically advantageous, and where the social system does not make the bearing and rearing of children a near-imperative.

THE FUTURE POPULATION

The present rate of growth of the world's population cannot be sustained for any extended time period, but in the shorter term—twenty-five, fifty, or even one hundred years—the range of possibilities is much greater. The art of anticipating the demographic future has engaged many population scholars in the past, but it is a hazardous undertaking because as time passes the predictions are confronted by the facts. In this concluding section there will be no attempt to make numerical predictions about the world's future population; instead the focus will be on the elements that will determine what that population will be.

Doomsday versus Transition

The idea that "nothing can be done about population growth," or, the opposing notion, that "the population problem will solve itself" are both wrong and potentially dangerous. Some writers have given the impression that the world is moving inexorably toward a population of many billions, and an inevitable "doomsday." These writers imply that almost nothing can be done to stop the present high rate of population growth. This view is not only theoretically incorrect but, worse, it may be disastrous in practice, since it could lead to inaction and a fatalistic response to population growth. If it is assumed that continued rapid population growth is inevitable, it might happen that only ineffectual efforts will be made to curb such growth. Certainly, if little action is taken, the population will continue to grow at a high rate, probably until some disaster occurs.

On the other hand, a kind of blind faith in the "demographic transition" can be equally perilous. The European and American transition experiences do not provide assurances that fertility declines will occur in the countries now experiencing the most rapid population growth. Indeed, without concerted action, there is a great danger that fertility will not drop soon enough to avoid a population crisis.

Neither a resigned acceptance of an inevitable doomsday nor a blind faith in the comforting idea of the demographic transition are rational responses to the population problem. All evidence points to the fact that it is the nature of the human institutions that determines the vital rates of the society, particularly the fertility rates. Since human institutions are modifiable, it follows that the vital rates of any society are also capable of being changed. Therefore, the appropriate question is *not,* Can world population growth be stopped? The question is, What steps should be taken if world population growth is to be stopped? This in turn leads to a quite different question about the future: What are the chances that appropriate efforts will be made by particular countries, and by enough countries, to slow the rate of world population growth?

Demographers' Views of the Future

Not many years ago demographers were nearly alone in their concern about the problem of a rapidly growing world population. Sometimes it seemed that the danger of a world population that was doubling every thirty-five to forty years was going unheeded by all but a handful of people. Most world and national political leaders were either unconcerned or disbelieving. The average citizen was not yet aware of what was already being called by some a "population explosion." Gradually, in the decade of the 1960s—perhaps convinced by the crowded conditions in their own urban environment—many people suddenly became aware of the "population problem" and accepted it as real. While the problem has now been recognized by many people, it is doubtful that the nature of the solution has yet become clear to most.

Among the population specialists, considerable disagreement has developed over the outlook for world-population growth. Roughly speaking, some demographers are predicting that world-population growth will reach the zero point around the year 2000, while others are convinced that current efforts will not even slow the rate of growth. A consideration of the various positions on this issue will help to highlight the factors that must be taken into account.

One polar position on world-population growth has been taken by Bogue, who is extremely optimistic about stopping rapid population growth. He has stated that by the year 2000 the growth rate of the world population will not be at its present high of nearly 2 percent per year, but will be more nearly zero. His position is expressed in the assertion that "it is quite reasonable to assume that the world population crisis is a phenomenon of the 20th century, and will be largely if not entirely a matter of history when humanity moves into the 21st century."[33]

While allowing that in the year 2000 there might still be a few places in the world with excessive populations and continuing growth, Bogue believes that such conditions will be confined to small areas in only a few nations.

There may be particular ethnic, economic, or religious groups that will not have received or accepted fertility control, but these will be relatively small pockets of resistance and of no great demographic significance. Since other areas in the same region or nation might have less-than-replacement growth, the over-all effect will be a zero growth rate for all major world regions.

This strikingly optimistic conclusion is based on a number of conditions, the most important of which is that there will be an "all-out 'crash program' to make the widest and most intensive use of the medical, sociological, and psychological knowledge now available. . . ." Population control, through fertility control, is not going to happen in some spontaneous or mysterious way. It will occur only when great efforts have been made to extend and fulfill the already existing programs of fertility control. On this point almost everyone—whether optimist or pessimist—is in agreement.

Bogue outlined several reasons for believing that there will be continued efforts to decrease fertility, and that these efforts will be increasingly successful:

1. *Grass-roots approval.* Surveys have shown that most families are interested in fertility control, and do not have major active objections to the principle of family planning.

2. *Aroused political leadership.* The leadership of most nations with a population problem openly accepts family planning as a moral and rational solution.

3. *Accelerated professional and research activity.* There has been increasing support for, and research activity on, family planning by medical and scholarly personnel.

4. *Sociological and psychological knowledge.* The findings of social and psychological research in the last thirty years are increasingly useful for promoting family planning.

5. *Improved contraceptives.* The research on contraceptive techniques has already produced oral contraceptives and intrauterine devices which have proved to be highly effective. Continued research is likely to produce still more easy-to-use and inexpensive fertility-control techniques.

One more factor can be added to Bogue's reasons for expecting population control. Since mortality is approaching its lowest possible level in many countries, there is less possibility of population growth through further death control.

Many observers, including Bogue, see much cause for optimism in the results of some already functioning family-planning programs, because these programs demonstrate that there is already a widespread acceptance of the concept of family planning throughout the world.

The key elements in the optimistic position are that the people, and the leaders, of the world accept the idea of family planning; that contraceptive technology exists and will continue to be improved; and that there is sufficient scientific knowledge about human behavior to implement effective fertility-control programs. Granting these assumptions, it simply remains for the all-out crash effort to be made and fertility will be brought under control during this century.

Other demographers have expressed a similar hope about controlling population growth, but their optimism is more cautious. For example, Coale made predictions covering a much shorter period of time. Writing in 1967, he estimated that there would be a 25 percent decline in fertility in Korea, China, India, and Pakistan within a decade. He estimated that Latin America would experience similar declines by 1980.[34]

Coale based his prediction on several developments, including the already established success of government-sponsored family-planning programs in Taiwan and South Korea. He also noted that there was an increasing recognition of the importance of reduced fertility by the governments of many of the less developed countries, by international agencies, and by world opinion generally. Finally, the technological advance represented by the successful use of the intrauterine device was seen as a most favorable development. This technique of fertility control was considered particularly important because it required only a low level of motivation to limit the number of births.

Notestein has also taken a mildly optimistic position about the possibility of population control, but he has made no specific predictions. Instead, he concluded, "We now have a basis for expecting that a rapid decline in birth rates can be achieved in the next decades."[35] He expressed the hope that the problems could be solved "by a world fully alert to the dangers and willing to devote serious resources and energy to attacking them."[36] Notestein's reasons for believing that a decline in fertility could be achieved rested upon the success of the family-planning programs in Taiwan, South Korea, Hong Kong, and Singapore; the developments in contraceptive technology—especially the intrauterine device—and the interest in family planning being shown by both governments and the people.

The similarity of the arguments of these more optimistic writers leaves the impression that there is reason for considerable hope. Perhaps, it may be thought, the dangers of overpopulation have been overstressed, or even exaggerated. But it must be remembered that each writer is basing his optimism largely on an assumption about action that is *yet to be taken*. Notestein put it best when he said, "We cannot argue that the solution is in sight, but we can argue that the prerequisites for a solution are at hand."[37]

These prerequisites include the willingness and the ability to implement family planning around the world. But is that enough? One clear negative voice has been heard in answer to this question. Davis has argued that present-day thinking about family planning is seriously inadequate for the task of population control.[38] To comprehend fully the extent of the problem and the action required for a solution, it is important to understand Davis's argument.

Davis has several reasons for being skeptical about the effectiveness of present population-control programs. He first attacks the idea that the terms "population control," "fertility control," and "family planning" are interchangeable. The programs in existence today, particularly those in the less developed nations, are generally called "family-planning programs." Family planning is usually a euphemism for contraception. The family-planning approach to population limitation typically concentrates on providing new and efficient contraceptives on a national basis and under public-health auspices. The existing family-planning programs are thus very limited in scope, and cannot be called population-control programs or even fertility-control programs. A true population-control program would involve deliberate control over all aspects of population, "including its age-sex structure, geographical distribution, racial composition, genetic quality, and total size."[39] The term fertility control is misleading because the programs in existence use only a very limited approach to control fertility. The programs are aimed at reducing fertility by increasing the use of contraceptive techniques, but this does not bring any changes in the most important determinants of human fertility—the motivations produced by the social system. If fertility behavior is shaped by the social system, then the social forces that motivate people to have children must be given attention in any fertility-control program. A family-planning program that focuses only on the distribution of contraceptive techniques in order that families may have the number of children they want is narrowly conceived, and will very likely fail to curb population growth.

Davis's position is based on the well-established point that childbearing and rearing is behavior that is "socially motivated, like other forms of behavior, by being a part of the system of rewards and punishments that is built into human relationships, and thus is bound up with the individual's economic and personal interests. . . ." The obvious implication of this fact is that if there are to be changes in fertility there must be changes in the social and economic structure of the society. In particular, changes must be made with regard to the position and the role of the family in society. This point is a sensitive one, however, for the family is the most sacrosanct of social institutions, and to suggest even some modest changes in its position is to risk censure. Perhaps for this reason, family-planning programs have usually had the expressed goal of *strengthening* the family. But this objective may be directly contrary to what is needed today as far as fertility is concerned.

Blake considered the question of fertility motivation by reviewing the desired and ideal family sizes of American and European populations. She concluded that even in these largely urban and industrially developed countries the existing social systems lead to family-size desires that exceed the two children that would replace the parents.[40] Blake concluded, "In order for it [family size] to stablize at low levels, we believe that the population must experience a major change in the institutional structure supporting the [larger family size] ideals—namely, the family and the set of roles articulating with reproduction as a social insitution."[41]

The existing family-planning programs do not, by and large, exert pressure that would change the rewards for producing children. Indeed, they usually take the opposite approach. Again and again family-planning programs emphasize that family planning is designed to allow the couple to have *the number of children they desire*. It is illogical to assume that by allowing individual couples, through contraception, to have the number of children they desire, the rate of population growth will be in any way controlled. All existing evidence about desired family size, in both underdeveloped and developed societies, indicates that people generally desire more children than are needed if the population-growth rate is to be zero. It is fairly obvious that most couples *must not* have the desired three, four, or more children if the population size is to be stable. Whether the three or more children are planned or unplanned, whether birth-control techniques are used or not used, it makes little difference. As Davis has emphasized, *"Contraception is compatible with high fertility."*[42]

Existing programs of family planning may succeed in reducing fertility, for as they provide people with a knowledge of contraceptives and actually make them available, there should be less and less unwanted fertility. This is clearly what has been happening in much of the Western world and what has begun to happen in Japan, Taiwan, South Korea, Puerto Rico, and various other places. But the reduction or elimination of unwanted fertility will not alone stop population growth in most societies. The positive rewards for having children are so firmly a part of most existing value systems and institutional structures that changes in the social orders of most societies will be necessary before fertility is reduced to the point at which a stable population size results.

Controlling Population Growth

The differences of opinion between the optimists and the pessimists about population do not mean that their views are necessarily incompatible. A combination of their positions provides a total view of what must be done if the societies are to reduce present rates of population growth to zero or near zero. From this synthesis, four broad features necessary for a successful program of fertility control emerge:

1. *A recognition by the leadership that population growth is excessive.* The *sine qua non* of any successful fertility-control program is a recognition on the

part of the power holders of the society that continued growth because of high fertility is detrimental to the well-being of the society. This point clearly introduces a value question, for "well-being" may not be the same for all individuals and strata in the social system. It is, however, "well-being" as construed by the power holders of the society that will make the crucial difference. From an objective standpoint it matters little what goals cause the leaders of a society to want to reduce population growth. They may want to reduce in order to lessen the problems of overcrowding, poverty, or contamination of the environment. Their aim may be to hasten economic development or to increase the country's power position in international affairs. The leaders of a country may want to reduce population growth in an effort to avert a popular revolution. Whatever personal, political, economic, or nationalistic reasons they may have, the people in the society who hold the political, economic, and religious power must want a reduction in fertility in order for it to occur.

It may seem strange that so much emphasis is placed on a recognition of the problem by the leaders of the society rather than by the people. The reason is quite simple. Individual couples have children or refrain from having them on the basis of what they define as their own personal well-being. They do not bear children on the basis of the needs of the society, and they do not stop bearing them simply because there is no societal need for more. Even the occasional couples who claim that they do not have children because "the world (or the country) is already overcrowded" are saying in effect that the value they place on having a child does not exceed the negative costs of rearing and being responsible for that child in the world as it is today. Fertility-control programs may operate to produce such values among the population, but these programs are not likely to grow out of a popular demand.

2. *Contraceptive technology.* The role of contraceptive technology in a successful fertility-control program is important, but it is easy to overstress its importance. Fertility limitation has occurred in many places throughout history without the help of the modern-day contraceptive techniques. However, the fact that there are now a number of effective contraceptives can be very important to the success of fertility-control programs. Other, even more effective, techniques are likely to be forthcoming as research in the area of reproduction control produces results.

3. *Social-scientific knowledge.* An essential counterpart to contraceptive technology is the social and psychological knowledge necessary for dispensing such technology. In the last three decades there has been a considerable amount of social-scientific research on the process by which people adopt innovations, including birth-control techniques. Such research on the communication and adoption process has convinced most authorities that the techniques and approaches for disseminating information about birth control,

even to nonliterate populations, are sufficiently well known so that it can be done successfully.[43]

4. *Modifications in the social structure.* The fourth essential feature of any effective program of fertility control involves social structures directly: Some efforts must be made to modify the social institutions of the society so that people may receive as much social reward for not having children as they now generally receive for having them. This element is the least discussed, and is therefore also the least developed factor in existing programs. The extent to which changes in social institutions become a part of existing programs will be a key factor in determining the future success of fertility control in this century.

The Outlook for Population Control

What are the chances that sufficient and appropriate efforts will be made by particular countries, and by enough countries, to slow the rate of world-population growth? The answer lies in three areas: (1) the desires of the holders of power, (2) the availability of scientific knowledge, and (3) the willingness of the leadership to make changes in the structure of social and economic life.

The availability of scientific knowledge is the easiest to affirm. The production of effective contraceptive techniques and the knowledge about how to disseminate them are both clearly within the scope of man's ability. Whatever knowledge is yet needed can be obtained whenever the leaders of societies are willing to allocate the resources necessary for research and development.

The willingness of the leaders of societies to allocate the resources necessary for successful population-control programs is more problematic. First, granting that they know what is necessary for meeting their objectives, the more fundamental question is, Can the power holders of the society get what they want? The evidence available indicates that they generally do, by allocating sufficient resources. Not only are their wishes attainable, but they are attainable in quick order. The best examples are in the scientific-technical realm. The American production of an atomic weapon in the years during World War II is a striking example of the advances that can be made when a society engages in a "crash" program. A reading of the details of the Manhattan Project is an awesome revelation of what can be accomplished when scientific, technological, and production personnel are given nearly unlimited resources. Starting largely with only theoretical knowledge in 1942, the United States government recruited large numbers of people and provided untold amounts of material to the directors of the Manhattan Project. The outcome of this extraordinary effort was the production of two workable atomic weapons, produced in time to be used in the war against Japan in 1945. The American space program is another illustration of a scientific-technological advance resulting from an intensive national effort. It took less than a decade for the United States to land a manned vehicle on the moon after government leaders set that goal in the early 1960s. Both examples show how quickly objectives can be achieved when the leadership of a modern society chooses to provide the necessary resources.

If there are scientific, technical, or distribution problems remaining to be solved in the efforts toward controlling world-population growth, it would surely be within the economic capabilities of the nations of the world to solve them. On a world-wide basis, the money spent on military systems approaches 200 billion dollars per year. It would probably require only a small fraction of this amount to finance all the research still necessary in order to carry out a successful worldwide population-control program.

But the leaders of societies do not yet seem willing to allocate the necessary resources for population-control programs. Most governments, even those strongly committed to population control, are far less willing to allocate funds for population-control programs than they are for their military programs. Since no Latin American or Sub-Sahara African country has any appreciable population-control program at present, this statement most assuredly holds true for those two continents. The Indian case is a good test of the proposition, since India has had a population-control program since 1953. Yet in the fiscal year 1961–1962, before the Chinese-Indian border dispute and before the 1965 war with Pakistan, India had a defense budget of over 3 *billion* rupees. In the same year expenditures on the family-planning program were about 14 *million* rupees. This was nearly ten years after the beginning of India's population-control program, yet its budget was less than one-half of one percent of the military budget. The new intensive family-planning program in India provides 2.3 billion rupees for five years. This is an average yearly expenditure of about 460 million rupees (U.S. $100 million based on the official exchange rate for 1961–1965) compared with a defense budget of about ten times that much.[44]

The fact is that at present most national leaders are willing to spend only a tiny proportion of total governmental expenditures for family-planning programs. This is true even in those countries where overpopulation is officially recognized as a national problem. One must infer from this information that *most national and world leaders are not yet truly convinced about the dangers of overpopulation.* Ultimately, then, from this perspective the population problem is not scientific; it is political.

It will probably require some dramatic events before the necessary action will be taken in most countries. As the world population continues to grow rapidly through the 1970s and 1980s there will very likely be tragic crises caused by overpopulation. World and national leaders will be appalled at millions of deaths resulting from famines, epidemics, civil disorder, or wars caused by excessive populations. Events of this nature will be dramatic enough so that, belatedly, actions will be taken to slow down or stop population growth.

Changes in the Social Structure

Probably very few deliberate efforts will be made to change the social structure in order to reduce population growth. There may be some deliberate changes in the structure of social institutions, but they will be for reasons other than reducing fertility. There will also be some naturally occurring changes that come as concomitants of technical and economic change. Despite the essential validity of the argument that the present institutional supports for the family and childbearing must be reduced, it will not be heard by enough people and it will not be received objectively by many of those who do hear it. Most of the suggestions to reduce the importance and primacy of the family, marital sex roles, and reproduction will be met by adamant opposition. At present, even the advocates of family planning are interested in *strengthening* the role of the family in society, not weakening it. As an example, but only one of a multitude, the Director of the Central Family Planning Institute in New Delhi, India has described the purpose of India's family-planning program as one that is "ultimately to promote, as far as possible, the growth of the family as a unit of society. . . ."[45]

Two basic institutional approaches to controlling fertility have been suggested: The delay of marriage and the limitation of births within marriage.[46] Either by law or custom most societies do set a minimum age for marriage; it therefore follows that laws could be introduced to prohibit marriage until some more advanced age—say, twenty years. However, the difficulties involved in enforcement and the latent effects of such regulations are both deterrents to this course of action. On the other hand, *indirect* factors can cause the postponement of marriage, and in many societies they have proved to be very effective. In some agrarian societies, the necessity of paying a bride price or meeting some other economic prerequisite to marriage causes many people to marry late. In industrial societies, the high cost of housing or education can often act as a deterrent to marriage.

Within marriage, the cost connected with having children could be increased. This would be a distinct change from the present, for most societies now have either direct or indirect benefits accruing to families with children. Even if benefits were only reduced, people might be deterred from having children. For example, governments could

cease taxing single persons more than married ones; stop giving parents special tax exemptions; abandon the income-tax policy that discriminates against couples when the wife works; reduce paid maternity leaves; reduce family allowances; stop awarding public housing on the basis of family size; stop granting fellowships and other educational aids (including special allowances for wives and children) to married students; cease outlawing abortions and sterilizations; and relax rules that allow use of harmless contraceptives only with medical permission.[47]

Other more sensational suggestions include the government paying the cost of all abortions, high fees for marriage licenses, and a requirement that illegitimate pregnancies be aborted.

Although some of these actions may eventually be taken with the direct aim in view of reducing fertility, most direct changes will be for other purposes. For example, while abortion may become available and more widely used in societies, it is more likely to be accepted because of its consonance with new values about personal freedom. Or, abortion will be accepted for the protection it gives to the health and well-being of women. Rarely will the explicit aim of liberalized abortion practices be to reduce the number of children born in the society.

Economic equality for women would also be a social structural change that could decrease fertility, but if it comes, it will come in the context of greater equality for all citizens, not as an explicit measure to reduce fertility.

Mainland China—A Harbinger of What Might Be

The task of reducing the rapid population growth of the world often seems impossible because there are so many obstacles yet to be overcome. Particularly discouraging is the thought of trying to reduce population growth in those countries and areas where the economy is largely agricultural, where many of the people are uneducated, and where the traditions of family and childbearing are deeply rooted in the culture. Often these very conditions prevail among the extremely large population groups of the world—the national populations that run to several hundred million people. But if world-population growth is to diminish, fertility must go down in precisely these populations.

One might point to the fertility declines that have occurred in Japan, South Korea, or Taiwan as the basis for optimism, but while the fertility rates in these countries have dropped, they have done so in the context of increasing urbanization-industrialization. It is therefore possible that the family-planning programs in these countries have not in themselves had such a pronounced effect upon fertility as has sometimes been supposed. There is, however, one country that may provide a demonstration of how a large, agrarian population with a very traditional culture can control population growth. The country is mainland China, the largest national population in the world, with over 700 million people. It is quite possible that the Chinese have already controlled their population growth through the reduction of fertility. If this is so, it should be possible for any country to limit the growth rate of its population.

Unfortunately, demographic information on China is not available, at least not in the West. It is doubtful that even the Chinese leaders have very up-to-date data on their population. One can only examine the available evidence, and, on the basis of what is known about population dynamics, draw the most reasonable conclusions.

After the 1949 Communist revolution dramatic efforts were made to break the strength of the traditional Chinese family.[48] Apparently these original efforts were deemed necessary in order to secure the revolution. It does not appear that these changes were directly aimed at reducing fertility, but somewhat later, during the middle 1950s, a birth-control movement did begin in China. This campaign reached a peak of activity in 1957.[49] Thereafter it diminished very rapidly, but this abrupt ending of the birth-control movement was prompted more by political in-fighting among the Chinese leaders than by a belief that fertility control was no longer necessary. Throughout the 1960s there have been indications that the Chinese have continued their efforts to control population by lowering fertility. Birth-control devices are both imported into China and manufactured there. Birth control has been encouraged in significant Chinese periodicals, and various techniques of birth control are frequently discussed in the Chinese medical journals.[50]

But most important, the Chinese system since the revolution has been clearly consistent with low fertility. The official Communist Party position has changed the role of women from one of subservience to one of equality. Women have been urged to dedicate their lives to their work, the Communist Party, and the State. Occupations and professions that might previously have been restricted to men have now been widely opened to women. (Taeuber and Orleans report that "½ of the graduates of medical schools are women."[51]) Childbearing is only one of the possible avenues to a satisfying life, according to the official Chinese ideology. The marriage and family ideal in China calls for couples to marry in their late twenties and then to have only one or two children.

If the Chinese young people are following the norm of late marriage, the the long-term consequences for population growth may be as important as the short-term effects. The immediate result of late marriage is the reduction of fertility, since women remain unmarried and childless through many of their most fecund years. Such a delay in childbearing will almost always result in a lower total number of children born to the individual couple. From a long-run societal view, the fact that people marry later has the additional effect of slowing population growth, because the time interval from generation to generation increases.

If all of these factors have reduced fertility in China, the resultant population-growth rate may already have diminished. Even with the declining mortality that has occurred in China, the reduction of the birth rate may have been sufficient to lower the population-growth rate. The availability of birth-control techniques, the increasing use of abortion,[52] and most of all the changed family structure, supported by the values embodied in the official ideology, all point to the possibility of a substantially reduced rate of growth for the Chinese population.

Specifically, one might suppose that China, a developing country with a large population, has been able to keep its growth rate much below the estimated 2 percent of a few years ago, and in the next decade, under the existing regime and ideology, it could reduce that rate of growth even more. If this reduction occurs, it will have several important implications. A low fertility rate, leading to a low population-growth rate, could allow China to make dramatic economic progress. That progress could in turn redistribute the balance of world power. From the standpoint of world population, what happens in China will affect the world total, since the Chinese represent about one-fifth of that total at present. But more importantly it will stand as an example of the kind of change that can occur in a large underdeveloped society with a traditional culture. It will show that patterns of fertility that have prevailed for millenia can be suddenly and dramatically reversed. While in China these changes have been concomitants of a political revolution, there is no intrinsic connection. Equally effective programs and social-structural changes could be introduced in other countries experiencing excessive population growth.

The next two decades will be a crucial time for many of these countries. During these years the necessary efforts and changes could be made, and crises that would be caused by overpopulation could be averted. But these crucial years may be wasted on ineffectual action and substantial amounts of rhetoric. If they are, human tragedy may be the result.

Summary

In the long history of man the growth of the world's population has been very very slow. Only in the past three hundred years has the rate of growth quickened, and only in the last fifty has the rate increased so rapidly that the "population problem" has taken on dramatic new dimensions. With an ever-larger world population, and a rate of growth that is higher than ever before, there is now a distinct possibility that an excessive human population will threaten man's existence.

It is possible to understand the dynamics of the recent population growth by understanding the fundamental features of the modern demographic transition. Transition theory, as it is often called, focuses on the relationship between modernization and the changing vital rates of a society. As a society begins the transition from a rural-agrarian economy to an urban-industrial economy, there is an early decline in the mortality rate while the fertility rate remains high. As long as high birth rates and low death rates prevail there will be a high rate of population growth. European countries experienced this transition, but over a relatively long period of time. While population growth did occur in Europe, the growth rate was much less rapid than that being experienced by many underdeveloped countries today. These latter countries, often with populations of hundreds of millions, have been able to adopt the death-control measures of the developed countries and thus bring about decreases in mortality without decreasing fertility in any appreciable way.

Population growth can be reduced only by balancing, or nearly balancing, birth and death rates. Since no one seriously suggests raising death rates, the only alternative is fertility control. Fertility control can occur if the leaders of the society recognize a need for it and allocate the necessary resources to the task. When they do so, the necessary scientific and technical knowledge—including the social-scientific knowledge—will be available, or within reach. A successful program to reduce fertility may have as its core the introduction and distribution of birth-control techniques, but if the program is to be truly successful, and successful in a relatively short time, it must give attention to the features of the social structure and culture that promote fertility. This will require a recognition of the simple proposition that fertility behavior is socially produced, and as long as there are significant social inducements for having children, fertility in most societies will continue to be excessive.

The population problem produced by excessive population growth is not something that will solve itself—except in a most unpleasant way. But it is not a problem that is incapable of solution. The means of solution are available. It remains to be seen whether man will use them.

: : SELECTED READINGS AND MATERIALS

General

American Academy of Political and Social Science. "World Population." *The Annals*, Vol. 365, 1967.

Berelson, Bernard, *et al. Family Planning and Population Programs.* Chicago, University of Chicago Press, 1969.

Ehrlich, Paul R., and Anne H. Ehrlich. *Population, Resources and Environment.* San Francisco, W. H. Freeman, 1970.

Ford, Thomas R., and Gordon DeJong, editors. *Social Demography.* Englewood Cliffs, N.J., Prentice Hall, 1970. Part 5, "Demographic Transition and the Socioeconomic Development of Societies."

Kammeyer, Kenneth C. W., editor. *Population Studies: Selected Essays and Research.* Chicago, Rand-McNally, 1969. Section VI, "World Population."

Nam, Charles B., editor. *Population and Society: A Textbook of Selected Readings.* Boston, Houghton-Mifflin, 1968. Chapter 2, "Population Growth: Theory and Fact" and Chapter 15, "Population and the Polity."

Sauvy, Alfred. *Fertility and Survival: Population Problems from Malthus to Mao Tse-Tung.* New York, Criterion Books, 1961.

Sheps, Mindel C., and Jeanne Clare Ridley. *Public Health and Population Change: Current Research Issues.* Pittsburgh, University of Pittsburgh Press, 1965.

Periodicals and Journals

The following publications regularly provide current and authoritative information on existing family-planning programs. The major emphasis is on family planning through the dissemination of birth-control techniques.

Reports on Population/Family Planning. Published by the Population Council and the International Institute for the study of Human Reproduction. 245 Park Avenue, New York, New York, 10017.

Studies in Family Planning. Published by the Population Council. 245 Park Avenue, New York, New York 10017.

: : NOTES

1. S. L. Washburn, "Thinking About Race," in *This Is Race,* Earl W. Count, ed. (New York: Henry Schuman, 1950), pp. 691–702.

2. Annabelle Desmond, "How Many People Have Ever Lived on Earth?" *Population Bulletin,* 18: 1–18 (1962).

3. Some of the more recently published books are: Paul R. Ehrlich, *The Population Bomb* (New York: Ballantine Books, 1968); Paul R. Ehrlich and Anne H. Ehrlich, *Population, Resources, Environment* (San Francisco: W. H. Freeman, 1970); William Paddock and Paul Paddock, *Famine 1975* (Boston: Little Brown, 1967); Lincoln H. Day and Alice Taylor Day, *Too Many Americans* (Boston: Houghton Mifflin, 1964). The last book directs attention specifically to the population growth of the United States. The Days emphasize that the American growth rate is sufficiently high to create problems in the United States. Ehrlich has repeatedly emphasized that in relation to resource consumption the American population can be particularly threatening, since each American consumes so much more than does a person in a less developed economy.

4. Nathan Keyfitz, "How Many People Have Lived on Earth?" *Demography,* 3: 581–582 (1966).

5. Desmond, pp. 1–19.

6. Desmond, p. 1.

7. The claim is one that is typically made verbally, and thus is not usually found in a writing, but a recent appearance of the assertion is found in Gore Vidal's novel *Myra Breckinridge.* Author Vidal (who is concerned with world-population growth) has his hero(ine) make the claim. Gore Vidal, *Myra Breckinridge* (New York: Bantam Books, 1968), p. 153.

8. Donald Bogue, *Principles of Demography* (New York: John Wiley & Sons, 1969), p. 48.

9. William Petersen, *Population,* 2nd edition (New York: Macmillan, 1969), p. 11.

10. Warren S. Thompson, "Population," *American Journal of Sociology*, 34:959–975 (1929).

11. Donald Cowgill, "The Theory of Population Growth Cycles," *The American Journal of Sociology*, 55: 163–170 (1949); "Transition Theory as General Population Theory," *Social Forces*, 41: 270–274 (1963).

12. Cowgill, "Transition Theory," p. 271.

13. Cowgill, "Transition Theory," p. 270; see Thomas Robert Malthus, *An Essay of the Principle of Population as it Affects the Future Improvement of Society, with Remarks on the Speculations of Mr. Godwin, M. Condorcet and Other Writers* (London: Printed for J. Johnson in St. Pauls Churchyard, 1798). Reprinted by Macmillan, London, 1926).

14. Cowgill, "The Theory of Population Growth Cycles," p. 170.

15. The Scandinavian countries have remarkably good population data covering the early stages of their modernization, and provide good examples of the early decline in mortality. See Michael Drake, *Population and Society in Norway 1735–1865* (Cambridge, Cambridge University Press, 1969), pp. 42–49; Alva Myrdal, *Nation and Family* (Cambridge, Mass: M.I.T. Press, 1968), pp. 17–28; Kenneth C. W. Kammeyer, "A Re-examination of some Recent Criticisms of Transition Theory," *The Sociological Quarterly*, 11: 500–510 (1970).

16. Dennis Wrong, *Population and Society*, 3rd edition (New York: Random House, 1967), p. 19.

17. Robert Gutman, "In Defense of Population Theory," *American Sociological Review*, 25: 331 (1960).

18. Leighton Van Nort, "On Values in Population Theory," *The Milbank Memorial Fund Quarterly*, 38: 387-395 (1960).

19. Joyce O. Hertzler, *The Crisis in World Population* (Lincoln, Nebr.: University of Nebraska Press, 1956), p. 45.

20. Thomas McKeown and R. G. Brown, "Medical Evidence Related to English Population Changes in the Eighteenth Century," in *Population in History: Essays in Historical Demography*, edited by D. V. Glass and D. E. L. Eversly (Chicago: Aldine, 1965), p. 306.

21. Frank W. Notestein, "Population—the Long View," *Food for the World*, edited by Theodore W. Schultz (Chicago: University of Chicago Press, 1945), p. 39. See also Hertzler, p. 47.

22. Notestein, p. 40.

23. Hertzler, p. 48.

24. Hertzler, p. 49.

25. Petersen, p. 420.

26. Norman B. Ryder and Charles F. Westoff, "The United States: The Pill and the Birth Rate, 1960–1965," *Studies in Family Planning*, 20: 3 (1967).

27. See Mary Douglas, "Population Control among Primitive Groups," *British Journal of Sociology*, 17: 263–273 (1966); Kingsley Davis and Judith Blake, "Social Structure and Fertility: An Analytic Framework," *Economic Development and Cultural Change*, 4: 211-235 (1956).

28. Petersen, p. 503.

29. Kingsley Davis, *Human Society* (New York: Macmillan, 1948), pp. 599-600.

30. Kingsley Davis, "The Theory of Change and Response in Modern Demographic History," *Population Index*, 29: 345–365 (1963).

31. Davis, "The Theory of Change," p. 349

32. Davis, "The Theory of Change," p. 362

33. Donald J. Bogue, "The End of the Population Explosion," *The Public Interest*, 7: 11–20 (1967).

34. Ansley Coale, "Voluntary Control of Fertility," *Proceedings of the American Philosophical Society*, 3:169 (1967).

35. Frank Notestein, "The Population Crisis: Reasons for Hope," *Foreign Affairs*, 46:170 (1967).

36. Notestein, p. 170.

37. Notestein, p. 170.

38. Kingsley Davis, "Population Policy: Will Current Programs Succeed?" *Science*, 158: 730–739 (1967)

39. Davis, p. 731.

40. Judith Blake, "Demographic Science and the Redirection of Population Policy," *Journal of Chronic Disease* (1965), pp. 1181–1200; "Income and Reproductive Motivation," *Population Studies*, 21: 185–206 (1967).

41. Blake, "Income and Reproductive Motivation," p. 205.

42. Davis, p. 753.

43. J. Mayone Stycos, "Obstacles to Programs of Population Control," *Marriage and Family Living*, 25: 9–13 (1963); Bernard Berelson, "On Family Planning Communication," *Demography*, 1: 94–105 (1964).

44. Government of India Ministry of Finance, Department of Economic Affairs, *India Pocket Book of Economic Information* (1962), p. 134.

45. B. L. Raina, "India," in Bernard Berelson, *et al.*, *Family Planning and Population Programs* (Chicago: University of Chicago Press, 1966), p. 113.

46. Davis, pp. 737, 738.

47. Davis, p. 738.

48. C. K. Yang, *Chinese Communist Society: The Family and the Village* (Cambridge, Mass.: The M.I.T. Press, 1959), Chapters I–XIII.

49. H. Yuan Tien, "Birth Control in Mainland China: Ideology and Politics," *Milbank Memorial Fund Quarterly*, 41: 269–290 (1963).

50. Tien, p. 209; Leo A. Orleans, "Evidence from Chinese Medical Journals on Current Population Policy," *The China Quarterly*, 40:137–146 (1969).

51. Irene B. Taeuber and Letta Orleans, "Mainland China" in Berelson, p. 43.

52. Leo Orleans, pp. 139–141.

Appendices

POPULATION REFERENCE MATERIALS

1. Glossary
2. 1970 World Population Data Sheet
3. World Map: Population-Growth Rates—1970
4. Inquiries for the 1970 Census of Population and Housing
5. The United States Census—1970

153

1. Glossary

Age-sex pyramid (population pyramid). A graphic method of showing the age-sex composition of the population. Age groups are arranged in strata, with the youngest at the bottom and the oldest at the top. (See Chapter 3, Figure 2.)

Age-specific birth rate. Number of live births to women in a specific age group per 1,000 females in that age group at mid-year.

Age-specific death rate. Number of deaths in a specific age group per 1,000 individuals in that age group at mid-year.

Birth rate (or crude birth rate). Number of live births in one year per 1,000 people in the mid-year population.

Cohort. A group of persons all of whom enter some stage of the life cycle simultaneously. A birth cohort consists of all the males, females, or both, who were born in a given year. A marriage cohort consists of all the men, women, or both who were married in a given year.

Death rate (or crude death rate). Number of deaths in one year per 1,000 people in the mid-year population.

Dependency ratio (or age-dependency ratio). The number of persons under 15 years of age plus the number of persons 65 and over per 1,000 persons aged 15 to 64.

Fecundity. The biological capacity of a woman (or couple) to reproduce.

Fertility. The actual number of births occurring to a particular woman, couple, or population aggregate.

General fertility rate. Number of live births in one year per 1,000 females of childbearing age (usually defined as the age 15 to 49, or 15 to 45).

Growth rate. Increase or decrease in a population during a year (expressed as a percentage of the original population), as determined by births, deaths, and net migration.

Infant-mortality rate. The number of infants (children under one year of age) who die during a year per 1,000 live births in that year.

Life expectancy. Under given mortality conditions (that is, age-specific death rates), the average number of years of life remaining to males or females of a specified age. Often expressed as the average number of years of life expected at birth.

Sources of these and other population terms include: *Population Bulletin*, "A Sourcebook on Population," 25: 5, 1969 (principal source for this glossary); George W. Barclay, *Techniques of Population Analysis* (New York: John Wiley & Sons, 1958); Donald J. Bogue, *Principles of Demography* (New York: John Wiley & Sons, 1969); Robert D. Grover and Alice M. Hetzel, *Vital Statistics Rates in the United States, 1940–1960* (Washington, D.C.: U.S. Department of Health, Education and Welfare, U.S. Government Printing Office, 1968); William Petersen, *Population*, 2nd edition (New York: Macmillan, 1969).

Life table (or mortality table). The application of age-specific death rates to a cohort of 100,000 people, showing the probability of surviving from any age to any subsequent age.

Maternal-mortality rate. The number of female deaths caused by the complications of pregnancy and childbirth per 100,000 live births.

Morbidity. The incidence and prevalence of disease and illness in a population.

Natural increase (or decrease). The difference between births and deaths in a given population in a given period of time.

Neonatal mortality rate. The number of deaths occurring among children under 28 days of age during a year per 1,000 live births in that year.

Net migration. In a given population, the difference between the number of persons entering and leaving through migration.

Sex ratio. Number of males per 100 females in a population.

Stable population. A population whose rate of growth or decline is constant, and in which the birth rate, death rate, and age-sex structure are also constant.

Stationary population. A stable population which does not increase or decrease in size.

2. 1970 WORLD POPULATION DATA SHEET

POPULATION INFORMATION FOR 142 COUNTRIES

Region or Country	Population Estimates Mid-1970 (Millions) †	Births per 1,000 population ‡	Deaths per 1,000 population ‡	Current Rate of Population Growth	Number of Years to Double Population □	Infant Mortality Rate (Deaths under one year per 1,000 live births) ‡	Population under 15 Years (Percent) ▲	Population Projections to 1985 (Millions) †	Per Capita Gross National Product (U.S.$) §	Population Increase 1965-1970 (Millions) †
WORLD	**3,632**¹	**34**	**14**	**2.0**	**35**		**37**	**4,933**		**343**
AFRICA	**344**²	**47**	**20**	**2.6**	**27**		**44**	**530**		**41**
NORTHERN AFRICA	**87**	**47**	**16**	**3.1**	**23**		**45**	**140**		**12.1**
Algeria	14.0	44	14	3.2	22		47	23.9	250	2.1
Libya	1.9			3.1	23		44	3.1	720	0.3
Morocco	15.7	46	15	3.3	21	149	46	26.2	190	2.4
Sudan	15.8	52	18	3.2	22		47	26.0	90	2.2
Tunisia	5.1	45	16	3.0	24		44	8.3	210	0.7
UAR	33.9	43	15	2.8	25	117	43	52.3	160	4.4
WESTERN AFRICA	**101**	**49**	**23**	**2.5**	**28**		**44**	**155**		**11.7**
Dahomey	2.7	54	26	2.6	27	110	46	4.1	80	0.3
Gambia	0.4	39	21	1.9	37		38	0.5	90	0.03
Ghana	9.0	47	20	2.9	24	156	45	14.9	200	1.3
Guinea	3.9	49	26	2.3	31	216	44	5.7	90	0.4
Ivory Coast	4.3	50	25	2.4	29	138	43	6.4	230	0.5
Liberia	1.2	44	25	1.9	37	188	37	1.6	190	0.1
Mali	5.1	50	25	2.4	29	120	46	7.6	80	0.6
Mauritania	1.2	45	25	2.2	32	187		1.7	130	0.1
Niger	3.8	52	25	2.9	24	200	46	6.2	70	0.5
Nigeria	55.1	50	25	2.6	27		43	84.7	80	6.4
Senegal	3.9	46	22	2.4	29		42	5.8	190	0.4
Sierra Leone	2.6	44	22	2.3	31	136		3.9	140	0.3
Togo	1.9	50	24	2.6	27	127	48	2.8	100	0.2
Upper Volta	5.4	49	28	2.1	33	182	42	7.7	50	0.5
EASTERN AFRICA	**98**	**47**	**21**	**2.6**	**27**		**44**	**149**		**11.4**
Burundi	3.6	46	26	2.3	31	150	47	5.3	50	0.4
Ethiopia	25.0			2.1	33			35.7	60	2.4
Kenya	10.9	50	20	3.1	23		46	17.9	120	1.5
Madagascar	6.9	46	22	2.7	26	102	46	10.8	100	0.9
Malawi	4.4			2.5	28	148	45	6.8	60	0.5
Mauritius	0.9	31	9	2.5	28	70	44	1.2	220	0.1
Mozambique*	7.7	47		2.1	33			11.1	180	0.7
Reunion*	0.5	37	4	3.1	23	59		0.7	560	0.1
Rwanda	3.6	52	22	2.9	24	137		5.7	60	0.5
Somalia	2.8			2.4	29			4.2	50	0.3
Southern Rhodesia*	5.0	48	14	3.4	21	122	47	8.6	230	0.8
Tanzania	13.2	47	22	2.6	27	163	42	20.3	80	1.6
Uganda	8.6	43	18	2.6	27	160	41	13.1	100	1.0
Zambia	4.3	51	20	3.0	24	259	45	7.0	180	0.6
MIDDLE AFRICA	**36**	**46**	**23**	**2.2**	**32**		**42**	**52**		**3.6**
Angola*	5.7			2.1	33		42	8.1	190	0.5
Cameroon (West)	5.8	50	26	2.2	32	137	39	8.4	130	0.6
Central African Republic	1.5	48	25	2.2	32	190	42	2.2	120	0.2
Chad	3.7	45	23	2.4	29	160	46	5.5	70	0.4
Congo (Brazzaville)	0.9	41	24	2.2	32	180		1.4	190	0.1
Congo (Democratic Republic)	17.4	43	20	2.2	32	104	42	25.8	90	1.8
Equatorial Guinea	0.3			1.3	54			0.4	240	0.02
Gabon	0.5	35	25	0.9	78	229	36	0.6	410	0.02

[Footnotes are on p. 159]

Region or Country	Population Estimates Mid-1970 (Millions) †	Births per 1,000 population ‡	Deaths per 1,000 population ‡	Current Rate of Population Growth	Number of Years to Double Population □	Infant Mortality Rate (Deaths under one year per 1,000 live births) ‡	Population under 15 Years (Percent) ▲	Population Projections to 1985 (Millions) †	Per Capita Gross National Product (U.S.$) §	Population Increase 1965-1970 (Millions) †
SOUTHERN AFRICA	23	41	17	2.4	29		40	34		2.5
Botswana	0.6			2.2	32		43	0.9	90	0.1
Lesotho	1.0	40	23	1.8	39	181	43	1.4	60	0.1
South Africa	20.1	40	16	2.4	29		40	29.7	590	2.2
Southwest Africa (Namibia) *	0.6			2.0	35		40	0.9		0.1
Swaziland	0.4			3.0	24			0.7	280	0.1
ASIA	2,056 2	38	15	2.3	31		40	2,874		223
SOUTHWEST ASIA	77	44	15	2.9	24		43	121		10.3
Cyprus	0.6	25	7	0.9	78	28	35	0.7	780	0.02
Iraq	9.7	48	15	3.4	21		45	16.7	230	1.5
Israel	2.9	26	7	2.4	29	26	33	4.0	1,200	0.3
Jordan	2.3	47	16	3.3	21		46	3.9	250	0.3
Kuwait	0.7	47	6	8.3	9	31	38	2.4	3,490	0.2
Lebanon	2.8			3.0	24			4.3	520	0.4
Saudi Arabia	7.7			2.8	25			12.2	350	1.0
Southern Yemen	1.3			2.8	25			2.0	130	0.2
Syria	6.2	47	15	3.3	21		46	10.5	180	0.9
Turkey	35.6	43	16	2.7	26	155	44	52.8	290	4.4
Yemen	5.7			2.8	25			9.1	70	0.7
MIDDLE SOUTH ASIA	762	44	16	2.7	26		43	1,137		96.9
Afghanistan	17.0			2.5	28			25.0	70	1.9
Bhutan	0.8			2.2	32			1.2	60	0.1
Ceylon	12.6	32	8	2.4	29	53	41	17.7	160	1.4
India	554.6	42	17	2.6	27	139	41	807.6	90	67.9
Iran	28.4	48	18	3.0	24		46	45.0	280	3.8
Nepal	11.2	41	21	2.2	32		40	15.8	70	1.2
Pakistan	136.9	50	18	3.3	21	142	45	224.2	90	20.6
SOUTHEAST ASIA	287	43	15	2.8	25		44	434		37.6
Burma	27.7			2.3	31		40	39.2	70	3.0
Cambodia	7.1	50	20	3.0	24	127	44	11.3	130	1.0
Indonesia	121.2	49	21	2.9	24	125	42	183.8	100	16.3
Laos	3.0	42	17	2.5	28			4.4	90	0.4
Malaysia (East and West)	10.8	35	8	2.8	25	48	44	16.4	290	1.4
Philippines	38.1	50		3.4	21	72	47	64.0	180	5.8
Singapore	2.1	25	6	2.4	29	25	43	3.0	600	0.2
Thailand	36.2	46	13	3.3	21		43	57.7	130	5.4
North Vietnam	21.2			2.1	33			28.2	100	2.2
South Vietnam	18.0			2.1	33			23.9	120	1.8
EAST ASIA	930	30	13	1.8	39		36	1,182		78.1
China (Mainland)	759.6	34	15	1.8	39			964.6	90	64.6
China (Taiwan)	14.0	29	6	2.3	31	21	44	19.4	250	1.6
Hong Kong*	4.2	21	5	2.5	28	23	40	6.0	620	0.5
Japan	103.5	19	7	1.1	63	15	25	121.3	1,000	5.5
Korea (North)	13.9	39	11	2.8	25			20.7	230	1.8
Korea (South)	32.1	36	11	2.5	28		42	45.9	160	3.7
Mongolia	1.3	40	10	3.1	23		44	2.0	410	0.2
Ryukyu Islands*	1.0	22	5	1.7	41		39	1.3	540	0.1
NORTHERN AMERICA	228 2	18	9	1.1	63		30	280		13.2
Canada	21.4	17.7	7.4	1.7	41	22.0	33	27.3	2,380	1.8
United States 3	205.2	17.6	9.6	1.0	70	21.2	30	241.7	3,670	11.4

[Footnotes are on p. 159]

Region or Country	Population Estimates Mid-1970 (Millions) †	Births per 1,000 population ‡	Deaths per 1,000 population ‡	Current Rate of Population Growth	Number of Years to Double Population □	Infant Mortality Rate (Deaths under one year per 1,000 live births) ‡	Population under 15 Years (Percent) ▲	Population Projections to 1985 (Millions) †	Per Capita Gross National Product (U.S.$) §	Population Increase 1965-1970 (Millions) †
LATIN AMERICA	**283**²	**38**	**9**	**2.9**	**24**		**42**	**435**		**37**
MIDDLE AMERICA	**67**	**43**	**9**	**3.4**	**21**		**46**	**112**		**10.5**
Costa Rica	1.8	45	8	3.8	19	70	48	3.2	410	0.3
El Salvador	3.4	48	13	3.4	21		45	5.9	270	0.5
Guatemala	5.1	46	16	2.9	24	89	46	7.9	310	0.7
Honduras	2.7	49	16	3.4	21		51	4.6	240	0.4
Mexico	50.7	44	10	3.4	21	64	46	84.4	490	8.0
Nicaragua	2.0	47	16	3.0	24		48	3.3	360	0.3
Panama	1.5	42	10	3.3	21	43	43	2.5	550	0.2
CARIBBEAN	**26**	**35**	**11**	**2.2**	**32**		**40**	**36**		**2.7**
Barbados	0.3	29	9	0.8	88	54	38	0.3	420	0.01
Cuba	8.4	28	8	1.9	37	38	37	11.0	330	0.8
Dominican Republican	4.3	48	15	3.4	21	73	47	7.3	260	0.7
Guadeloupe*	0.4	32	8	2.4	29		42	0.5	470	0.04
Haiti	5.2	45	20	2.5	28		42	7.9	70	0.6
Jamaica	2.0	39	8	2.1	33	30	41	2.6	460	0.2
Martinique*	0.4	30	7	2.0	35		42	0.5	540	0.03
Puerto Rico*	2.8	25	6	1.4	50	28	39	3.4	1,210	0.2
Trinidad and Tobago	1.1	30	8	1.8	39	42	43	1.3	790	0.1
TROPICAL SOUTH AMERICA	**151**	**39**	**9**	**3.0**	**24**		**43**	**236**		**20.8**
Bolivia	4.6	44	20	2.4	29		44	6.8	170	0.5
Brazil	93.0	39	11	2.8	25	170	43	142.6	250	12.3
Colombia	21.4	44	11	3.4	21	78	47	35.6	300	3.3
Ecuador	6.1	47	13	3.4	21	90	48	10.1	210	1.0
Guyana	0.7	40	10	2.9	24	40	46	1.1	330	0.1
Peru	13.6	44	12	3.1	23	62	45	21.6	350	1.9
Venezuela	10.8	46	10	3.4	21	46	46	17.4	880	1.6
TEMPERATE SOUTH AMERICA	**39**	**26**	**9**	**1.8**	**39**		**33**	**51**		**3.4**
Argentina	24.3	22	8	1.5	47	58	29	29.6	800	1.7
Chile	9.8	34	11	2.3	31	100	40	13.6	470	1.1
Paraguay	2.4	45	12	3.4	21	52	45	4.1	220	0.4
Uruguay	2.9	24	9	1.2	58	43	28	3.4	550	0.2
EUROPE	**462**²	**18**	**10**	**0.8**	**88**		**25**	**515**		**18**
NORTHERN EUROPE	**81**	**18**	**11**	**0.6**	**117**		**24**	**90**		**2.3**
Denmark	4.9	16.8	9.7	0.8	88	15.8	24	5.5	1,950	0.2
Finland	4.7	16.0	9.6	0.4	175	14.0	27	5.0	1,660	0.1
Iceland	0.2	20.9	6.9	1.8	39	14.1	34	0.3	1,690	0.02
Ireland	3.0	20.9	11.3	0.7	100	24.4	31	3.5	910	0.1
Norway	3.9	17.6	9.7	0.9	78	12.8	25	4.5	1,860	0.2
Sweden	8.0	14.3	10.4	0.8	88	12.9	21	8.8	2,500	0.3
United Kingdom	56.0	17.1	11.9	0.5	140	18.8	23	61.8	1,700	1.4
WESTERN EUROPE	**149**	**17**	**11**	**0.8**	**88**		**24**	**163**		**5.5**
Austria	7.4	17.2	13.1	0.4	175	25.5	24	8.0	1,210	0.2
Belgium	9.7	14.8	12.8	0.4	175	22.9	24	10.4	1,740	0.2
France	51.1	16.8	11.0	0.8	88	20.4	25	57.6	1,950	2.4
West Germany	58.6	19.7	11.9	0.6	117	22.8	23	62.3	1,750	1.7
Luxembourg	0.4	14.2	12.3	1.2	58	16.7	22	0.4	2,000	0.02
Netherlands	13.0	18.6	8.2	1.1	63	13.6	28	15.3	1,520	0.7
Switzerland	6.3	17.1	9.3	1.1	63	16.1	23	7.4	2,310	0.3
EASTERN EUROPE	**104**	**17**	**10**	**0.8**	**88**		**25**	**116**		**4.0**
Bulgaria	8.5	16.9	8.6	0.8	88	28.3	24	9.4	690	0.3
Czechoslovakia	14.7	14.9	10.7	0.7	100	22.1	25	16.2	1,110	0.5
East Germany	16.2	14.3	14.3	0.3	233	20.4	22	16.9	1,300	0.2
Hungary	10.3	15.1	11.2	0.4	175	35.8	23	11.0	900	0.1
Poland	33.0	16.2	7.6	0.9	78	33.4	30	38.2	780	1.5
Romania	20.3	26.3	9.6	1.3	54	59.5	26	23.3	720	1.3

[Footnotes are on p. 159]

Region or Country	Population Estimates Mid-1970 (Millions) †	Births per 1,000 population ‡	Deaths per 1,000 population ‡	Current Rate of Population Growth	Number of Years to Double Population □	Infant Mortality Rate (Deaths under one year per 1,000 live births) ‡	Population under 15 Years (Percent) ▲	Population Projections to 1985 (Millions) †	Per Capita Gross National Product (U.S.$) §	Population Increase 1965-1970 (Millions) †
SOUTHERN EUROPE	128	19	9	0.9	78		27	146		5.7
Albania	2.2	35.6	8.0	2.7	26	86.8		3.3	320	0.3
Greece	8.9	18.2	8.3	0.8	88	34.4	25	9.7	700	0.3
Italy	53.7	17.6	10.1	0.8	88	32.8	24	60.0	1,120	2.1
Malta	0.3	16.1	9.0	−0.8		27.4	32	0.3	570	−0.01
Portugal	9.6	20.5	10.0	0.7	100	59.2	29	10.7	420	0.3
Spain	33.2	20.5	8.7	1.0	70	32.0	27	38.1	680	1.6
Yugoslavia	20.6	18.9	8.6	1.1	63	61.4	30	23.8	530	1.1
U.S.S.R.	242.6	17.9	7.7	1.0	70	26.5	28	286.9	970	12.1
OCEANIA	19²	25	10	2.0	35		32	27		2.0
Australia	12.5	20.0	9.1	1.9	37	18.3	29	17.0	1,970	1.1
New Zealand	2.9	22.6	8.9	1.7	41	18.7	33	3.8	1,890	0.2

WORLD AND REGIONAL POPULATION (Millions)

	WORLD	AFRICA	ASIA	NORTH AMERICA	LATIN AMERICA	EUROPE	OCEANIA	USSR
MID-1970	3,632	344	2,056	228	283	462	19	243
2000 PROJECTIONS, U.N. CONSTANT FERTILITY	7,522	860	4,513	388	756	571	33	402
2000 PROJECTIONS, U.N. MEDIUM ESTIMATE	6,130	768	3,458	354	638	527	32	353

FOOTNOTES

† Estimates from United Nations. *World Population Prospects, 1965-85, As Assessed in 1968,* United Nations Population Division Working Paper No. 30, December 1969.

‡ Latest available year. Except for North American rates computed by PRB, world and regional estimates are derived from *World Population Prospects* (see footnote †). The country estimates are essentially those available as of October, 1969 in United Nations *Population and Vital Statistics Report,* Series A, Vol. XXI, No. 4, with some adjustments which were necessary in view of the deficiency of registration in some countries.

▲ Latest available year. Derived from *World Population Prospects* (see footnote †) and United Nations *Demographic Yearbook, 1967.*

§ 1967 data supplied by the International Bank for Reconstruction and Development.

□ Assuming continued growth at current annual rate.

* Non-sovereign country.

1 Total reflects United Nations adjustments of discrepancies in international migration data.

2 Regional population totals take into account small areas not listed on the Data Sheet.

3 U.S. figures are based on data from the U.S. Bureau of the Census and the National Center for Health Statistics. The total mid-year population has not been adjusted to accommodate the estimated 5.7 million "undercount" of the U.S. population in the 1960 census.

NOTE: In general, for many of the developing countries, the demographic data including total population, age reporting and vital rates are subject to deficiencies of varying degrees. In some cases, the data are estimates of the United Nations Secretariat.

The Population Reference Bureau, Inc. was founded in 1929 to educate the public about the implications of population growth and other demographic trends. With the advice of demographers, ecologists, economists, sociologists, political scientists and other scholars, the Bureau issues Population Bulletins, Profiles, Selections, ancillary textbooks, an annual World Population Data Sheet and other publications. It consults with other groups in the United States and abroad and operates an information service, library and international program with emphasis on Latin America. A list of publications is available from the Population Reference Bureau, 1755 Massachusetts Avenue, N.W., Washington, D. C. 20036. Regular Membership $5.00; Teacher or Student Membership $3.00; Library Subscription $3.00.

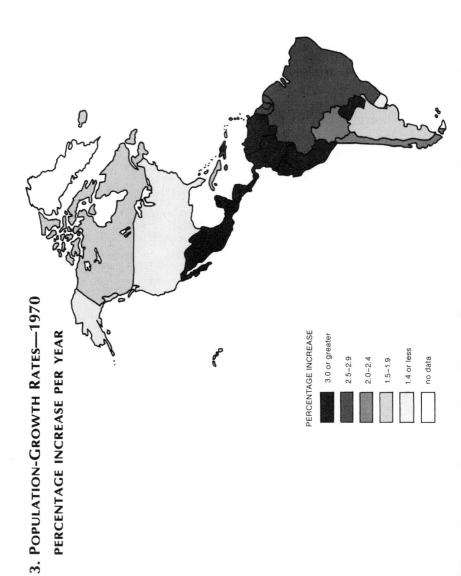

3. POPULATION-GROWTH RATES—1970

PERCENTAGE INCREASE PER YEAR

PERCENTAGE INCREASE

3.0 or greater

2.5–2.9

2.0–2.4

1.5–1.9

1.4 or less

no data

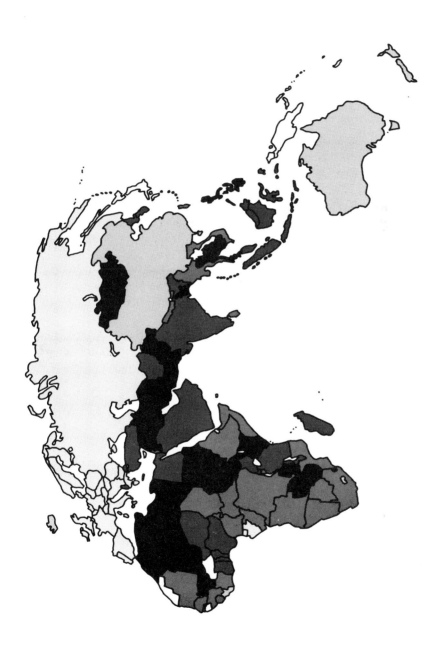

4. INQUIRIES FOR THE 1970 CENSUS OF POPULATION AND HOUSING

U.S. DEPARTMENT OF COMMERCE, BUREAU OF THE CENSUS

Listed below are the subject items included in the 1970 Census. Some of these items are asked of 100-percent of the people and households; others are asked of a sample of 20 percent, 15 percent, or 5 percent. Whether a question is asked on a 100-percent basis or on a sample basis depends on the size of the area for which statistics are needed. Information required for apportioning representation in Congress or other law-making bodies, and that needed for city blocks is collected from all households; information to be tabulated for such areas as census tracts and most counties is collected on a 15- or 20-percent sample basis. The 5-percent sample will provide statistics for larger cities, standard metropolitan statistical areas, larger counties, and States. The samples are scientifically selected in such a way that every person and every household has an equal chance of being included.

The law requires that a person answer the census questions to the best of his knowledge. The same law also provides that all information given to the Census Bureau must be held in confidence and may be used only for statistical purposes. It may be released only in the form of statistical tables such as the one shown below. No statistics may be released which might disclose information about any individual or household.

On the following pages there are short summary statements describing some of the reasons why the subjects are included. The year shown in parentheses for each item refers to the first census in which information about that item was collected.

• • • • • • •

NEED FOR ITEMS ON THE CENSUS SCHEDULE

Population Items

Name and address--100 percent (1790)
This information is needed to be sure a person is counted, but counted only once. Name and address are dropped when information goes into the Census Bureau computers.

Relationship to head of household--100 percent (1880)
Because most government programs aimed at helping people deal with families or households, it is important to know how may households and families there are in each area.

Color or race--100 percent (1790)
It is not enough to know the number of people and the number of families. Lawmakers and administrators of programs aimed at improved incomes, more jobs,

This material is a partial reproduction of a United States Department of Commerce publication.

better housing, better schools, etc., need information about the numbers, characteristics, and location of the racial groups they are trying to serve.

Age and sex--100 percent (1790)

Men and women, the old and the young have different needs. Information by age and sex is essential if the figures on employment, unemployment, school enrollment, income and other characteristics of the population are to have meaning.

Marital status--100 percent (1880)

This question produces information on how many persons are married, divorced, separated, widowed, or never married. It is needed for such purposes as determining how many married and unmarried men are unemployed; how many married women have paid jobs; and the number of dependent widows.

State or country of birth--20 percent (1850)

Facts about country of birth are needed to guide in the development of immigration laws and regulations. The information on State of birth is useful in measuring the migration from certain regions of the country to other regions, for example, Negroes from the South to the big cities of the North and West. In rapidly growing States and metropolitan areas, much of the growth results from people moving in from other areas. State and local governments need information about new arrivals in order to meet their needs for schools, housing, and other services.

Years of school completed--20 percent (1940)

This information indicates to employment officials the educational levels of workers in a neighborhood, city, or county, and provides a guide to the kinds of manpower training programs that are likely to be most needed.

Number of children ever born--20 percent (1890)

This information is necessary for calculating trends in population growth and understanding how the makeup of the population is changing through differences in numbers of children born to various population groups. It is essential in making projections of future population which are important to plans of Federal, State, and local governments.

Employment status and hours worked / Weeks worked last year / Last year in which worked } 20 percent (1880)

Answers to these questions provide the only information for each State, city, county, or metropolitan area about people who have jobs, are looking for jobs or have stopped working. This information guides industries to areas with available skills and helps governments plan the training of workers, and necessary welfare programs.

Occupation, industry, and class of worker--20 percent (1840)

Officials of every State and local government need to know how many people work as typists, carpenters, steamfitters, journalists, etc.; and what kinds of jobs are provided in the steel industry or in the clothing industry, etc. They also need to know how many people work for themselves, how many work for wages or salaries, or are unpaid family workers. This type of information is needed in planning for new industries, and new training programs, which, in turn, can mean new jobs.

Activity 5 years ago--20 percent (1970)

This information will make it possible to know how many people changed from jobs or college to the Armed Forces, how many went from the Armed Forces into jobs and what kind of jobs, how many people started or stopped working and what they were doing previously.

Income--20 percent (1940)

There is no better way of measuring how well the people of a city or county are doing economically than by asking for information about income. Census information about income, especially the proportion of families with low incomes, is used to guide the allocation of several billion dollars a year under Federal programs to improve job opportunities, education, and health in local communities throughout the Nation. Although many people report their incomes to the Internal Revenue Service, the information from the tax returns cannot provide the basis for many federal programs, such as aid to education. One reason is that not all people have to file tax returns.

Country of birth of parents--15 percent (1870)

This helps to identify the so-called "foreign neighborhoods." Communities with large numbers of first and second generation immigrants who may not have adjusted to American life often have special problems in relation to schools, welfare programs, and other public services.

Mother tongue--15 percent (1910)

This information will be used especially to learn how many Mexican-American, Puerto Rican, and other Spanish-speaking persons there are in each State, county or city and in neighborhoods in cities. Local school, health, welfare, and employment officials need this information to help meet the special problems which these people may have.

Year moved into this house--15 percent (1960)
Place of residence 5 years ago--15 percent (1940)

Officials of cities need to know how many and what kinds of people are moving into and out of their localities in order to help plan programs to deal with problems resulting from migration.

School or college enrollment--15 percent (1850)

Education is big. Its cost represents about 40 percent of all costs of State and local governments. About 30 percent of the population are students. This census question will tell officials and citizens of each city what share of the school-age population is enrolled in school, and also how many young people are school dropouts.

Veteran status--15 percent (1840)

The Federal government and many State governments that administer programs to benefit veterans need information about all veterans, not just those who have kept in touch with the Veterans Administration.

Place of work
Means of transportation to work } 15 percent (1960)

Traffic planners need to know where people work in relation to where they live; and whether they get back and forth by car, bus, or other means.

Mexican or Spanish origin or descent--5 percent (1970)

This question will provide information on the number of persons and families whose ancestry is Mexican or Spanish. It will tell the States, counties and cities where there are large numbers of persons who identify themselves as of Mexican, Cuban, Puerto Rican, Central or South American, or other Spanish origin. This will help the government develop programs for more jobs, better housing and improved education for these people.

Citizenship--5 percent (1820)

More than 5 million immigrants have come to the United States since 1950. Answers to this question combined with those to other questions will help show how well aliens and foreign-born citizens have adjusted to American life.

Year of immigration--5 percent (1890)

Information from this question will be used by lawmakers and other government officials to study the jobs and living conditions of recent immigrants and to plan programs to help immigrants adapt to American life.

When married--5 percent (1900)

The growth of the population is influenced by the average age at which people marry (recently it has risen), the length of marriage, and the number of widowed or divorced persons who have remarried.

Vocational training completed--5 percent (1970)

Does a man who has had vocational training earn more money and have a better job than one without such training? Where should new vocational schools be located? This census item will help answer these questions for the benefit of officials planning school and employment programs.

Presence and duration of disability--5 percent (1830)

Governments and volunteer agencies are spending billions of dollars each year to help disabled persons. Information from this census item will help allocate the resources more wisely, and guide local health-workers.

Occupation-industry 5 years ago--5 percent (1970)

This will help to measure, for the first time, the "pull" of job opportunities and the "push" which may cause people to leave depressed areas, low paying jobs or low paying industries. Employment officials concerned need this information to study the rate at which workers shift jobs and the type of work they do.

Housing Items

Number of units at this address--100 percent (1970)

This is to help the census taker find apartments or other housing units which might otherwise be missed.

Telephone--100 percent (1960)

This is to help the census taker: in many instances an incomplete questionnaire can be completed with a telephone call, which is quicker and cheaper than a personal visit.

Private entrance to living quarters--100 percent (1960)
Complete kitchen facilities--100 percent (1970)

The answers to the two questions determine whether or not the particular living quarters is a separate housing unit. To be counted as a housing unit, the living quarters must have a direct entrance (that is, not through someone else's living quarters) or complete kitchen facilities (stove, refrigerator, and sink with running water).

Number of rooms--100 percent (1940)

Local housing officials need information on crowding. A measure of crowding is provided by combining number of rooms with number of persons.

Water supply
Flush toilet $\left.\right\}$ 100 percent (1940)
Bathtub or shower

These facilities are important indicators of housing quality. If some or all are used by more than one household, the quality of housing is lower than if the facilities are for the use of only one household. If one or more is lacking, housing quality is even lower. Federal, State, and local governments spend several billion dollars each year to improve low quality housing and need census data to make a wise allocation of this money.

Basement--100 percent (1960)

The Office of Civil Defense uses this information in developing fallout shelter programs.

Tenure--100 percent (1890)

Agencies concerned with housing need to know what proportions of homes in a community are owned or rented by their occupants and to know the characteristics of the occupants, as shown by census statistics.

Commercial establishment on property--100 percent (1940)

This information is needed by the Census Bureau to exclude properties with business establishments in calculating value of single family homes.

Value
Contract rent $\left.\right\}$ 100 percent (1930)

Value of owner-occupied homes and rent paid by tenants are significant measures of housing quality and level of living in an area, and of increase or decrease in the cost of housing in the Nation or any of its communities.

Vacancy status--100 percent (1940)
Months vacant--100 percent (1960)

Federal and local agencies concerned with planning, building, and lending money for housing need to know how many houses and apartments are vacant and available for sale or rent, what kinds of housing are staying vacant longest, and what types of housing are in greatest demand.

Components of gross rent--20 percent (1940)

Gross rent means total cost of shelter: rent plus the cost of electricity, water, and fuels for heating and cooking. Some tenants get only space for their rental payments; others also get heat or utilities or both. Housing officials need facts which put all rent on a comparable basis. Gross rent as a percent of income shows the relationship between housing costs and income for various income groups in the Nation or in a city.

Heating equipment--20 percent (1940)

Officials of local governments concerned with levels of living, health, and safety all want to know what share of homes in a community are heated by furnaces, or by stoves, or fireplaces, and if there are homes with no heating equipment.

Year structure built--20 percent (1940)

The age of a house when related to other characteristics of housing gives an indication of quality. Old housing which also is deficient in plumbing may be a candidate for improvement or replacement as a part of government housing programs. Information from this question in different censuses tells local officials if new housing is being built to keep up with needs or if on an average the housing in the community is getting older.

Number of units in structure--20 percent (1940)
Trailers--20 percent (1950)
Local officials responsible for schools, traffic, parking, water and other utilities need to know how many households live in one-family houses or in apartment buildings of different sizes. The same officials need to know about numbers of trailers and characteristics of the people who live in them. In recent years, trailers have represented about one-fifth of the new homes in the Nation.

Farm residence--20 percent (1890)
How many people live on farms? This is important to the Agriculture and Housing and Urban Development Departments and to local officials.

Source of water ⎫ 15 percent (1960)
Sewage disposal ⎭
This information will be used in planning to deal with pollution and diseases of many kinds. Public works officials need the information to tell them if water and sewage facilities are adequate. This is particularly important in rapidly growing suburban areas and in rural areas.

Number of bathrooms--15 percent (1960)
Federal housing officials need this information to measure quality of housing, especially in areas applying for urban renewal.

Air conditioning--15 percent (1960)
This information helps utility officials plan to avoid electric power failures. The information also is an indicator of quality of housing and level of living.

Number of automobiles--15 percent (1960)
Local officials concerned with traffic, streets, highways, and parking asked for this information in the 1960 census, and increased congestion makes it more important in 1970.

Number of stories ⎫ 5 percent (1960)
Elevator in structure ⎭
Local zoning officials in particular need this information to establish or modify zoning codes and regulations.

Fuel for heating, cooking, water-heating--5 percent (1940)
Important in measuring air pollution. The extent to which electricity is used is important in planning for enough power at all times.

Number of bedrooms--5 percent (1960)
The number of bedrooms related to size of family gives local housing authorities important information about the need for more housing in an area. This is a better measure of crowding than a count of all rooms in buildings where living, dining and kitchen space may not be divided into rooms.

Clothing washing machine--5 percent (1960)
Clothes dryer--5 percent (1960)
·Dishwasher--5 percent (1970)
This information tells local officials if additional water sewage and electric or gas lines may be needed in an area.

Home food freezer--5 percent (1960)

Households with food freezers generally are considered to have a higher level of living than homes without freezers. Civil Defense officials use information from this item in calculating food supplies available in emergencies.

Television--5 percent (1950)
Radio--5 percent (1930)

The Federal Communications Commission is concerned with the number and share of households in each area with television sets, especially those that can receive UHF. Federal and local officials need to know how many families have battery-operated radios, so they can receive information during emergencies.

Second home--5 percent (1970)

Vacation homes, such as a cottage at the lake or an apartment overlooking the ocean, are becoming increasingly numerous. Federal and local officials concerned with housing and utilities need this information to guide their plans for the future.

5. UNITED STATES CENSUS—1970

EXPLANATORY NOTES

This leaflet shows the content of the 1970 census questionnaires. The content was determined after review of the 1960 census experience, extensive consultation with many government and private users of census data, and a series of experimental censuses in which various alternatives were tested.

Three questionnaires are being used in the census and each household has an equal chance of answering a particular form.

80 percent of the households answer a form containing only the questions on pages 2 and 3 of this leaflet.

15 percent and **5 percent** of the households answer forms which also contain the specified questions on the remaining pages of this leaflet. The 15-percent form does not show the 5-percent questions, and the 5-percent form does not show the 15-percent questions. On both forms, population questions 13 to 41 are repeated for each person in the household but questions 24 to 41 do not apply to children under 14 years of age.

The same sets of questions are used throughout the country, regardless of whether the census in a particular area is conducted by mail or house-to-house canvass. An illustrative example is enclosed with each questionnaire to help the householder complete the form.

[Page 2]

┌──────────────────────────────────────┐
│ 80, 15, and 5 percent (100 percent) │
└──────────────────────────────────────┘

---

1. WHAT IS THE NAME OF EACH PERSON
who was living here on Wednesday, April 1, 1970 or
who was staying or visiting here and had no other home?

*Print
names
in this
order*

{ *Head of the household*
  Wife of head
  Unmarried children, oldest first
  Married childen and their families
  Other relatives of the head
  Persons not related to the head }

Line No.

[Questions 2 through 12 appear on the following two pages. Items 2 through 8 under questions 1 through 8 are identical with item 1 and have therefore been omitted in this reproduction.]

(1) Last name

First name   Middle initial

Reprinted from a leaflet showing the content of the questionnaires used in the 1970 Census of Population and Housing. U.S. Department of Commerce, Bureau of the Census, Form D-60.

[Page 2]

2. HOW IS EACH PERSON RELATED TO THE HEAD OF THIS HOUSEHOLD?

Fill one circle.

If "Other relative of head," also give exact relationship, for example, mother-in-law, brother, niece, grandson, etc.

If "Other not related to head," also give exact relationship, for example, partner, maid, etc.

○ Head of household
○ Wife of head
○ Son or daughter of head
○ Other relative of head— *Print exact relationship →*

○ Roomer, boarder, lodger
○ Patient or inmate
○ Other not related to head— *Print exact relationship*

3. SEX

Fill one circle

4. COLOR OR RACE

Fill one circle.

If "Indian (American)," also give tribe.

If "Other," also give race.

Male ○	○ White
	○ Negro or Black
Female ○	○ Indian (Amer.) *Print tribe →*

○ Japanese
○ Chinese
○ Filipino

○ Hawaiian
○ Korean
○ Other— *Print race*

DATE OF BIRTH

8. WHAT IS EACH PERSON'S MARITAL STATUS?

5. Month and year of birth and age last birthday

Print

Month _ _ _ _ _

Year _ _ _ _ _

Age _ _ _ _ _

6. Month of birth

Fill one circle

○ Jan.-Mar.
○ Apr.-June
○ July-Sept.
○ Oct.-Dec.

7. Year of birth

Fill one circle for first three numbers

○ 186-   ○ 192-
○ 187-   ○ 193-
○ 188-   ○ 194-
○ 189-   ○ 195-
○ 190-   ○ 196-
○ 191-   ○ 197-

Fill one circle for last number

○ 0   ○ 5
○ 1   ○ 6
○ 2   ○ 7
○ 3   ○ 8
○ 4   ○ 9

Fill one circle

○ Now married
○ Widowed
○ Divorced
○ Separated
○ Never married

[Page 2]

---

9. *If you used all*
8 *lines* **—Are there**
any other persons
in this household?

○ Yes   No
↘
Do not list the others; we will
call to get the information.

---

10. Did you leave anyone out of Question 1 because
you were not sure if he should be listed—for
example, a new baby still in the hospital, or
a lodger who also has another home?

○ Yes   No
↘
On back page, give name(s)
and reason left out.

---

11. Did you list anyone in Question 1
who is away from home now—
for example, on a vacation or
in a hospital?

○ Yes   ○ No
↘
On back page, give name(s)
and reason person is away.

---

12. Did anyone stay here
on Tuesday, March 31,
who is not already
listed?

Yes   No
↘
On back page, give name of each visitor for
whom there is no one at his <u>home address</u>
to report him to a census taker.

[Page 3]

80, 15, and 5 percent (100 percent)

<u>A.</u> **How many living quarters, occupied and vacant, are**
at this address?

○ One
○ 2 apartments or living quarters
○ 3 apartments or living quarters
○ 4 apartments or living quarters
○ 5 apartments or living quarters
○ 6 apartments or living quarters
○ 7 apartments or living quarters
○ 8 apartments or living quarters
○ 9 apartments or living quarters
○ 10 or more apartments or living quarters
○ This is a mobile home or trailer

Answer these questions for your living quarters

H1. Is there a telephone on which people in your living
quarters can be called?

○ Yes ——➤ **What is**
○ No   **the number?** _ _ _ _ _ _ _ _ _ _ _ _ _ _
                        Phone number

[Page 3]

H2. Do you enter your living quarters—

○ Directly from the outside or through
   a common or public hall?
○ Through someone else's living quarters?

H3. Do you have complete kitchen facilities?
*Complete kitchen facilities are a sink with piped
water, a range or cook stove, and a refrigerator.*

○ Yes, for this household only
○ Yes, but also used by another household
○ No complete kitchen facilities for this household

H4. How many rooms do you have in your living quarters?
*Do not count bathrooms, porches, balconies, foyers,
halls, or half-rooms.*

○ 1 room   ○ 6 rooms
○ 2 rooms   ○ 7 rooms
○ 3 rooms   ■   ○ 8 rooms
○ 4 rooms   ○ 9 rooms or more
○ 5 rooms

H5. Is there hot and cold piped water in this building?

○ Yes, hot and cold piped water in this building
○ No, only cold piped water in this building
○ No piped water in this building

H6. Do you have a flush toilet?

○ Yes, for this household only
○ Yes, but also used by another household
○ No flush toilet

■

H7. Do you have a bathtub or shower?

○ Yes, for this household only
○ Yes, but also used by another household
○ No bathtub or shower

H8. Is there a basement in this building?

○ Yes
○ No, built on a concrete slab
○ No, built in another way *(include mobile homes
   and trailers)*

[Page 3]

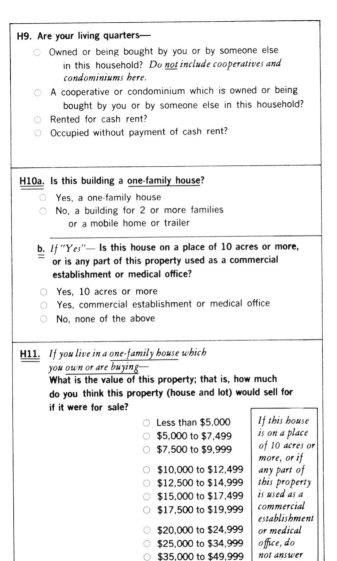

H9. Are your living quarters—

○ Owned or being bought by you or by someone else in this household? *Do not include cooperatives and condominiums here.*

○ A cooperative or condominium which is owned or being bought by you or by someone else in this household?

○ Rented for cash rent?

○ Occupied without payment of cash rent?

H10a. Is this building a <u>one-family house</u>?

○ Yes, a one-family house

○ No, a building for 2 or more families or a mobile home or trailer

b. *If "Yes"—* **Is this house on a place of 10 acres or more, or is any part of this property used as a commercial establishment or medical office?**

○ Yes, 10 acres or more

○ Yes, commercial establishment or medical office

○ No, none of the above

H11. *If you live in a one-family house which you own or are buying—*
What is the value of this property; that is, how much do you think this property (house and lot) would sell for if it were for sale?

○ Less than $5,000
○ $5,000 to $7,499
○ $7,500 to $9,999

○ $10,000 to $12,499
○ $12,500 to $14,999
○ $15,000 to $17,499
○ $17,500 to $19,999

○ $20,000 to $24,999
○ $25,000 to $34,999
○ $35,000 to $49,999
○ $50,000 or more

If this house is on a place of 10 acres or more, or if any part of this property is used as a commercial establishment or medical office, do not answer this question.

[Page 3]

H12. *Answer this question if you pay rent for your living quarters.*
  a. *If rent is paid by the month—*

What is the monthly rent ?

Write amount here → $ _ _ _ _ _ _ _ _ _ .00 *(Nearest dollar)*

and

Fill one circle

○ Less than $30
○ $30 to $39
○ $40 to $49
○ $50 to $59

○ $60 to $69
○ $70 to $79
○ $80 to $89 ■
○ $90 to $99

○ $100 to $119
○ $120 to $149
○ $150 to $199
○ $200 to $249
○ $250 to $299
○ $300 or more

b. *If rent is not paid by the month—*
What is the rent, and what period of time does it cover?

$ _ _ _ _ _ _ _ _ _ _ _ .00 per _ _ _ _ _ _ _ _ _ _ _ _
        (Nearest dollar)   *(Week, half-month, year, etc.)*

80, 15,
and 5
percent

[Page 4]

The 15-percent form contains the questions shown on page 4. The 5-percent form contains the questions shown in the first column of page 4 [through H18] and the questions on page 5.

H13. *Answer question H13 if you pay rent for your living quarters.*

In addition to the rent entered in H12, do you also pay for—

a. Electricity?

○ Yes, average monthly cost is ➤ $ _____ .00
○ No, included in rent   *Average monthly cost*
○ No, electricity not used

b. Gas?

○ Yes, average monthly cost is ➤ $ _____ .00
○ No, included in rent   *Average monthly cost*
○ No, gas not used

c. Water?

○ Yes, yearly cost is ⟶ $ _____ .00
○ No, included in rent or no charge   *Yearly cost*

d. Oil, coal, kerosene, wood, etc.?

○ Yes, yearly cost is ⟶ $ _____ .00
○ No, included in rent   *Yearly cost*
○ No, these fuels not used

15 and 5 percent

H14. How are your living quarters heated?

Fill one circle for the kind of heat you use most.

○ Steam or hot water system
○ Central warm air furnace with ducts to the individual rooms, or central heat pump
○ Built-in electric units *(permanently installed in wall, ceiling, or baseboard)*

○ Floor, wall, or pipeless furnace
○ Room heaters **with** flue or vent, burning gas, oil, or kerosene
○ Room heaters **without** flue or vent, burning gas, oil, or kerosene *(not portable)*

○ Fireplaces, stoves, or portable room heaters of any kind

In some other way—*Describe* ⟶ _____

○ None, unit has no heating equipment

[Page 4]

H15. About when was this building originally built? *Mark when the building was first constructed, not when it was remodeled, added to, or converted.*

- ○ 1969 or 1970
- ○ 1965 to 1968
- ○ 1960 to 1964
- ○ 1950 to 1959
- ■ 1940 to 1949
- ○ 1939 or earlier

H16. Which best describes this building?
Include all apartments, flats, etc., even if vacant.

- ○ A one-family house detached from any other house
- ○ A one-family house attached to one or more houses
- ○ A building for 2 families
- ○ A building for 3 or 4 families
- ○ A building for 5 to 9 families
- ■ A building for 10 to 19 families
- ○ A building for 20 to 49 families
- ○ A building for 50 or more families

- ○ A mobile home or trailer

Other—
Describe _____

15 and 5 percent

H17. Is this building—

- ○ On a city or suburban lot?— *Skip to H19*
- ○ On a place of less than 10 acres?
- ○ On a place of 10 acres or more?

H18. Last year, 1969, did sales of crops, livestock, and other farm products from this place amount to—

- ■ Less than $50 (or None)
- ○ $50 to $249
- ○ $250 to $2,499
- ○ $2,500 to $4,999
- ○ $5,000 to $9,999
- ○ $10,000 or more

H19. Do you get water from—

- ○ A public system *(city water department, etc.)* or private company?
- ○ An individual well?
- ○ Some other source *(a spring, creek, river, cistern, etc.)*?

15 percent

H20. Is this building connected to a public sewer?

- ○ Yes, connected to public sewer
- ○ No, connected to septic tank or cesspool
- ○ No, use other means

[Page 4]

H21. **How many bathrooms do you have?**
A complete bathroom is a room with flush toilet, bathtub or shower, and wash basin with piped water.

A half bathroom has at least a flush toilet or bathtub or shower, but does not have all the facilities for a complete bathroom.

    ○ No bathroom, or only a half bathroom

    ○ 1 complete bathroom
    ○ 1 complete bathroom, plus half bath(s)

    ○ 2 complete bathrooms
    ○ 2 complete bathrooms, plus half bath(s)

    ○ 3 or more complete bathrooms

15 percent

H22. **Do you have air-conditioning?**
    ○ Yes, 1 individual room unit
    ○ Yes, 2 or more individual room units
    ○ Yes, a central air-conditioning system
    ○ No

H23. **How many passenger automobiles are owned or regularly used by members of your household?**
Count company cars kept at home.
    ○ None
    ○ 1 automobile
    ○ 2 automobiles
    ○ 3 automobiles or more

[Page 5]

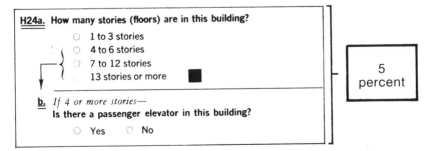

H24a. **How many stories (floors) are in this building?**
    ○ 1 to 3 stories
    ○ 4 to 6 stories
    ○ 7 to 12 stories
        13 stories or more

5 percent

b. *If 4 or more stories—*
Is there a passenger elevator in this building?
    ○ Yes ○ No

[Page 5]

H25a. Which fuel is used most for cooking?

Gas { From underground pipes serving the neighborhood. ○
{ Bottled, tank, or LP .... ○
Electricity .... ○
Fuel oil, kerosene, etc. .... ○

Coal or coke ○
Wood ...... ○
Other fuel .. ○
No fuel used ○

b. Which fuel is used most for house heating?

Gas { From underground pipes serving the neighborhood. ○
{ Bottled, tank, or LP .... ○
Electricity .... ○
Fuel oil, kerosene, etc. .... ○

Coal or coke ○
Wood ...... ○
Other fuel .. ○
No fuel used ○

c. Which fuel is used most for water heating?

Gas { From underground pipes serving the neighborhood. ○
{ Bottled, tank, or LP .... ○
Electricity .... ○
Fuel oil, kerosene, etc. .... ○

Coal or coke ○
Wood ...... ○
Other fuel .. ○
No fuel used ○

H26. How many bedrooms do you have?
Count rooms used mainly for sleeping even if used also for other purposes.

○ No bedroom   ○ 3 bedrooms
○ 1 bedroom   ○ 4 bedrooms
○ 2 bedrooms   ○ 5 bedrooms or more

H27a. Do you have a clothes washing machine?

○ Yes, automatic or semi-automatic
○ Yes, wringer or separate spinner
○ No

b. Do you have a clothes dryer?

○ Yes, electrically heated
○ Yes, gas heated
○ No

c. Do you have a dishwasher *(built-in or portable)***?**

○ Yes   ○ No

d. Do you have a home food freezer which is separate from your refrigerator?

○ Yes   ○ No

5 percent

[Page 5]

H28a. **Do you have a television set?** *Count only sets in working order.*

   ○ Yes, one set
   ○ Yes, two or more sets
   ○ No

b. *If "Yes"—* **Is any set equipped to receive UHF broadcasts, that is, channels 14 to 83?**

   ○ Yes   ○ No   ■

H29. **Do you have a battery-operated radio?**
Count car radios, transistors, and other battery-operated sets in working order or needing only a new battery for operation.

   ○ Yes, one or more   ○ No

H30. **Do you (or any member of your household) own a second home or other living quarters which you occupy sometime during the year?**

   ○ Yes   ○ No

> 5 percent

[Page 6]

> The 15-percent and 5-percent forms contain a pair of facing pages for each person in the household (as listed on page 2 [question 1]). Shown on each pair of pages in the 15-percent form are the questions designated as 15-percent here on pages 6, 7, and 8. Shown on each pair of pages in the 5-percent form are the questions designated as 5-percent here on pages 6, 7, and 8.

Name of person on line ① of page 2

Last name   First name   Initial

13a. **Where was this person born?** *If born in hospital, give State or country where mother lived. If born outside U.S., see instruction sheet; distinguish Northern Ireland from Ireland (Eire).*

   ○ This State

   OR

   (Name of State or foreign country; or Puerto Rico, Guam, etc.)

> 15 and 5 percent

b. **Is this person's origin or descent—** *(Fill one circle)*

   ○ Mexican   ○ Central or South American
   ○ Puerto Rican ○ Other Spanish
   ○ Cuban   ○ No, none of these

> 5 percent

14. **What country was his father born in?**

   ○ United States
   OR _____
   (Name of foreign country; or Puerto Rico, Guam, etc.)

> 15 percent

[Page 6]

<table>
<tr>
<td>

15 percent

</td>
<td>

15. What country was his mother born in?

○ United States
OR —
(Name of foreign country; or Puerto Rico, Guam, etc.)

</td>
</tr>
<tr>
<td>

5 percent

</td>
<td>

16. _For persons born in a foreign country—_
a. Is this person naturalized?

○ Yes, naturalized ■
○ No, alien
○ Born abroad of American parents

b. When did he come to the United States to stay?

○ 1965 to 70	○ 1950 to 54	○ 1925 to 34
○ 1960 to 64	○ 1945 to 49	○ 1915 to 24
○ 1955 to 59	○ 1935 to 44	○ Before 1915

17. What language, other than English, was spoken in this person's home when he was a child? _Fill one circle._

○ Spanish ■   ○ Other—
○ French   _Specify_ _ _ _ _ _ _ _ _ _ _ _ _ _
○ German   ○ None, English only

</td>
</tr>
<tr>
<td>

15 percent

</td>
<td>

18. When did this person move into this house (or apartment)? _Fill circle for date of last move._

○ 1969 or 70	○ 1965 or 66	○ 1949 or earlier
○ 1968	○ 1960 to 64	○ Always lived in
○ 1967 ■	○ 1950 to 59	this house or apartment

19a. Did he live in this house on April 1, 1965? _If in college or Armed Forces in April 1965, report place of residence there._

○ Born April 1965 or later ⎱ _Skip to 20_
○ Yes, this house . . . . ⎰
○ No, different house

b. Where did he live on April 1, 1965?

(1) State, foreign country,
    U.S. possession, etc. _ _ _ _ _ _ _ _ _ _ _ _ _ _ _ _ _ _

(2) County _

(3) Inside the limits of a city, town, village, etc.?

    ○ Yes   ○ No

(4) _If "Yes,"_ name of city,
    town, village, etc. _ _ _ _ _ _ _ _ _ _ _ _ _ _ _ _ _

</td>
</tr>
</table>

[Page 6]

---

20. Since February 1, 1970, has this person attended regular
school or college at any time? *Count nursery school,
kindergarten, and schooling which leads to an elementary
school certificate, high school diploma, or college degree.*

○ No ■

○ Yes, public

○ Yes, parochial

○ Yes, other private

> 15 percent

**21. What is the highest grade (or year) of regular school
he has ever attended?**
Fill one circle. If now attending, mark grade he is in.

○ Never attended school— *Skip to 23*

○ Nursery school ■

○ Kindergarten

Elementary through high school (grade or year)

| 1 | 2 | 3 | 4 | 5 | 6 | | 7 | 8 | | 9 | 10 | 11 | 12 |
| ○ | ○ | ○ | ○ | ○ | ○ | | ○ | ○ | | ○ | ○ | ○ | ○ |

College (academic year)

| 1 | 2 | 3 | 4 | 5 | 6 or more |
| ○ | ○ | ○ | ○ | ○ | ○ |

> 15 and 5 percent

---

22. Did he finish the highest grade (or year) he attended?

○ Now attending this grade (or year)

○ Finished this grade (or year)

○ Did not finish this grade (or year)

---

23. When was this person born?

○ Born before April 1956— *Please go on with
questions 24 through 41.*

○ Born April 1956 or later— *Please omit questions 24 through
41 and go to the next page
for the next person.*

• ■   ■

---

24. *If this person has ever been married—*

a. Has this person been married more than once?

○ Once   ○ More than once

———— ▼ ————   ———— ▼ ————

**b. When did he   When did he get married
get married?   for the first time?**

― ― ― ― ― ― ― ― ― ―   ― ― ― ― ― ― ― ― ― ―
Month   Year   Month   Year

c. *If married more than once—* **Did the first marriage end
because of the death of the husband (or wife)?**

○ Yes   ○ No   ■

> 5 percent

[Page 6]

15 and 5 percent

25. *If this is a girl or a woman—*
How many babies has she ever had, not counting stillbirths?
Do not count her stepchildren or children she has adopted.

1 2 3 4 5 6 7 8
○ ○ ○ ○ ○ ○ ○ ○

9 10 11 12 or   None
            more
○ ○ ○ ○   ○

15 percent

26. *If this is a man—*
a. **Has he ever served in the Army, Navy, or other Armed Forces of the United States?**

○ Yes
○ No

b. **Was it during—** *(Fill the circle for each period of service.)*

Vietnam Conflict *(Since Aug. 1964)* ··········· ○
Korean War *(June 1950 to Jan. 1955)* ·········· ○
World War II *(Sept. 1940 to July 1947)* ········· ○
World War I *(April 1917 to Nov. 1918)* ········· ○
Any other time ························· ○

[Page 7]

5 percent

27a. Has this person ever completed a vocational training program?
For example, in high school; as apprentice; in school of business, nursing, or trades; technical institute; or Armed Forces schools.

○ Yes   ○ No— *Skip to 28*

b. **What was his main field of vocational training?** *Fill one circle.*

○ Business, office work
○ Nursing, other health fields
○ Trades and crafts *(mechanic. electrician. beautician. etc.)*
○ Engineering or science technician; draftsman
○ Agriculture or home economics
○ Other field— *Specify*

[Page 7]

28a. Does this person have a health or physical condition which limits the <u>kind</u> or <u>amount</u> of work he can do at a job?
If 65 years old or over, skip to question 29.

○ Yes
○ No

---

b. Does his health or physical condition keep him from holding <u>any</u> job at all?

○ Yes
○ No

5 percent

---

c. *If "Yes" in a or b*— How long has he been limited in his ability to work?

○ Less than 6 months   ○ 3 to 4 years
○ 6 to 11 months   ○ 5 to 9 years
○ 1 to 2 years   ○ 10 years or more

QUESTIONS 29 THROUGH 41 ARE FOR ALL PERSONS BORN BEFORE APRIL 1956 INCLUDING HOUSEWIVES, STUDENTS, OR DISABLED PERSONS AS WELL AS PART-TIME OR FULL-TIME WORKERS

29a. Did this person work at any time <u>last week</u>?

○ Yes– *Fill this circle if this person did full- or part-time work. (Count part-time work such as a Saturday job, delivering papers, or helping without pay in a family business or farm; and active duty in the Armed Forces)*

○ No– *Fill this circle if this person did not work, or did only own housework, school work, or volunteer work.*

Skip to 30

15 and 5 percent

---

b. How many hours did he work <u>last week</u> (at all jobs)?
Subtract any time off and add overtime or extra hours worked.

○ 1 to 14 hours   ○ 40 hours
○ 15 to 29 hours   ○ 41 to 48 hours
○ 30 to 34 hours   ○ 49 to 59 hours
○ 35 to 39 hours   ○ 60 hours or more

[Page 7]

c. Where did he work <u>last week</u>?

If he worked in more than one place, print
where he worked most last week.
If he travels about in his work or if the place does not
have a numbered address, see instruction sheet.

(1) Address *(Number*
and street name) _

(2) Name of city,
town, village, etc. _

(3) Inside the limits of this city, town, village, etc.? ·

○ Yes

○ No

(4) County _

(5) State   (6) ZIP
          Code _ _ _ _ _ _ _ _ _ _

15 percent

d. How did he get to work <u>last week</u>? *Fill one circle for chief*
means used on the last day he worked at the address given in 29c.

○ Driver, private auto   ○ Taxicab
○ Passenger, private auto   ○ Walked only
○ Bus or streetcar   ○ Worked at home
○ Subway or elevated   ○ Other means—*Specify*
○ Railroad

After completing question 29d, skip to question 33.

30. Does this person have a job or business from which he was temporarily absent or on layoff <u>last week</u>?

○ Yes, on layoff

○ Yes, on vacation, temporary illness, labor dispute, etc.

○ No

31a. Has he been looking for work during the past 4 weeks?

○ Yes   ○ No— *Skip to 32*

15 and 5 percent

b. Was there any reason why he could not take a job <u>last week</u>?

○ Yes, already has a job

○ Yes, because of this person's temporary illness

○ Yes, for other reasons (in school, etc.)

○ No, could have taken a job

32. When did he last work at all, even for a few days?

○ In 1970 ┊ ○ 1964 to 1967 ┊ ○ 1959 or earlier ┊ *Skip*
○ In 1969 ┊ ○ 1960 to 1963 ┊ ○ Never worked ┊ *to 36*
○ In 1968

[Page 8]

33–35. Current or most recent job activity

Describe clearly this person's chief job activity or business last week, if any. If he had more than one job, describe the one at which he worked the most hours.

If this person had no job or business last week, give information for last job or business since 1960.

33. Industry

    a. For whom did he work? *If now on active duty in the Armed Forces, print "AF" and skip to question 36.*

_____
(Name of company, business, organization, or other employer)

    b. What kind of business or industry was this?
    Describe activity at location where employed.

_____
(For example: Junior high school, retail supermarket, dairy farm, TV and radio service, auto assembly plant, road construction)

    c. Is this mainly— *(Fill one circle)*

    ○ Manufacturing   ○ Retail trade
    ○ Wholesale trade   ○ Other *(agriculture, construction, service, government, etc.)*

34. Occupation

    a. What kind of work was he doing?

_____
(For example: TV repairman, sewing machine operator, spray painter, civil engineer, farm operator, farm hand, junior high English teacher)

    b. What were his most important activities or duties?

_____
(For example: Types, keeps account books, files, sells cars, operates printing press, cleans buildings, finishes concrete)

    c. What was his job title?
_____

15 and 5 percent

[Page 8]

35. Was this person— *(Fill one circle)*

Employee of <u>private</u> company, business, or
individual, for wages, salary, or commissions... ○

Federal <u>government</u> employee .... ○
State <u>government</u> employee................. ○
Local <u>government</u> employee *(city. county. etc.)*... ○

<u>Self-employed</u> in own business,
professional practice, or farm—
    Own business not incorporated .... ○
    Own business incorporated .... ○

Working <u>without pay</u> in family business or farm ○

15 and 5 percent

36. In April 1965, what State did this person live in?

○ This State

OR

_____
(Name of State or foreign country; or Puerto Rico, etc.)

5 percent

37. In April 1965, was this person— *(Fill three circles)*

a. **Working at a job or business** *(full or part-time)*?
    ○ Yes   ○ No

b. **In the Armed Forces?**
    ○ Yes   ○ No

c. **Attending college?**
    ○ Yes   ○ No

15 and 5 percent

38. *If "Yes" for "Working at a job or business" in question 37—*
Describe this person's chief activity or business in April 1965.

a. **What kind of business or industry was this?**

_____

b. **What kind of work was he doing (occupation)?**

_____

c. **Was he—**
An employee of a private company or government agency... ○
Self-employed or an unpaid family worker .... ○

5 percent

[Page 8]

39a. Last year (1969), did this person work at all, even for a few days?

      ○ Yes ○ No— *Skip to 41*

b. How many weeks did he work in 1969, either full-time or part-time?
Count paid vacation, paid sick leave, and military service.

  ○ 13 weeks or less ■ ○ 40 to 47 weeks
  ○ 14 to 26 weeks   ○ 48 to 49 weeks
  ○ 27 to 39 weeks   ○ 50 to 52 weeks

40. Earnings in 1969— *Fill parts a, b, and c for everyone who worked any time in 1969 even if he had no income.*
  (If exact amount is not known, give best estimate.)

a. How much did this person earn in 1969 in wages, salary, commissions, bonuses, or tips from all jobs?
(Before deductions for taxes, bonds, dues, or other items.)

 $ _____ .00
 (Dollars only)
 OR ○ None

b. How much did he earn in 1969 from his own nonfarm business, professional practice, or partnership?
(Net after business expenses. If business lost money, write "Loss" above amount.) ■

 $ _____ .00
 (Dollars only)
 OR ○ None

c. How much did he earn in 1969 from his own farm?
(Net after operating expenses. Include earnings as a tenant farmer or sharecropper. If farm lost money, write "Loss" above amount.)

 $ _____ .00
 (Dollars only)
 OR ○ None

> 15 and 5 percent

41. Income other than earnings in 1969— *Fill parts a, b, and c.*
  (If exact amount is not known, give best estimate.)

a. How much did this person receive in 1969 from Social Security or Railroad Retirement?

 $ _____ .00
 (Dollars only)
 OR ○ None

b. How much did he receive in 1969 from public assistance or welfare payments?
Include aid for dependent children, old age assistance, general assistance, aid to the blind or totally disabled.
Exclude separate payments for ■
hospital or other medical care.

 $ _____ .00
 (Dollars only)
 OR ○ None

c. How much did he receive in 1969 from all other sources?
Include interest, dividends, veterans' payments, pensions, and other regular payments.
(See instruction sheet.)

 $ _____ .00
 (Dollars only)
 OR ○ None

INDEX

Abortion, 7, 146
Accidents, as cause of death, 85–86
  automobile, 85
Age at marriage, 20
Age composition, 1, 3–4, 33–44, 51
  and crime rate, 36–37
  as dependent variable, 34–35
  and mortality, 37–38
Age-dependency ratio, 154
Age heaping, 42–43
Age-sex composition, 154
Age-sex pyramid, 41–44, 154
Age-specific birth rate, 154
Age-specific death rate, 154, 155
Akers, Donald S., 53
Anderson, Theodore, 73
Antonovsky, Aaron, 81–82, 92
Aristotle, 5–7, 15
Arriaga, Eduardo E., 80, 92
Atomic weapon production, as "crash" program, 143
Automobile. See Accidents, as cause of death

"Baby boom," 39, 44
Back, Kurt W., 15, 32, 74, 114, 121, 124
Banks, J. A., 107, 121, 123
Barclay, George W., 30, 92, 154
Bauder, Ward, 75
Becker, Gary, 110–113, 123–124
Bell, Wendell, 74
Bendix, Reinhard, 92, 123
Berardo, Felix, 67, 71, 75
Berelson, Bernard, 149, 152
Beresford, John C., 53
Beshers, James M., 62–63, 73–74, 121
  theory of migration, 62
Bills of Mortality, 9, 16
Biological theories of fertility, 95–96
Birth control:
  devices in China, 147
  governmental, 7
  oral contraceptive ("the pill"), 134
  techniques, 149
  See also Births, limitation of; Contraception; Family planning; Family-planning programs; Population
Birth rate (defined), 154
Birth statistics, 23–24
Births, limitation of, 145–146
Black population. See Negro population

Blacks, fertility of:
  and Black pride, 99
  and Black revolution, 99, 102–103
  compared to White, 99–102
  in Nation of Islam (Black Muslims), 105
  in nineteenth century, 99
  and urbanization, 100–102
  See also Fertility
Blake, Judith, 22, 32, 52, 111–113, 123–124, 140–141, 151–152
Blau, Peter M., 52
Blumenthal, Hans, 75
Bogue, Donald J., 14, 29–30, 32, 52, 91, 92, 96–98, 122, 127, 137–138, 150, 151, 154
Bright, Margaret, 73
Broom, Leonard, 16
Brown, James S., 73–74
Brown, R. G., 133, 151
Burchinal, Lee, 75
Burgess, Ernest W., 92

Campbell, Arthur A., 122, 123, 124
Campbell, Flann, 53
Cardiovascular-renal diseases, 84–85
Catholics, fertility of, 103–105
  influenced by Catholic education, 104
  and minority status, 104–105
  in Ireland, 105
  compared to Protestant, 122
Causes of death, 84–86
  by sex and age, 85
Census, 2, 21–22
  as military secret, 25
  de facto, 26–27
  de jure, 26–27
  history of, 24–25
  in Great Britain, 25
  in Quebec, 25
  in Sweden, 25
  modern, 25–26
  self-enumeration, 27
  See also Census, United States
Census, United States, 25–26
  and canvasser method, 27
  Congress and, 26
  and Constitution, 23, 26
  errors in, 27–30
  history of, 24–26
  and householder method, 27

189